THE SAYINGS GOSPEL Q
IN GREEK AND ENGLISH

THE SAYINGS GOSPEL Q IN GREEK AND ENGLISH

WITH PARALLELS FROM THE GOSPELS OF MARK AND THOMAS

Edited by

James M. Robinson
Paul Hoffmann
John S. Kloppenborg

Managing Editor

Milton C. Moreland

Fortress Press
Minneapolis

THE SAYINGS GOSPEL Q IN GREEK AND ENGLISH
With Parallels from the Gospels of Mark and Thomas

This Fortress Press edition published in collaboration with Peeters Publishers (Leuven, Belgium).

Cover design: Jessica Thoreson

ISBN 0-8006-3494-2

Manufactured in Belgium by Peeters Publishers (Leuven)

07 06 05 04 03 02 1 2 3 4 5 6 7

CONTENTS

PREFACE

The Sayings Gospel Q in Greek and English with Parallels from the Gospels of Mark and Thomas is basically an abbreviation and simplification of *The Critical Edition of Q: Synopsis including the Gospels of Matthew and Luke, Mark and Thomas with English, German, and French Translations of Q and Thomas*, edited by James M. Robinson, Paul Hoffmann, and John S. Kloppenborg (Managing Editor: Milton C. Moreland), which was published in 2000 by Fortress Press for North America and by Peeters Publishers in Leuven, Belgium for Europe. A small booklet *The Sayings of Jesus: The Sayings Gospel Q in English*, without the Greek text at all, has already been published in 2001 by Fortress Press.

The critical text of Q, the result of almost two decades of ongoing work by the members of the International Q Project, is presented here on facing pages, with the Greek text on the left and its English translation on the right. Both use the simplified format that was already published in *The Critical Edition of Q*, where it was highlighted at the bottom of each left-hand page for ready reference. This format frees the user from the large battery of sigla that were necessary in carrying through the reconstruction of the critical text itself. For only those sigla are present now that are needed to suggest the degree of certainty ascribed to the text at any given place (see Sigla below, p. 73-74).

John S. Kloppenborg's Concordance of the vocabulary of Q, present in full detail in *The Critical Edition of Q*, is here reproduced in a more convenient format, in that only the significant vocabulary is included, but augmented with the English translation of each Greek term.

The massive databases prepared by the International Q Project, on which the reconstruction of the critical text of Q is based, are being published in a series of many volumes: Documenta Q: Reconstructions of Q Through Two Centuries of Gospel Research Excerpted, Sorted, and Evaluated (Leuven: University Press and Peeters, 1996 ff.).

ACKNOWLEDGEMENTS

An expression of gratitude is due first of all to the members of the International Q Project, who have amassed and sorted the Databases, prepared the Evaluations, participated in the discussions and voting of the meetings, and thereby provided the foundation upon which *The Sayings Gospel Q in Greek and English* is built: Josef E. Amon, Stanley D. Anderson, William E. Arnal, Jon Ma. Asgeirsson, Ulrich Bauer, Sterling G. Bjorndahl, M. Eugene Boring, Stefan H. Brandenburger, Shawn Carruth, Amos (Joon Ho) Chang, Jon B. Daniels, Robert A. Derrenbacker, Jr., Rees Conrad Douglas, Claudio Ettl, Harry T. Fleddermann, Albrecht Garsky, Heinz O. Guenther, Patrick J. Hartin, Christoph Heil, Thomas Hieke, Paul Hoffmann, Michael Humphries, Clayton N. Jefford, Steven R. Johnson, Ronald L. Jolliffe, Neal Kelsey, Alan Kirk, John S. Kloppenborg, Helmut Koester, Bradley H. McLean, Milton C. Moreland, Stephen J. Patterson, Ronald A. Piper, Jonathan L. Reed, James M. Robinson, Andreas Schmidt, Philip H. Sellew, Saw Lah Shein, Daniel A. Smith, Ky-Chun So, Michael G. Steinhauser, Darla Dee Turlington, Risto Uro, Leif E. Vaage, John Y. H. Yieh, and Linden E. Youngquist.

The Greek text is that of the *Novum Testamentum Graece*, [27]1993, edited by Barbara Aland et al., Deutsche Bibelgesellschaft, Stuttgart. We thank Barbara Aland and Joachim Lange for their cooperation in this undertaking.

The English translation of Q has been provided by James M. Robinson.

Parallels from the *Gospel of Thomas* have been provided by the Berliner Arbeitskreis für koptisch-gnostische Schriften under the responsibility of Hans-Gebhard Bethge, published in the *Synopsis Quattuor Evangeliorum: Locis parallelis evangeliorum apocryphorum et patrum adhibitis edidit Kurt Aland* (Stuttgart: Deutsche Bibelgesellschaft, 15. revidierte Aufl. 1996, 2. korrigierter Druck 1997, see the *Vorwort* to the fifteenth edition by Barbara Aland xi, and the appendix Evangelium Thomae Copticum, *Vorbemerkung* by Hans-Gebhard Bethge, pp. 517-518, and the text of the *Gospel of Thomas*, pp. 519-546). We wish to express to all involved our appreciation for permission to make use of these texts.

T. C. Skeat and Harold W. Attridge collaborated in making important improvements in the transcription and translation of *Gos. Thom.* 36 in P. Oxy 655, 10-15 at Q 12:27, 25: κ̣[αὶ] / ἓν ἔχο̣ντ[ες ἔ]νδ[υ]/μα, τί ἐν[.....].αι / ὑμεῖς; τίς ἂν προσθ<εί>η / ἐπὶ τὴν εἱλικίαν / ὑμῶν; αὐτὸ[ς δ]ώσει ὑμεῖν τὸ ἔνδυμα ὑμῶν. "[And] having *one* clothing, … you …? Who might add to your stature? That one will [give] you your clothing!" In other regards the text and translation of *Gos. Thom.* 36 in P. Oxy 655 at Q 12:22b, 25, 27, 28 is that of Harold W. Attridge, in *Nag Hammadi Codex II,2-7 together with XIII,3*, Brit. Lib. Or. 4926(1), and P. Oxy. 1, 654, 655* (ed. Bentley Layton; NHS 20; Leiden: Brill, 1989) 1. 121-122, 127.

Joseph Verheyden has worked through the text with great penetration, careful detail, and substantive suggestions that have led to many improvements in the published volume. Charles M. Beck has proofread the text with minute care and a very sharp eye. We are all very much in their debt for this expert and kind assistance.

Q TEXTS IN MATTHEAN ORDER

tthew	Matthean Doublet	Mark	Q (Luke)	Thomas	Page
0⟧			3:⟦0⟧		76-77
, 5	3:13b	1:4-5a	3:2b-3a		76-77
7-10	7:19	1:5	3:7-9		76-77
11-12		1:7-8	3:16b-17		78-79
16-17⟧	17:5b-c	1:9-11	3:⟦21b-22⟧		78-79
1-11		1:12-13	4:1-4, 9-12, 5-8, 13		78-81
3		6:1	4:16		80-81
-4, 6	4:25		6:20-21	54; 69.2	80-83
11-12			6:22-23	69.1a; 68.1	82-83
13		9:49-50a	14:34-35		138-39
15		4:21b-c	11:33	33.2-3	110-11
18	24:35	13:30-31	16:17		140-41
25-26			12:58-59		128-29
32	19:9	10:11b-12	16:18		140-41
39b-40	5:42b		6:29		84-85
⟦41⟧			6:⟦29↔30/Matt 5:41⟧		84-85
42	5:40		6:30	95	84-85
44			6:27-28		82-83
45	5:48		6:35c-d		82-83
46, 47	5:47, 46		6:32, 34	95	84-85
48	5:45		6:36		86-87
9-13a			11:2b-4		102-03
19-21	19:21b	10:21b	12:33-34	76.3	120-21
22-23			11:34-35	24.3	110-13
24			16:13	47.2	138-39
:25-33			12:22b-31	36	122-25
1-2		4:24b-e	6:37-38		86-87
3-5			6:41-42	26	88-89
:7-11			11:9-13	92.1; 94	104-05
:12	22:40		6:31	6.3	84-85
:13-14			13:24		130-31
:16b			6:44b	45.1	88-89
:18			6:43		88-89
:21	12:50a	3:35a	6:46		90-91
:22-23			13:26-27		130-31
:24-27			6:47-49		90-91
:28a			7:1a		90-91
:5-10, ?13?		2:1	7:1b, 3, 6b-9, ?10?		90-93
:11-12			13:29, 28		132-33
:19-22			9:57-60	86	96-97

Matthew	Matthean Doublet	Mark	Q (Luke)	Thomas	Pa
9:32-34	12:22-24	3:22	11:14-15		104
9:37-38			10:2	73	96
10:7-8	4:17	6:12-13	10:9	14.4c	98-
10:9-10a		6:8-9	10:4		98-
10:10b-11	10:12	6:10c	10:7-8	14.4a-b	98-
10:12-13	10:11	6:10b	10:5-6		98-
10:14		6:11	10:10-11		100-
10:15	11:24		10:12		100-
10:16			10:3		96-
10:19		13:9-11	12:11-12		120-
10:24-25a			6:40		86-
10:26		4:22	12:2	5.2 = 6.5	116-
10:27			12:3	33.1	116-
10:28			12:4-5		116-
10:29-31			12:6-7		118-
10:32-33	16:27	8:38	12:8-9		118-
—	10:34		12:⟦49⟧	10	126-
10:34			12:51	16.1-2	126-
10:35		13:12	12:53	16.3b	126-
10:37	19:29a	10:29b	14:26	55; 101.1-2	136-
10:38	14:24b	8:34b	14:27	55.2	136-
10:39	16:25	8:35	17:33		138-
10:40	18:5	9:37	10:16		100-
11:2-6			7:18-19, 22-23		92-
11:7-10		1:2	7:24-27	78	92-
11:11			7:28	46	92-
11:12-13			16:16		140-
11:16-19			7:31-35		94-
11:21-24	10:15		10:13-15		100-
11:25-26			10:21		102-
11:27			10:22	61.3b	102-
12:25-28		3:23-26	11:17-20		104-
12:⟦29⟧		3:27	11:⟦21-22⟧	35	106-
12:30		9:40	11:23		106-
12:32a-b	12:31, 32c	3:28-29	12:10	44	118-
12:33b	7:20b=16a		6:44a	45.1	88-
12:34-35			6:45	45.2-4	88-
12:38-40	16:1, 2a, 4	8:11-12	11:16, 29-30		108-
12:41-42			11:32, 31		110-
12:43-45			11:24-26		108-
—			11:?27-28?	79.1-2	108-
13:16-17			10:23b-24		102-
13:31-32		4:30-32	13:18-19	20	128-
13:33			13:20-21	96.1-2	130-
15:14			6:39	34	86-
16:⟦2-3a⟧			12:⟦54-55⟧		126-

atthew	Matthean Doublet	Mark	Q (Luke)	Thomas	Page
:⟦3b⟧			12:⟦56⟧	91.2	126-29
:20b	21:21	11:22b-23	17:6	48	144-45
:6-7		9:42	17:2, 1		140-43
:12-13	18:10		15:4-5a, 7	107	142-43
	18:10, 12-14		15:⟦8-10⟧		142-43
:15, 21			17:3-4		142-43
:28			22:28, 30		150-51
:⟦16⟧	19:30	10:31	13:⟦30⟧	4.2	132-33
:⟦32⟧	21:25c, 29		7:⟦29-30⟧		94-95
:2-5, ?6?, 7-10			14:16-18, ?19-20?, 21, 23	64	134-35
:?1-2a?			11:?39a?		112-13
:4			11:46b		114-15
:6-7		12:38c-39	11:43		112-13
:⟦12⟧	18:4		14:⟦11⟧		134-35
:13			11:52	39.1-2	114-15
:23			11:42		112-13
:25, 26b			11:39b, 41	89.1	112-13
:27			11:44		112-13
:29-32			11:47-48		114-15
:34-36			11:49-51		114-15
:37-39	21:9b	11:9c	13:34-35		132-33
			17:⟦20⟧	113.1-2	144-47
:⟦23⟧	24:26	13:21	17:⟦21⟧	113.3-4; 3	144-47
:26-27	24:23	13:21	17:23-24	3.1-2	146-47
:28			17:37		146-47
:37-39a			17:26-27		148-49
			17:?28-29?		148-49
:39b			17:30		148-49
:40-41	24:18	13:16	17:34-35	61.1	148-49
:43			12:39	21.5; 103	124-25
:44	24:42	13:35a-b	12:40		124-25
:45-51	25:21b	13:36	12:42-46		124-27
:10-12			13:25		130-31
:14-15b, 19-28		13:34	19:12-13, 15-24		148-51
:29	13:12	4:25	19:26	41	150-51

DIVERGENCES FROM THE LUKAN SEQUENCE

It has been generally assumed that Matthew tended to rearrange the sequence of Q in order to create the longer Matthean discourses, but that Luke tended to retain the sequence of Q. In preparing *The Critical Edition of Q*, such divergences of sequence between Matthew and Luke were examined when they occur. Indeed, in most cases, the Lukan rather than the Matthean order did seem to reflect that of Q. Hence one can normally follow Lukan sequence to find a text in *The Sayings Gospel Q*.[1] But in cases where it became clear that the Matthean rather than the Lukan order is that of Q, it is this reconstructed sequence of Q, rather than the Lukan sequence, that is followed.

Instances where the Lukan sequence is not that of Q are as follows:[2]

Q 4:5-8:	Between Q 4:9-12 and Q 4:13.
Q 6:35c-d:	Between Q 6:27-28 and Q 6:29, ⟦29↔30/ Matt 5:41⟧, 30-32, 34.
Q 11:16:	Between Q 11:17-20, ⟦21-22⟧, 23-26, ?27-28? and Q 11:29-30.
Q 11:42:	Between Q 11:34-35, ?39a? and Q 11:39b, 41.
Q 11:52:	Between Q 11:46b and Q 11:47-51; 12:2-3.
Q 12:33-34:	Between Q 12:2-12 and Q 12:22b-31.
Q 13:29:	Between Q 13:27 and Q 13:28, ⟦30⟧.
Q 17:33:	Between Q 14:26-27 and Q 14:34-35.
Q 15:4-5a, 7, ⟦8-10⟧:	Between Q 17:1-2 and Q 17:3-4.
Q 17:37:	Between Q 17:23-24 and Q 17:26-27.

The positions of Q 6:39 and Q 6:40 are very uncertain. As a convention, they are presented in their Lukan position.

1 This is the justification for the now widely accepted convention of quoting Q by Lukan chapter and verse numbers, a policy first introduced in the initial planning for *The Critical Edition of Q*. See James M. Robinson, "The Sermon on the Mount/Plain: Work Sheets for the Reconstruction of Q," SBL.SP 22 (1983) 451-54: 451-52, quoted below, p. 66, n. 162, in the Introduction.

2 See the discussion in James M. Robinson, "Instances of Matthew = Q Order," a section in "The Sequence of Q: The Lament over Jerusalem," in *Von Jesus zum Christus: Christologische Studien. Festgabe für Paul Hoffmann zum 65. Geburtstag* (ed. Rudolf Hoppe and Ulrich Busse; BZNW 93; Berlin and New York: de Gruyter, 1998) 225-60: 227-32.

Material considered for inclusion in Q that is only in Matthew, but not in Luke, is put in the sequence of the adjoining Matthean material that does have a Lukan parallel from Q, as its hypothetical position in Q:

Matt 5:⟦41⟧: Between Q 6:29 and Q 6:30.

INTRODUCTION

James M. Robinson

The purpose of this Introduction is to document the major turning points in the history of Q research, from which the present status of the study of Q emerges. Particular attention is paid to the way in which, over the years, the impediments to establishing a critical text of Q have been resolved.[1]

Throughout the nineteenth century, the study of Q was facilitated by a cluster of factors that succeeded in accrediting Q as the most viable solution to the so-called "Synoptic problem": How is it that Matthew, Mark, and Luke tell much the same story in much the same order, whereas John has a completely different procedure? Answer: Matthew and Luke used the same two sources, Mark and a no-longer-extant collection of sayings, commonly called "Q".

Yet the way this solution first came to expression made it very difficult even to conceive of the possibility of reconstructing a critical text of Q. For the point of departure of Q studies was the assumption that Q had been composed by the apostle Matthew in Aramaic, of which nothing has survived. This view, though theologically quite appealing, since it guaranteed apostolicity, turned out to make it quite impossible to gain access to Q itself. For one could hardly move behind the canonical Greek Gospels of Matthew and Luke to a purely hypothetical Aramaic source, attested at best by an occasional "Aramaism" sensed to lurk behind the Greek text. The Aramaic text of Q itself would forever remain undocumented and unattainable. On these terms, Q would never be more than a hypothesis. One could never really quote Q itself.

[1] For a more detailed presentation see John S. Kloppenborg Verbin, *Excavating Q: The History and Social Setting of the Sayings Gospel* (Minneapolis: Fortress, and Edinburgh: T & T Clark, 2000). For a focussed presentation limited to the twentieth century, see the 1996 Toronto dissertation of his student, Alan Kirk, *The Composition of the Sayings Source: Genre, Synchrony, and Wisdom Redaction in Q* (NovTSup 91; Leiden: Brill, 1998), "Compositional Analysis of Q in the History of Scholarship," 2-64. See also David R. Catchpole, *The Quest for Q* (Edinburgh: T & T Clark, 1993), "Did Q Exist?" 1-59, and Christopher M. Tuckett, *Q and the History of Early Christianity: Studies on Q* (Edinburgh: T & T Clark, and Peabody, Mass.: Hendrickson, 1996), "Introduction: The Existence of Q," 1-39.

Only gradually, especially in the latter part of the twentieth century, were such arguments, whose tenacious appeal lay in their apologetic value, completely replaced by objective criteria, based on empirical observation of Matthean and Lukan redactional traits. For once these are inferred from their redaction of Mark, they can be applied to the sayings of Q.[2] Now Q need no longer remain purely hypothetical, a mere postulate lurking unattainably behind Matthew and Luke. The result in more recent times has been a multiplication of reconstructions of the Greek text of Q, in whole or in part. *The Sayings Gospel Q* presented here in Greek and English is based on the collaboration of a team of scholars who, since 1985, have been working together as the International Q Project.

1 Papias's Aramaic λόγια

There are two terms, both from the same root, that have often been understood as referring to Jesus' sayings: *logia* (Greek λόγια, sg. λόγιον), and *logoi* (Greek λόγοι, sg. λόγος). Since one, λόγια, is used in the early second century by Papias in referring to Matthew, it was initially taken to be referring to Q. It was only with the discovery of the *Gospel of Thomas*, which uses λόγοι of Jesus' sayings, that the shift away from λόγια as a designation for Q was initiated. This turned out to be more than an insignificant debate about terminology, since hidden underneath was an apologetic interest: the issue was the Matthean and hence apostolic authorship of Q.

[2] This argument, though greatly expanded over the last generation as a result of redaction criticism, is in principle not new. See Kirsopp Lake, "The Date of Q," *The Expositor*, Seventh Series, 7 (1909) 494-507: 495-96:

> If we look at their treatment of Mark, we can see that Matthew and Luke both used it with a considerable degree of fidelity, except in small points of diction, such as altering the characteristic historic present of Mark to the more literary past tense. It is unusual for them both to alter Mark at the same place in the same way, and the number of places where they seem to do so ought probably to be considerably reduced by textual criticism. Therefore we have good reason for believing that as a rule the original Q is preserved either in Matthew or Luke, and an intelligent criticism ought to enable us generally to be right in our discrimination between the two.

1.1. *Papias's λόγια as an Aramaic Collection of Sayings by Matthew* *Friedrich Schleiermacher*

In 1832 Friedrich Schleiermacher interpreted Papias of the early second century[3] to the effect that his term λόγια referred to Jesus' sayings. For Papias wrote a work entitled Λογίων κυριακῶν ἐξήγησις, which Schleiermacher took to mean a work entitled *Exegesis of the Lord's Sayings*. There Papias reported: Ματθαῖος μὲν οὖν Ἑβραΐδι διαλέκτῳ τὰ λόγια συνετάξατο, ἡρμήνευσεν δ' αὐτὰ ὡς ἦν δυνατὸς ἕκαστος, which Schleiermacher interpreted to mean that "Matthew composed the sayings in the Hebrew dialect [= Aramaic], and each interpreted them as one was able." Schleiermacher argued that the Aramaic source was not the canonical Gospel of Matthew (as Papias mistakenly thought), but a lost Aramaic source written by the apostle Matthew lying behind (and thus giving its apostolic name and authority to) the Greek canonical Gospel of Matthew. It consisted of "λόγια," (mis)understood by Schleiermacher as referring to "sayings":

> Matthew wrote a collection of utterances of Christ, be they individual sayings, or longer discourses, or both, as is doubtless most probable. For the expression of Papias itself cannot have meant anything else.[4]

Since Schleiermacher thought the sayings collection used by Matthew was not used by the other canonical Gospels, and hence not by Luke,[5] he does not deserve credit for having discovered Q. But, building on such early patristic evidence, he did suggest the collection had apostolic authorship. The weight of this argument throughout the nineteenth century is hard to exaggerate. And he launched Papias's term λόγια as the (inaccurate) technical term for what only much later came to be known as Q.

[3] Eusebius, *Hist. eccl.* 3.39.16 (ed. E. Schwartz), GCS 9: 1. The Papias texts have been made available in *Synopsis Quattuor Evangeliorum* (ed. Kurt Aland; Stuttgart: Deutsche Bibelgesellschaft, 15. redivierte Aufl. 1996, 2. korrigierter Druck 1997) 547.

[4] Friedrich Schleiermacher, "Ueber die Zeugnisse des Papias von unsern beiden ersten Evangelien," *TSK* 5 (1832) 735-68: 738.

[5] Schleiermacher, "Ueber die Zeugnisse des Papias von unsern beiden ersten Evangelien," 757.

1.2 *"The Genuine Matthew" also Used by Luke*
Christian Hermann Weisse

In 1838 the Leipzig philosopher Christian Hermann Weisse first presented the argument basic to establishing the existence of Q, to the effect that both Matthew and Luke used, in addition to Mark, a sayings collection:

> If we maintain of this just-mentioned work [the Gospel of Luke], that it stands in a similar relation to Mark as does the Gospel of Matthew, that it, like the latter [Matthew], only even more freely, and seeking a certain pragmatism of narration, wove into the thread of Mark's narrative the λόγια of Matthew, and in addition an impressive series of other communications, yet in the process remaining completely independent of our Gospel of Matthew, as [Matthew] of [Luke] – one will find no preliminary *external* justification needed for this view, insofar as it stands in no contradiction with the historical reports about the Gospel of Luke. Luke himself tells us in the opening words of his work that he has used outside communications about the life history of the Redeemer which stand nearer the first source [Mark]. ... But after all that has been noted thus far, it lies so near at hand to presuppose that among the sources he used were to be found the writings of Mark and of the genuine Matthew [i.e. Q], that we would have to be extremely surprised, if it had not been the case. Hence we can confidently pursue further the path we have entered upon, in relation to Luke as well, with the consciousness that precisely in this way we remain in the best possible agreement with the historical witnesses.[6]
>
> This leads us to reflect briefly on the mutual relationship of the two other Synoptics to one another apart from their shared connection to Mark. We have already noted that we regard this relationship as an independent one, independent, that is to say, in the use of the common sources by each of the two, but not in the sense that each of them, throughout or for the most part, had used sources that the other had not used. It is our most certain conviction that not only Mark but also Matthew's collection of sayings is a source common to both.[7]

[6] Christian Hermann Weisse, *Die evangelische Geschichte kritisch und philosophisch bearbeitet* (2 vols.; Leipzig: Breitkopf und Härtel, 1838) 1: 55-56.

[7] Weisse, *Die evangelische Geschichte kritisch und philosophisch bearbeitet*, 1: 83. This is the decisive passage for the origin of the Q hypothesis quoted by Werner Georg Kümmel, *Das Neue Testament: Geschichte der Erforschung seiner Probleme* (Orbis Academicus 3.3: Problemgeschichten der Wissenschaft in Dokumenten und Darstellungen; Freiburg and Munich: Karl Alber, 1958) 185. ET: *The New Testament: The History of the Investigation of Its Problems* (Nashville and New York: Abingdon, 1972) 151. (The English translation is here edited to render it more precise.)

1.3 *Λ, "L," for λόγια*
Heinrich Julius Holtzmann

In 1863 Heinrich Julius Holtzmann presented a detailed comparison of the sayings in Matthew and Luke in such a convincing way as to gain for Q general acceptance.[8] For, in spite of various continuing minority views, it has remained the dominant position, of course improved in various regards, down to the present.

Holtzmann, still in deference to Papias's *λόγια*, designated this sayings source as Λ, "L":

> Rather, we stay with the quite simple assumption of a further Greek source shared by Matthew and Luke, which we, pending the demonstration of its more precise nature, want to indicate in what follows with the *siglum* Λ (λόγια).[9]

2 The λόγοι of the Gospel of Thomas

2.1 *P. Oxy. 1*
Bernhard P. Grenfell and Arthur S. Hunt

In 1897, the publication by Bernard P. Grenfell and Arthur S. Hunt of *P. Oxy.* 1, fragments from an unknown sayings collection (which we now know to be the *Gospel of Thomas*), as ΛΟΓΙΑ ΙΗΣΟΥ, illustrated the broadly based acceptance of the designation λόγια for such a sayings collection. They summarized the initial reception of their publication in its republication a year later:

> Lastly, with regard to the questions of origin and history, we stated in our edition our belief in four points: (1) that we have here part of a collection of sayings, not extracts from a narrative gospel; (2) that they were not heretical; (3) that they were independent of the Four Gospels in their present shape; (4) that they were earlier than 140 A.D., and might go back to the first century. These propositions, especially the first, have, as is natural, been warmly disputed. Attempts have been made to show that the "Logia" were extracts from the Gospel according to the Egyptians (Harnack), the Gospel according to the Hebrews (Batiffol), or the Gospel of the Ebionites

[8] Heinrich Julius Holtzmann, *Die synoptischen Evangelien: Ihr Ursprung und geschichtlicher Charakter* (Leipzig: Engelmann, 1863).

[9] Holtzmann, *Die synoptischen Evangelien,* 128.

(Zahn); and Gnostic, mystic, Ebionite, or Therapeutic tendencies, according to the point of view, have been discovered in them. On the other hand our position has received the general support of critics such as Swete, Rendel Harris, Heinrici, and Lock; and so far the discussion has tended to confirm us in our original view.[10]

2.2 *Remembering Jesus' λόγια/λόγοι*
J. Rendel Harris and Walter Lock

P. Oxy. 1 did of course create considerable discussion. J. Rendel Harris drew attention to the quotation formula repeated with each saying, λέγει Ἰ(ησοῦ)ς, "Jesus says," for he related it to the quotation formula in Acts 20:35: μνημονεύειν τε τῶν λόγων τοῦ κυρίου Ἰησοῦ ὅτι αὐτὸς εἶπεν, "to remember the sayings of the Lord Jesus, how he said...." Since almost the same formula occurs in 1 *Clem.* 13.1; 46.7 and Pol. *Phil.* 2.3, he concluded:

> Here we have the same peculiarity – viz., a quotation of *Logia*, not from our Gospels, with a prologue about the remembrance of what He said. And we have noticed the phenomenon four times. We conclude that it was the introductory formula of the book, which must have run something like this:
> "We ought to remember what things our Lord said in His teaching, for He said ..." and then probably follows the first *Logion*.[11]

Although the remembrance formula turned out to be absent from the opening line of the *Gospel of Thomas*, Rendell Harris was right to sense that the standard quotation formula that introduces each saying was picked up in that opening line. But he overlooked completely the fact that this remembrance formula only speaks of λόγοι, never λόγια (though Pol. *Phil.* 2.3 uses neither). But Walter Lock, also stimulated by *P. Oxy.* 1, published the same year a very similar position, while conjecturing more logically as the title Λόγοι Ἰησοῦ:

> Further, there are two points on which I would enter a caveat, – a caveat which the history of the discussion seems to render necessary. I think first that we should sit loosely to the exact title Λόγια; I do

[10] Bernard P. Grenfell and Arthur S. Hunt, *ΛΟΓΙΑ ΙΗΣΟΥ: Sayings of our Lord* (London: Henry Frowde for the Egypt Exploration Fund, 1897), republished as "**1.** ΛΟΓΙΑ ΙΗΣΟΥ" in *The Oxyrhynchus Papyri*, Part I (London: Egyptian Exploration Fund, 1898) 1-3: 2.

[11] J. Rendell Harris, "The Logia and the Gospels," *Contemporary Review* (1897) 346-48: 348.

> not say that it is wrong, but we need to remember that it has no authority as the title of this document; many will think it a very probable suggestion, but considering that the phrase λόγια Ἰησοῦ never occurs, that the phrase λόγια or τὰ λόγια with Θεοῦ or τοῦ Κυρίου or Κυριακά most frequently seems to mean both in the first and second centuries *either* the Old Testament *or* the whole Gospel message, and considering such passages as Acts xx.35, Apoc xxi.5, Clem. Rom. xiii, and the πιστοὶ λόγοι of the Pastoral Epistles, it seems to me at least as probable that the real title was Λόγοι Ἰησοῦ. At any rate if Logia is right, "Sayings" is scarcely an adequate translation; "Solemn Utterances" or "Oracles" would better reproduce the authoritative associations of the word.[12]

2.3 *λόγια as "Question-Begging"*
J. Armitage Robinson

Thereupon, already in 1902, J. Armitage Robinson rejected the use of λόγια for Q as "question-begging," in that it suggested that Q is to be identified with Papias's Matthean λόγια:

> I would here put in a warning, which is sorely needed, against the confusion introduced by the attempt to give this lost document a name. ... We have no evidence that there ever was a book entitled *Logia*, and to apply this name to the document which we are considering is to beg the question and prejudice our study. We must be content to speak of our lost document as the non-Marcan Greek document which was used by St Matthew and St Luke. *Logia* is a question-begging name: I could wish that we might hear no more of it in this connection.[13]

This criticism of the label λόγια as "question-begging" has been repeated sufficiently[14] that the term is no longer used to refer to Q in English-language scholarship, though it continues in use in German scholarship.

[12] Walter Lock, "Interpretation of the Text," Ch. 3 in Walter Lock and William Sanday, *Two Lectures on the "Sayings of Jesus" Recently Discovered at Oxyrhynchus* (Oxford: Clarendon, 1897) 15-27: 16.

[13] J. Armitage Robinson, *The Study of the Gospels* (London, New York, Bombay, and Calcutta: Longmans, Green, and Co., 1902, fifth impression [quoted here] 1909), 68-70.

[14] The criticism of "question-begging" was repeated by Benjamin W. Bacon, "A Turning Point in Synoptic Criticism," *HTR* 1 (1908) 55 and *Studies in Matthew* (London: Henry Holt, 1930) 92, in criticism of Germans taking Papias's σύνταξις τῶν λογίων to designate Q as a "Spruchsammlung." See also (below, p. 24) John Caesar Hawkins, *Horae Synopticae* (Oxford: Clarendon, 1899, second edition revised and supplemented 1909, reprinted 1968), 107.

2.4 *P. Oxy. 654: λόγοι*

The publication in 1904 of *P. Oxy*. 654, containing the opening of the same sayings collection already attested by *P. Oxy*. 1 (thereby showing it to be the *Gospel of Thomas*), made the rejection of λόγια in favor of λόγοι inescapable.[15] For the opening of *P. Oxy*. 654 uses λόγοι: ο<ὗ>τοι οἱ {οι} λόγοι οἱ [ἀπόκρυφοι οὓς ἐλά-]λησεν Ἰη(σοῦ)ς ὁ ζῶν ... ("These are the [secret] sayings [which] the living Jesus [spoke ...]"). Thereupon Grenfell and Hunt, in view of the arguments of Rendell Harris and Lock, formally retracted the term λόγια they had used in the title of their first publication:

> There is considerable resemblance between the scheme of II. 1-3, "the words... which Jesus spake... and he said," and the formulae employed in introducing several of the earliest citations of our Lord's Sayings.
>
> ... all questions concerning the meaning of the latter term [*logia*] may therefore be left out of account in dealing with the present series of Sayings.[16]

Kirsopp Lake[17] immediately threw his support to this shift in terminology:

> ... few criticisms have ever been more completely justified. The title has been found, and it is *Logoi*, not *Logia*.

Adolf Harnack promptly proposed as the title of Q: Λόγοι τοῦ κυρίου Ἰησοῦ, "Sayings of the Lord Jesus."[18]

[15] To be sure, this was rendered difficult by two scribal errors in the Greek text that could have obscured the nature of the opening: ΟΙΤΟΙΟΙΟΙΛΟΓΟΙΟΙ[...], i. e. ο<ὗ>τοι οἱ {οι} λόγοι οἱ [...]. See Grenfell and Hunt, *New Sayings of Jesus and Fragment of a Lost Gospel from Oxyrhynchus* (London: Henry Frowde, and New York: Oxford University Press American Branch, 1904), republished as "**654**. New Sayings of Jesus," and "**655**. Fragment of a Lost Gospel," in *The Oxyrhynchus Papyri*, Part IV (London: Egyptian Exploration Fund, 1904), 1-22, 22-28. Grenfell and Hunt mistranscribed: {οἱ} τοῖοι οἱ λόγοι οἱ [...].

[16] Grenfell and Hunt, *New Sayings of Jesus and Fragment of a Lost Gospel from Oxyrhynchus*, 13, 25; *The Oxyrhynchus Papyri*, Part IV (where the Greek original, using λόγοι, rather than an English translation, is used), 13.

[17] Kirsopp Lake, "The New Sayings of Jesus and the Synoptic Problem," *HibJ* 3 (1905) 332-41: 333. For a full quotation of his quite definitive statement, see James M. Robinson, "The *Incipit* of the Sayings Gospel Q," *RHPR* 75 (1995) 9-33: 23-24.

[18] Adolf Harnack, *Sprüche und Reden Jesu: Die zweite Quelle des Matthäus und Lukas* (Beiträge zur Einleitung in das Neue Testament, 2; Leipzig: Hinrichs'sche Buchhandlung, 1907) 132. ET: *The Sayings of Jesus: The Second Source of St. Matthew and St. Luke* (London: Williams and Norgate, and New York: Putnam, 1908) 188. Harnack

2.5 *First Century Usage: λόγοι = "Sayings"*

One may summarize the documentation from the last half of the First Century for the usage of λόγοι, never λόγια, to designate sayings of Jesus, as follows:

1. The conclusion of the Inaugural Sermon in Q (Q 6:47-49), where one might expect something comparable to a title or appropriate opening line, contains the exhortation not only to hear but also to keep Jesus' λόγοι (πᾶς ὁ ἀκούων μου τοὺς λόγους καὶ [μὴ] ποιῶν αὐτούς ..., "everyone hearing my sayings and [not] doing them ..."). Clearly this is a designation for the immediately preceding "sayings" that constitute the Inaugural Sermon. This formulation is retained as the conclusion in Matthew's Sermon on the Mount (Matt 7:24-27) and Luke's Sermon on the Plain (Luke 6:47-49).

2. The formula of Q 7:1 (καὶ ἐγένετο ὅτε ἐπλήρωσεν τοὺς λόγους τούτους, "and it came to pass when he ended these sayings"), which was adopted by Matthew as a stereotypical conclusion for three of his five major discourses (Matt 7:28; 19:1; 26:1), uses the term λόγοι to designate these collections of Jesus' sayings. The Centurion's Faith in Jesus' Word, which immediately follows in Q, has its point in the Centurion's faith in the authority of Jesus' λόγος (Q 7:7).

3. Paul (1 Thess 4:15) uses λόγος in the quotation formula (ἐν λόγῳ κυρίου, "in a saying of the Lord") to introduce a saying he ascribes to the Lord.

4. Acts 20:35 uses λόγοι in what appears to have become a stereotypical formula for introducing sayings of Jesus: μνημονεύειν τε τῶν λόγων τοῦ κυρίου Ἰησοῦ ὅτι αὐτὸς εἶπεν ("to remember the sayings of the Lord Jesus, how he said ..."). It recurs 1 *Clem* 13,1: μεμνημένοι τῶν λόγων τοῦ κυρίου Ἰησοῦ, οὓς ἐλάλησεν ("remembering the sayings of the Lord Jesus which he spoke"), followed by the injunction (1 *Clem* 13,3) to be obedient to Jesus' "holy sayings" (τοῖς ἁγιοπρεπέσι λόγοις), where again Jesus' sayings are referred to as his λόγοι. Similarly 1 *Clem* 46,7: μνήσθητε τῶν λόγων τοῦ κυρίου Ἰησοῦ ("Remember the sayings of the Lord Jesus").

noted, 132, n. 1 (ET: 189, n. 1) that Rendell Harris and Lake had anticipated his view. Athanasius Polag, *Fragmenta Q: Textheft zur Logienquelle* (Neukirchen-Vluyn: Neukirchener Verlag, [1]1979, [2]1982) 28, followed Harnack. Ivan Havener, *Q: The Sayings of Jesus. With a Reconstruction of Q by Athanasius Polag* (GNS; Wilmington, Del.: Michael Glazier, 1987; reprinted Collegeville, Minn.: Liturgical Press, 1990) 123: "Sayings of the Lord Jesus."

5. Rev 22:6 refers to the resurrected Christ's revelation: καὶ εἶπεν μοι· οὗτοι οἱ λόγοι πιστοὶ καὶ ἀληθινοί ("And he said to me: These sayings are trustworthy and true").

6. *Did* 1,2-3a obtained its title by making use in its opening language of a formula for presenting sayings (designated λόγοι) followed by their interpretation (in this case their διδαχή, "teaching"). For the *Didache* begins with the core of Jesus' sayings (λόγοι), found, according to *Did* 1,2, in the combination of love of God and neighbor (Mark 12:30-31) with the (negative) Golden Rule (Q 6:31). This is followed by the formula: τούτων δὲ τῶν λόγων ἡ διδαχή ἐστιν αὕτη·, "Now the teaching of these sayings is this:" (*Did* 1,3a). This is much the same formula as is found in the similarly-placed introductory saying of the *Gospel of Thomas*: [ὃς ἂν τὴν ἑρμηνεί]αν τῶν λόγων τούτ[ων εὕρῃ, ...],[19] "whoever [finds] the [interpretation] of these sayings ...".[20] Indeed Rufinus' Latin translation of the term διδαχή in the opening of the *Didache* is *interpretatio*.[21]

7. The *incipit* of *P. Oxy*. 654 (*Gospel of Thomas*) surely belongs in this list in its use of λόγοι: ο<ὗ>τοι οἱ {οι} λόγοι οἱ [ἀπόκρυφοι οὓς ἐλά]/λησεν Ἰη(σοῦ)ς ὁ ζῶν ... ("These are the [secret] sayings [which] the living Jesus [spoke] ..."), followed immediately by the call for their "interpretation" (ἑρμηνεία). This formulation recurs, probably as a conscious imitation, as the *incipit* of the *Book of Thomas* (*the Contender*) (Nag Hammadi Codex II, Tractate 7). For it began: "The secret sayings that the savior spoke to Judas Thomas which I, even I Mathaias,

[19] The restoration of the lacunae is assured by the Coptic translation, here fully extant (Nag Hammadi II 2: 32.13), where the Greek ἑρμηνεία is used as a loan word, and the Coptic ϣⲁϫⲉ is the standard Sahidic translation of λόγος, for example both here and in the opening itself, where the Greek, λόγοι, is also extant in *P. Oxy*. 654.

[20] See also Mark 4:34, where the synonym ἐπίλυσις is presupposed, as the "resolution," i.e. explanation, of Jesus' obscure "parables": χωρὶς δὲ παραβολῆς οὐκ ἐλάλει αὐτοῖς, κατ' ἰδίαν δὲ τοῖς μαθηταῖς ἐπέλυεν πάντα ("And he did not speak to them without a parable, but privately to his own disciples he explained everything"). The technical term παρρησία is used for this plainness of speech on the higher level (Mark 8:32): καὶ παρρησίᾳ τὸν λόγον ἐλάλει ("and in openness he spoke the word"). John 16:25, 29 employs the similar contrast between παροιμία ("riddle") and παρρησία ("openness"), for Jesus' obscure sayings and their interpretation. The hermeneutical formula involved in the Pesher exegesis in Qumran is similar. The role this concept of interpreting Jesus' sayings played in the development of the genre of the Gospels is discussed in the "Einleitung," to James M. Robinson, *Messiasgeheimnis und Geschichtsverständnis: Zur Gattungsgeschichte des Markus-Evangeliums* (TB 81; Munich: Chr. Kaiser, 1989) v-ix: ix.

[21] Eusebius, *Hist. eccl.* 2.1.253.

wrote down, while I was walking, listening to them speak with one another." In both instances, the scribe is named. The roughly contemporary incipit of the Greek Baruch is similar: Καὶ οὗτοι οἱ λόγοι τοῦ βιβλίου, οὓς ἔγραψεν Βαρουχ υἱὸς Νηριου υἱοῦ Μαασαιου.

8. Much the same formula as that in *P. Oxy.* 654 is used by the resurrected Christ in Luke 24:44: οὗτοι οἱ λόγοι μου οὓς ἐλάλησα πρὸς ὑμᾶς ἔτι ὢν σὺν ὑμῖν.

The frequency of the use of λόγοι in this quasi-technical sense, and the complete absence of the use of λόγια for sayings of Jesus in the first century, make it clear that one should speak of Q as λόγοι rather than as λόγια.

2.6 *Second Century Usage: λόγια = "Oracles"*

For its part, λόγια is used in its standard meaning (Liddell and Scott: "oracle, esp. one preserved from antiquity, ... more freq. in pl.") in Rom 3:2; Acts 7:38; Heb 5:12; 1 Pet 4:11 – and presumably also in Papias.[22] Dieter Lührmann has made it clear that Papias with his term λόγια did not record the original terminology, but rather introduced a new meaning for the sayings of Jesus, and hence a new terminology:

> The thesis of this study is that at the beginning of Q-research there was a misunderstanding, namely Schleiermacher's interpretation of Papias's comments on the gospels of Matthew and Mark. The two-document hypothesis was developed in the 19th century in part independently of this, and in part appealing to it. At the end of the 19th century it became separated from this interpretation, but to some extent was now substantiated by new discoveries of apocryphal gospels....
>
> But in that Papias understood the sayings of Jesus as λόγια in the strict sense, he gave a new significance to *them*, not to the Greek word λόγιον. He thus stands at the beginning of a development which can be traced in the 2nd century....
>
> Papias was the first to understand the sayings of Jesus as oracles preserved from antiquity, but down to his own time found only poor or even false translations and/or interpretations of such oracles, and

22 Hawkins, *Horae Synopticae* ²1909, xiii, translated Papias's reference: "Matthew composed the oracles ...." Kirsopp Lake, *Eusebius: The Ecclesiastical History with an English Translation* (LCL, 2 vols; London: Heinemann, and Cambridge, MA: Harvard University Press, 1926, reprint 1959 [quoted here], 1: 291, 297), translated "Interpretation of the Oracles of the Lord," "Matthew collected the oracles ...."

> wished himself to supply the interpretation which with oracles is always necessary.[23]

In fact this is evident even in the usage of Papias himself. He uses λόγοι when referring to sayings, be they sayings of the presbyters (τοὺς τῶν πρεσβυτέρων ἀνέκρινον λόγους ["I inquired into the sayings of the presbyters"]), the apostles (τοὺς μὲν τῶν ἀποστόλων λόγους ["the sayings of the apostles"]) or Aristion's interpretation of Jesus' sayings (τῶν τοῦ κυρίου λόγων διηγήσεις ["interpretations of the sayings of the Lord"]).[24] Then Papias shifts to λόγια to refer to Peter's, and hence Mark's, lack of an arrangement of the Lord's oracles (οὐχ ὥσπερ σύνταξιν τῶν κυριακῶν ποιούμενος λογίων ["not making, as it were, an arrangement of the Lord's oracles"]).[25] Since the λόγια of Mark are surely not limited to Jesus' sayings, the immediately following reference to Matthew collecting the oracles (τὰ λόγια συνετάξατο ["he collected the oracles"]) should not be taken to refer to sayings only, but to the whole scope of the Gospel of Matthew.[26] Papias's book, which Eusebius referred to in terms of its title as Λογίων κυριακῶν ἐξηγήσεως ("Interpretation of the Oracles of the Lord"),[27] was not limited to sayings of Jesus, for it included "marvels and other details,"[28] including the resurrection of a corpse in connection with the daughters of Philip, another miracle associated with Justus Barsabas, and a millenarianism that offended the intelligence of Eusebius.[29] Hence Papias's vocabulary provides no valid reason to consider his reference to the Gospel of Matthew as consisting of λόγια to be a mistake on his part for what should have been a reference to a prior sayings collection. In brief, Papias provides no evidence that λόγια was used as a technical term for sayings of Jesus in primitive Christianity, which could then justify the use of λόγια in modern scholarship to designate the sayings source used by Matthew and Luke.

[23] Dieter Lührmann, "Q: Sayings of Jesus or Logia?" in *The Gospel behind the Gospels: Current Studies on Q* (ed. Ronald A. Piper; NovTSup 75; Leiden: Brill, 1995) 97-116: 97-98, 108, 111.

[24] Eusebius, *Hist. eccl.* 3.39.4, 7, 14.

[25] Eusebius, *Hist. eccl.* 3.39.4, 15.

[26] Eusebius, *Hist. eccl.* 3.39.16.

[27] Eusebius, *Hist. eccl.* 3.39.1.

[28] Eusebius, *Hist. eccl.* 3.39.8: παράδοξά τινα ἱστορεῖ καὶ ἄλλα.

[29] Eusebius, *Hist. eccl.* 3.39.9-13.

3 Q for "Quelle," "Source"

3.1 *Q instead of λόγοι*

Yet, in fact, neither the discovery of the formula of "remembering" Jesus' λόγοι by Rendell Harris and Lock, nor the discovery of the opening of the collection of Jesus' λόγοι by Grenfell and Hunt in *P. Oxy.* 654, which is in fact the opening of the *Gospel of Thomas*, nor Harnack's elevation of λόγοι into the title of Q, led to a replacement of *Logia* with *Logoi* as the technical term in scholarship. Instead, the designation Q emerged as a replacement for Holtzmann's Λ (which, after all, could have been redefined as an abbreviation for Λόγοι.)

"Q." (with a period making it clear that it was meant as an abbreviation, representing *Quelle*, "source") was first used in 1880,[30] but "Q" came to be used simply as a symbol first in the 1890s, beginning with Johannes Weiss:

> ... a dependence on Urmarkus (A) is excluded, since Luke is here not reflecting on Mark at all. By and large, both are following another shared source, namely Q.[31]

[30] The history of the designation Q has been worked out in debate with other suggested derivations by Frans Neirynck, "The Symbol Q (=Quelle)," *ETL* 54 (1978) 119-25; "Once More: The Symbol Q," *ETL* 55 (1979) 382-83, both republished in his collected essays *Evangelica: Gospel Studies–Études d'Évangile* (Leuven: University Press and Peeters, 1982) 683-89, 689-90, where the usage is traced back to Johannes Weiss in 1890, and then a "Note on the Siglum Q" in the second volume of collected essays, *Evangelica II: 1982-1991* (Leuven: University Press and Peeters, 1991) 474, tracing it back to Eduard Simons in 1880: *Hat der dritte Evangelist den kanonischen Matthäus benutzt?* (Bonn: Universitäts-Buchdruckerei von Carl Georgi). Simons used it as an abbreviation for *Quelle*, in a dissertation at the Kaiser-Wilhelm-Universität Strassburg that persuaded his professor, Heinrich Julius Holtzmann, to give up his Urmarkus theory: Holtzmann, *Lehrbuch der historisch-kritischen Einleitung in das Neue Testament* (Freiburg im Breisgau, [2]1886) 357, 363-65. Neirynck quotes Simons to make clear that Simons normally used Λ, especially when envisaging Holtzmann's position. But when the position of Bernhard Weiss is involved, Simons can speak of "Λ (resp. Q.)" (p. 29), "Λ (Q)" (p. 30), or just "Q. (Die apostolische Quelle nach W.)" (p. 22), "die W.'sche Q." (p. 95), or simply "Q." (p. 68). This would suggest that Bernhard Weiss had already introduced the designation"Q." But Weiss' source was much more extensive than what we now mean by Q, e.g. it included much narrative material: "Die Aufstellung der Matthäusquelle (Q)," *Die Quellen der synoptischen Überlieferung* (TU 32,3; Leipzig: J. C. Hinrichs'sche Buchhandlung, 1908) 1-75.

[31] Johannes Weiss, "Die Verteidigung Jesu gegen den Vorwurf des Bündnisses mit Beelzebul," *TSK* 63 (1890) 557, cited by Neirynck, "The Symbol Q (= Quelle)," 686, n. 17. The period had by then disappeared. See further Johannes Weiss, "Die Parabelrede bei Markus," *TSK* 64 (1891) 291; "Die Komposition der synoptischen Wiederkunftsrede," *TSK* 65 (1892) 248; *Die Predigt Jesu vom Reiche Gottes* (Göttingen: Vandenhoeck und

Paul Wernle then accepted this symbol in 1899: "Let this – hypothetical – source be denoted with Q."[32]

John Caesar Hawkins illustrates the way in which this shift to "Q" replaced a shift to λόγοι. For in 1909 he wrote:

> THE SOURCE LARGELY USED BY MATTHEW AND LUKE, APART FROM MARK. In the first edition of this book (1899) the title of the present Section was "The Logia of Matthew as a probable source." Since then the scholars of England and America have largely followed those of Germany in designating this source as Q (= *Quelle*). For it has been generally admitted that to call it "the Logia of Matthew" was unfairly "question-begging," as assuming that Matthew and Luke certainly used the document named by Papias .... But the abandonment of that name in favour of the neutral symbol Q need not involve any intention of begging the question in the other direction, by ignoring the reasons for holding that the only two documents named by the earliest writer who deals with sources at all are the two which bulk so largely in our First and Third Gospels.[33]

Yet from this it is clear that Hawkins still identified Papias's λόγια with Q. The "question-begging" simply went underground, hidden beneath the innocuously objective symbol Q. Indeed Hawkins still proposed as late as 1911 the title based on Papias, Κυριακὰ Λόγια.[34]

3.2 *The Irrelevance of Papias*

The result of this inconsistency of a century ago has been that the argument has needed to be repeated half a century later.[35] In 1965 Roger Gryson gave a full report on research on the Papias issue to conclude:

Ruprecht, 1892) 8; ET: *Jesus' Proclamation of the Kingdom of God* (Philadelphia: Fortress, 1971) 60. "Q" is then used by Bernhard and Johannes Weiss, *Die Evangelien des Markus und Lukas* (KEK 1: 2; Göttingen: Vandenhoeck und Ruprecht, [8]1892) iii-iv, 279-83.

32 Paul Wernle, *Die synoptische Frage* (Freiburg im Breisgau, Leipzig, Tübingen: Mohr-Siebeck, 1899) 44.

33 Hawkins, *Horae Synopticae* [2]1909, 107.

34 John Caesar Hawkins, "Probabilities as to the so-called Double Tradition of St. Matthew and St. Luke," in *Studies in the Synoptic Problem*: *By Members of the University of Oxford* (ed. William Sanday; Oxford: Clarendon, 1911) 95-140: 119.

35 James M. Robinson, "ΛΟΓΟΙ ΣΟΦΩΝ: Zur Gattung der Spruchquelle Q," in *Zeit und Geschichte: Dankesgabe an Rudolf Bultmann zum 80. Geburtstag* (ed. Erich Dinkler; Tübingen: Mohr-Siebeck, 1964) 77-96, then in a revised and enlarged edition in *Entwicklungslinien durch die Welt des frühen Christentums* (ed. Helmut Koester and James M. Robinson; Tübingen: Mohr-Siebeck 1971) 67-106. In English it was also revised and enlarged, and published as "*Logoi Sophon*: On the *Gattung* of Q," in *The*

> The result of these observations is that the usage of the word λόγιον in the fathers of the Second Century would not be able to serve to accredit the theories according to which, in the Testimony of Papias about Matthew, the words τὰ λόγια have in view sayings of Jesus or Old Testament oracles. It could be appealed to as an argument, on the other hand, by those who think that these words designate the ensemble of the material "put in order" by Matthew to compose his Gospel, and that these λόγια, like the κυριακὰ λόγια of which Mark has left us a remembrance in his work, are not only sayings of the Lord (τὰ λεχθέντα ["the things said"]), but also narrations of his deeds and actions (τὰ πραχθέντα ["the things done"]).[36]

That is to say, the language Eusebius uses (*Hist. eccl.* 3.39.15) with regard to the Gospel of Mark: οὐ μέντοι τάξει τὰ ὑπὸ τοῦ κυρίου ἢ λεχθέντα ἢ πραχθέντα ... οὐχ ὥσπερ σύνταξιν τῶν κυριακῶν ποιούμενος λογίων ["not, indeed, in order, the things said or done by the Lord ... not making, as it were, an arrangement of the Lord's oracles "], seems to make clear that λόγια would include both λεχθέντα and πραχθέντα, not just what was said but also what was done, and hence would not suggest a sayings collection when used in referring to the canonical Gospel of Matthew in the continuation that immediately follows (Eusebius, *Hist. eccl.* 3.39.16).

Hence, something approaching a consensus has tended to emerge regarding Papias and Q. Werner Georg Kümmel concluded:

Future of Our Religious Past: Essays in Honour of Rudolf Bultmann (ed. James M. Robinson; London: SCM, and New York: Harper and Row, 1971) 84-130, then as "LOGOI SOPHON: On the Gattung of Q," in *Trajectories through Early Christianity* (ed. James M. Robinson and Helmut Koester; Philadelphia: Fortress, 1971; paperback edition, 1979) 71-113. The concluding section, "Jewish Wisdom Literature and the Gattung LOGOI SOPHON," was reprinted in *The Shape of Q: Signal Essays on the Sayings Gospel*, 51-58.

36 Roger Gryson, "A propos du Témoignage de Papias sur Matthieu: Le sens du mot λόγιον chez les Pères du second siècle," *ETL* 41 (1965) 530-47: 547. A similar view was repeatedly advocated by Josef Kürzinger, "Das Papiaszeugnis und die Erstgestalt des Matthäusevangeliums," *BZ*, n.F. 4 (1960) 19-38; "Die Aussage des Papias von Hierapolis zur literarischen Form des Markusevangeliums," *BZ*, n.F. 21 (1977) 245-64; "Papias von Hierapolis: Zu Titel und Art seines Werkes," *BZ*, n.F. 23 (1979) 172-86: 176 (where he presents the same quotation from Gryson). These essays are reprinted in his collected essays: *Papias von Hierapolis und die Evangelien des Neuen Testaments: Gesammelte Aufsätze, Neuausgabe und Übersetzung der Fragmente, kommentierte Bibliographie* (Eichstätter Materialien, Abt. Philosophie und Theologie, 4; Regensburg: Pustet, 1983): *BZ* 1960 = 1983, 9-32; *BZ* 1977 = 1983, 43-67; *BZ* 1979 = 1983, 69-87: 73.

> It is in order to leave the Papias references out of consideration – in spite of their great age – when studying the literary relationships between the Gospels.[37]

Helmut Merkel agreed that Kümmel "must be reproducing the view widespread in the historical-critical camp":[38]

> There is surely agreement today that the interpretation, advocated again and again since Schleiermacher, as referring to the sayings source, is inaccurate; after all, the fragment about Mark speaks also of λόγια κυριακά.[39]

Dieter Lührmann concurs in this view:

> The modern solution of the Synoptic Problem thus freed itself from the early church tradition....
> Nobody today argues for the existence of Q on the basis of the Papias quotation in Eusebius. For all who follow the two-document hypothesis, it results from the analysis of the Synoptic Gospels.[40]

[37] Werner Georg Kümmel, *Einleitung in das Neue Testament* (Heidelberg: Quelle & Meyer, [20]1980) 29. ET: *Introduction to the New Testament* (Nashville: Abingdon, revised edition 1973) 55.

[38] Helmut Merkel, "Die Überlieferungen der alten Kirche über das Verhältnis der Evangelien," in *The Interrelations of the Gospels* (ed. David L. Dungan; BETL 95; Leuven: University Press and Peeters; Macon, Ga.: Mercer University Press, 1990) 566-90: 566.

[39] Merkel, "Die Überlieferungen der alten Kirche über das Verhältnis der Evangelien," 571.

[40] Lührmann, "Q: Sayings of Jesus or Logia?" 101. This is in spite of the fact that Lührmann disagreed (109, n. 20) with the dissertation of his pupil, Ulrich H. J. Körtner, *Papias von Hierapolis* (FRLANT 133; Göttingen: Vandenhoeck und Ruprecht, 1983), who argued from Papias's comments on Mark that λόγια refers not specifically to sayings, but to deeds as well. Frans Neirynck, "Q: From Source to Gospel," *ETL* 71 (1995) 421-34: 422, n. 7 (reprinted in *Evangelica* III; BETL 150; Leuven: University Press and Peeters, 2001, 419-31), though agreeing to exclude Papias from the discussion, points out that Lührmann's "nobody" is a slight exaggeration, with reference to Helmut Koester, *Einführung in das Neue Testament* (Berlin and New York: Walter de Gruyter, 1980) 608; ET: *Introduction to the New Testament*. Vol. 2, *History and Literature of Early Christianity* (Hermeneia, Foundations and Facets; Philadelphia: Fortress, and Berlin and New York: de Gruyter, 1982) 172. But in the second English edition (2000), 177, Koester shifts from Q as originally in Aramaic "with different Greek translations," to "originally composed in Greek," so that Papias might only be referring to Aramaic traditions behind Q. Koester, *Ancient Christian Gospels: Their History and Development* (London: SCM, and Philadelphia, Trinity Press International, 1990) translates Papias's title usually as "sayings" (pp. 33, 189, 316), but once "Interpretations of the Oracles of the Lord" (p. 337, n. 3).

4 An Aramaic Q?

4.1 *Different Recensions of a Greek Translation from Aramaic* *Julius Wellhausen*

The misinterpretation of the Papias reference as attestation for an Aramaic Q has been largely responsible for the widespread assumption that it would be futile to seek to reconstruct a Greek, much less an Aramaic, archetype behind the Q texts of the Matthean and Lukan communities. But once Papias is no longer a factor in the study of Q, one impediment to its reconstruction is for all practical purposes eliminated.

Yet Wellhausen had argued for an Aramaic origin of Q less on the authority of Papias than on his own authority in Semitic linguistics:

> If these sayings are derived from Q, this source must have been available to both Evangelists still in Aramaic. In addition they both, to a large extent, used one and the same Greek translation, whereby admittedly the degree of their agreement in the Greek wording fluctuates for whole pericopes. Whether it suffices as an explanation for this unusual situation to say that they at times repeated an available translation each according to one's assessment and preference, at times literally, at times somewhat altered, and at times replaced by a new translation from the original, strikes me as somewhat problematic.[41]

Wellhausen then gave up his concept of the Aramaic text of Q, seeking to make more sense out of "this unusual situation" that he had quite rightly recognized as "somewhat problematic" by appeal to diverging recensions of the Greek text of Q:

> That the pieces that agree in sequence in Matthew and Luke come from one source, i.e. from Q, must be retained, although the degree of their agreement in the Greek wording fluctuates, and some variants can be satisfactorily derived only from a different reading or interpretation of an Aramaic original. This fact is admittedly unusual, and in need of explanation: It is not to be assumed that the sources lay before both Evangelists in Greek (hence the agreement) as well as in Aramaic (hence the difference). Rather they both knew them only in Greek translation. This was originally one and the same, but it then separated into recensions, which arose from subsequent corrections, in part based on the Aramaic original, much as is the case, e.g., in the Septuagint. Matthew used a different recension than did Luke.[42]

[41] Wellhausen, *Einleitung in die drei ersten Evangelien* (Berlin: Reimer, [1]1905) 68.

[42] Wellhausen, *Einleitung in die drei ersten Evangelien*, [2]1911, the second revised edition reprinted with the same pagination in *Evangelienkommentare* (Berlin and New York: de Gruyter, 1987) 59-60.

4.2 *(Mis)translations from an Oral or Written Chreia Collection Matthew Black*

The English tradition shared the prevalent assumption of an Aramaic origin of Q, including the appeal to an Aramaic Q to explain the divergences between Matthew and Luke. Representative of the first half of the century was T. W. Manson.[43] In the second half of the century it was Matthew Black who most authoritatively presented the argument for an Aramaic origin of Q, by maintaining that Q reflected (mis)translations of Aramaic. Yet it is striking, to what a large extent he had already reduced the claims for an Aramaic origin, even though at the time he was the main advocate of this view:

> This evidence of "non-translation Greek" in Q is just as important as the evidence of translation; and it points to something more than minor editorial improvements by the Evangelists. In the light of it, it is doubtful if we are justified in describing Q, without qualification, as a translation of Aramaic. Certainly it seems clear that the most the Aramaic element can *prove* is an Aramaic origin, not always translation of an Aramaic original; and *it is the Greek literary factor which has had the final word with the shaping of the Q tradition.*
>
> The evidence from the Gospels themselves for the existence of an Aramaic document is necessarily speculative.[44]

John S. Kloppenborg drew the inference, constitutive of the current efforts to reconstruct a critical text of Q, that the divergences between Matthew and Luke in the wording of Q are not to be explained in terms of (mis)translations, but rather in terms of the Evangelists' redaction:

> While Black has convincingly demonstrated the presence of Semitisms in Q, the case for a mistranslation hypothesis is insecure at best. Moreover, this type of explanation hinges on so many imponderables – such as both Matthew and Luke knowing Aramaic, and only occasionally using that knowledge – that in comparison with the redactional solution it is clearly the more cumbersome one. To be convincing a translation hypothesis would have to explain not only the occasional variation but extensive portions of the Matthew-Luke

[43] H. D. A. Major, T. W. Manson, C. J. Wright, *The Mission and Message of Jesus: An Exposition of the Gospels in the Light of Modern Research* (New York: Dutton, 1938, [6]1953 [cited here]) 18.

[44] Matthew Black, *An Aramaic Approach to the Gospels and Acts* (Oxford: Clarendon, [1]1946, [2]1954, [3]1967 [quoted here]), "Synoptic Variants from Aramaic," 186-96: 191 (introduced first among the "Supplementary Notes" in [2]1954, 270-78: 274, i.e. absent in [1]1946); and "Mistranslation and Interpretation of Aramaic," 197-243, including "The Source Q," 203-08.

> disagreements. Moreover, it would have to show that the variations cannot be accounted for by the more proximate explanation, namely, redactional modification. In the absence of such demonstrations, we are obligated to conclude that while parts of Q betray a Semitizing Greek style, and possibly an origin in an Aramaic-speaking milieu, there is no convincing proof of a literary formulation in Aramaic.[45]

To this Black in turn responded, conceding that a written Aramaic source even for parts of Q may not be demonstrable:

> That this complicated issue is not so easily disposed of, I have argued in a recent article; Papias may well be referring to a "Hebrew", i.e. Aramaic Chreiae (Sayings, etc.) collection of which Q is the Greek equivalent and for which it is the main source....
>
> What I sought to do was to indicate those *parts* of Q which were originally composed in Aramaic; I would now add, parts transmitted *either* orally *or* in written form, and that this was the Aramaic *Vorlage* of Q. We may not be able to prove that there was an Aramaic Chreiae collection identical with parts of Q, but we cannot, as Kloppenborg does, reject the hypothesis altogether.[46]

Kloppenborg responded, with the conclusion:

> The thesis of an Aramaic original of Q is extraordinarily weak. The origin of the speculation, Papias's statement about Matthew, is legendary at best. The linguistic data employed to demonstrate an Aramaic origin is scant and what little there is admits of more economical explanations that avoid having to posit yet another document. Finally, the dazzlingly improbable logistics needed to account for Matthew's *and* Luke's occasional revision of their Greek Q by recourse to a *written* Aramaic version that *both* had (and could read!) reduce the likelihood of demonstrating an Aramaic Q to near zero.[47]

The trend away from interpreting Papias's reference to "Hebrew" λόγια as a reference to Jesus' λόγοι in Q and the dwindling number of (mis)translations from a postulated written Aramaic Q to which one could appeal to explain divergences of wording between Matthew and Luke, as well as Q's use of the LXX,[48] have led to the general abandonment of the

[45] John S. Kloppenborg, *The Formation of Q: Trajectories in Ancient Wisdom Collections* (Studies in Antiquity and Christianity; Philadelphia: Fortress, 1987; reprint, Trinity Press International, 2000), "The Original Language of Q," 51-64: 59.

[46] Matthew Black, "The Aramaic Dimension in Q with Notes on Luke 17.22 Matthew 24.26 (Luke 17.23)," *JSNT* 40 (1990) 33-41: 33-34, 36. He refers to his article, "The Use of Rhetorical Terminology in Papias on Mark and Matthew," *JSNT* 37 (1989) 31-41.

[47] Kloppenborg Verbin, *Excavating Q*, "The Language of Q," 72-80: 80.

[48] Siegfried Schulz, *Q: Die Spruchquelle der Evangelisten* (Zürich: Theologischer Verlag, 1972), "Die Septuaginta-Benutzung," 27-28, 49-50. For a critical review of Schulz' book see Paul Hoffmann, *BZ* 19 (1975) 104-15, and with regard to the exaggerated importance of the LXX, 108-9.

conjecture that Q was originally in Aramaic and then translated differently into Greek. Rather Q is a Greek text whose Greek archetype, lying behind both Matthew and Luke, one might well try to reconstruct.

5 Matthew Without Q: Jesus the Apocalypticist

5.1 *Matt 10 as Historical in its Smallest Detail* *Albert Schweitzer*

The logical consequence of rejecting the existence of Q was dramatically illustrated by Albert Schweitzer, who considered the two-document hypothesis, though carried through most successfully by his own professor at Strassburg, Heinrich Julius Holtzmann, to be only an evasive tactic to avoid the inevitable but painful conclusion that Jesus was a fanatic apocalypticist. Instead, Schweitzer preferred Ferdinand Christian Baur's prioritizing of Matthew:

> In its early days historical research was spared having to accept the full weight of the problem by accepting Mark as the original Gospel, under the influence of Christian Hermann Weisse's *Die Evangelienfrage* (1856) and Heinrich Julius Holtzmann's *Die synoptischen Evangelien* (1863), instead of Matthew, as held by Ferdinand Christian Baur (1792-1860) and the Tübingen school. The preference for this earlier Gospel prevented research from giving the significant material that Matthew offers above and beyond that of Mark its full importance. And it is precisely these discourses and narratives which demonstrate the dependence of Jesus upon the late-Jewish world of eschatological ideas – particularly the Sermon on the Mount (Matt. 5-7), the great discourse at the sending out of the disciples (Matt. 10), John the Baptist's question and Jesus' reply (Matt. 11), and the discourse on the coming of the Son of man and his judgment (Matt. 25)....
>
> The decisive point in the quest of the historical Jesus is not which of the two oldest Gospels could be a little older than the other. That, moreover, is a literary question which it is scarcely possible to answer. The historical problem of the life of Jesus cannot be recognized, much less solved, from the fragmentary record of Mark. The differing narratives of the two oldest Gospels are equally valuable, but Matthew's fullness gives it greater importance, and Baur and his school rightly gave it preference.[49]

[49] Albert Schweitzer, *Von Reimarus zu Wrede: Eine Geschichte der Leben-Jesu-Forschung* (Tübingen: Mohr-Siebeck, 1906). The second edition, entitled only *Die Geschichte der Leben-Jesu-Forschung* (Tübingen: Mohr-Siebeck, 1913), is considerably revised, especially in the concluding sections under discussion here. The references are to the first edition, with the pagination in the second edition, when parallel

Though Schweitzer was guarded in his statements, the position that he took on the sources only makes sense if he considered the canonical Gospel of Matthew to be the product of an eye-witness, which amounts to treating it as a definitive work of the apostle Matthew, the prevalent pre-critical view ever since Papias. He simply dismissed as absurd efforts to dismantle into its sources Matthew's Mission Instructions, whose detailed historicity was decisive for his own interpretation of Jesus' public ministry. Whereas one normally recognized, then as now, that in Matt 10 material from the Markan apocalypse had been interpolated into the Mission Instructions of Mark and Q, which were also conflated both with each other and with other Q and special Matthean material, Schweitzer maintained:

> Thus this discourse [Matt 10] is historical as a whole and down to the smallest detail precisely because, according to the view of modern theology, it must be judged unhistorical....
>
> That being so, we may judge with what right modern theology dismisses the great Matthean discourses out of hand as mere "composite discourses." Just let anyone try to show how the Evangelist, when he was racking his brains over the task of making a "discourse at the sending out of the disciples," half piecing it together out of sayings in the tradition and "community theology" and half inventing it, lit on the curious idea of making Jesus speak entirely of inopportune and unpractical matters, and of then going on to provide the evidence that they never happened.[50]

5.2 *The Apocalyptic Life of Jesus*
Albert Schweitzer

Schweitzer proposed going beyond Johannes Weiss' discovery of the eschatological nature of Jesus' preaching about the kingdom,[51] by carrying

(though, even then, copy-edited to produce a smoother text), given in parentheses, both according to [6]1951 and to the republication as Siebenstern-Taschenbuch 77/78, Munich, 1966. A retrospective "Vorrede," dated 1950, beginning with [6]1951, is cited, here, 1951, vi, xii and 1966, 30, 36. ET: *The Quest of the Historical Jesus: A Critical Study of Its Progress from Reimarus to Wrede* (New York: Macmillan, 1910, paperback edition 1961, reprint 1968), did not include this "Preface" of 1950. But it is present in the English translation of the second edition, *The Quest of the Historical Jesus: First Complete Edition* (ed. John Bowden; London: SCM, and Minneapolis, Minn.: Fortress, 2000) xxxv-xlv: xxxvi, xl. (The translation is edited to render it more literal, when needed to avoid misunderstanding.)

[50] Schweitzer, *Von Reimarus zu Wrede*, 360 (*Die Geschichte der Leben-Jesu-Forschung*, 1951, 410 and 1966, 420). ET: *The Quest of the Historical Jesus*, [1]1910, 363, [2]2000, 330-31.

[51] Weiss, *Die Predigt Jesu vom Reiche Gottes*. ET: *Jesus' Proclamation of the Kingdom of God*.

this eschatological interpretation consistently through all of Jesus' "life and work" (literally: "conduct and action") down to the very end of the public ministry:

> Johannes Weiss shows the thoroughly eschatological character of Jesus' preaching about the kingdom of God. My contribution is to find the eschatological clue, not only to his preaching, but also to his life and work.[52]

This led to Schweitzer's own "life of Jesus," with which his *Quest of the Historical Jesus* concluded. His point of departure is Jesus' fascination with parables of harvest:

> If this genuinely "historical" interpretation of the mystery of the kingdom of God is correct, Jesus must have expected the coming of the kingdom at harvest time. And that is just what he did expect. That in fact is why he sends his disciples out. They are to make known in Israel, as speedily as may be, what is about to happen.[53]

Jesus intended the Mission of the Twelve as his final act before the end:

> He tells them in plain words (Matt. 10. 23), that he does not expect to see them back in the present age. The parousia of the Son of man, which is logically and temporally identical with the dawn of the kingdom, will take place before they have completed a hasty journey through the cities of Israel to announce it.[54]

Schweitzer described "the significance of the sending forth of the disciples and the discourse which Jesus uttered upon that occasion" as follows:

> Jesus' purpose is to set in motion the eschatological development of history, to let loose the final woes, the confusion and strife, from which shall issue the Parousia, and so to introduce the supra-mundane phase of the eschatological drama.[55]

[52] Schweitzer, *Die Geschichte der Leben-Jesu-Forschung,* "Vorrede zur sechsten Auflage," 1951, viii and 1966, 32. ET: *The Quest of the Historical Jesus*, ^{2}2000, xxxvii.

[53] Schweitzer, *Von Reimarus zu Wrede*, 355 (*Die Geschichte der Leben-Jesu-Forschung*, 1951, 405 and 1966, 415). ET: *The Quest of the Historical Jesus*, ^{1}1910, 358 and ^{2}2000, 326.

[54] Schweitzer, *Von Reimarus zu Wrede*, 355 (*Die Geschichte der Leben-Jesu-Forschung*, 1951, 405 and 1966, 416). ET: *The Quest of the Historical Jesus*, ^{1}1910, 358-59 and ^{2}2000, 327.

[55] Schweitzer, *Von Reimarus zu Wrede*, 367. ET: *The Quest of the Historical Jesus*, ^{1}1910, 371. (The quotation is absent from the second and following editions.)

He was convinced that "at the time of their mission," Jesus "did not expect them to return before the Parousia."[56] But that is in fact just what happened:

> There followed neither the sufferings, nor the outpouring of the Spirit, nor the parousia of the Son of man. The disciples returned safe and sound and full of a proud satisfaction (Mark 6.30).[57]

Schweitzer drew the inevitable consequence:

> The actual history disavowed the dogmatic history on which the action of Jesus had been based. An event of supernatural history which had to take place, and to take place at that particular point of time, failed to come about. That was for Jesus, who lived wholly in the dogmatic history, the first "historical" occurrence, the central event which closed the former period of his activity and gave the coming period a new forward orientation.[58]

The failure of the apocalyptic end to come before the end of the mission must have been a terrible letdown for Jesus. He felt compelled to change his strategy:

> This change was due to the non-fulfillment of the promises made in the discourse at the sending forth of the Twelve. He had thought then that he was letting loose the final tribulation and so compelling the coming of the kingdom. But the cataclysm had not occurred. He still expected it after the return of the disciples....
>
> On leaving Galilee he abandoned the hope that the final tribulation would begin of itself. If it delayed, that meant that there was still something to be done, and that yet another of the violent had to lay violent hands upon the kingdom of God. The repentance movement had not been sufficient. When, in accordance with his commission, by sending forth the disciples with their message he hurled the firebrand which was to have kindled the fiery trials, the flame went out.[59]

56 Schweitzer, *Von Reimarus zu Wrede*, 383. ET: *The Quest of the Historical Jesus*, [1]1910, 386. (The quotation is absent from the second and following editions.)

57 Schweitzer, *Von Reimarus zu Wrede*, 360 (*Die Geschichte der Leben-Jesu-Forschung*, 1951, 411 and 1966, 421). ET: *The Quest of the Historical Jesus*, [1]1910, 364 and [2]2000, 331.

58 Schweitzer, *Von Reimarus zu Wrede*, 355 (*Die Geschichte der Leben-Jesu-Forschung*, 1951, 406 and 1966, 416). ET: *The Quest of the Historical Jesus*, [1]1910, 359 and [2]2000, 327.

59 Schweitzer, *Von Reimarus zu Wrede*, 385-86 (*Die Geschichte der Leben-Jesu-Forschung*, 1951, 434-35 and 1966, 442). ET: *The Quest of the Historical Jesus*, [1]1910, 389 and [2]2000, 347-48.

So Jesus determined to go to Jerusalem for Passover, in order to provoke there his own martyrdom as an alternate way to compel God to bring in the end:

> … his death must at last compel the coming of the kingdom.…
> For now Jesus identifies his natural condemnation and execution with the predicted pre-messianic tribulations. This imperious forcing of eschatology into history is also its destruction; at the same time its assertion and abandonment.[60]

This heroic resolve ended in a second, even more painful encounter with actual history, leading to his last anguished cry: "My God, my God, why have you abandoned me?"

> The Baptist appears, and cries: "Repent, for the Kingdom of Heaven is at hand." Soon after that comes Jesus, and in the knowledge that He is the coming Son of Man lays hold of the wheel of the world to set it moving on that last revolution which is to bring all ordinary history to a close. It refuses to turn, and He throws Himself upon it. Then it does turn; and crushes Him. Instead of bringing in the eschatological conditions, He has destroyed them. The wheel rolls onward, and the mangled body of the one immeasurably great Man, who was strong enough to think of Himself as the spiritual ruler of mankind and to bend history to His purpose, is hanging upon it still. That is His victory and His reign.[61]

Subsequent scholarship has shied away from Schweitzer's all-too-apocalyptic public ministry of Jesus. Such a picture of a deluded fanatic is hardly appetizing. Instead, it has preferred Weiss' limitation to the eschatological preaching of Jesus, exemplified perhaps most clearly in Rudolf Bultmann's *Jesus and the Word*.[62] But Schweitzer was in a sense correct, that such an apocalyptic message must have meant something in Jesus' actual practice, his "life and work."

[60] Schweitzer, *Von Reimarus zu Wrede*, 387-88 (*Die Geschichte der Leben-Jesu-Forschung*, 1951, 435, 437 and 1966, 443-44). ET: *The Quest of the Historical Jesus*, [1]1910, 390-91 and [2]2000, 348-49.

[61] Schweitzer, *Von Reimarus zu Wrede*, 367. ET: *The Quest of the Historical Jesus*, [1]1910, 370-71. This is present only in the first edition.

[62] Rudolf Bultmann, *Jesus* (Die Unsterblichen: Die geistigen Heroen der Menschheit in ihrem Leben und Wirken mit zahlreichen Illustrationen, 1; Berlin: Deutsche Bibliothek, n. d. [1926]; Tübingen: Mohr-Siebeck, [2]1929, with many subsequent reprints); ET: *Jesus and the Word* (New York: Scribner's Sons, 1934). In the "Translators' Preface to the New Edition" of 1958, Louise Pettibone Smith and Erminie Huntress Lantero explain the enlarged title:

> It was felt by both publishers and translators that the title, *Jesus and the Word*, would convey a more definite idea of the content and viewpoint of the book than the original title, *Jesus*. This change was made with the approval of the author.

Yet Schweitzer's position was untenable for ongoing critical scholarship, especially because his methodological presuppositions, such as the non-existence of Q, were already out of date. His attempt at a life of Jesus based on an eye-witness account by Matthew only serves to illustrate the price one pays for such a reversion from critical scholarship to a more traditional view of the sources, at least if one were to operate with the remorseless consistency of a genius such as Schweitzer.

6 The Essence of Christianity as Q or the Kerygma

6.1 *The Gospel of Jesus or the Apostolic Gospel* *Adolf Harnack vs. Julius Wellhausen*

Once William Wrede had removed Mark from the status of a historically accurate report on which the quest of the historical Jesus could confidently build,[63] it was Q to which critical scholarship had naturally turned. For it was upon the sayings of Jesus that Adolf Harnack had built his "essence of Christianity":

> If, however, we take a general view of Jesus' teaching, we shall see that it may be grouped under three heads. They are each of such a nature as to contain the whole, and hence it can be exhibited in its entirety under any one of them.
>
> *Firstly, the kingdom of God and its coming.*
> *Secondly, God the Father and the infinite value of the human soul.*
> *Thirdly, the higher righteousness and the commandment of love.*[64]
>
> But the fact that the whole of Jesus' message may be reduced to these two heads – God as the Father, and the human soul so ennobled that it

[63] William Wrede, *Das Messiasgeheimnis in den Evangelien* (Göttingen: Vandenhoeck & Ruprecht, 1901). ET: *The Messianic Secret* (Cambridge and London: Clarke, 1971).

[64] Adolf Harnack, *Das Wesen des Christentums: 16 Vorlesungen vor Studierenden aller Fakultäten im Wintersemester 1899/1900 an der Universität Berlin* (Leipzig: Hinrichs'-sche Buchhandlung, 1900) 33. A student, Walther Becker, took down the lectures in shorthand, which Harnack edited for publication. It was an immediate best-seller: [3]1900 (11th to 15th thousand), 45th to 50th thousand 1903, 56th to 60th thousand 1908, 70th thousand 1925; more recent reprints: Adolf Harnack, *Das Wesen des Christentums: Neuauflage zum fünfzigsten Jahrestag des ersten Erscheinens mit einem Geleitwort von Rudolf Bultmann* (Stuttgart: Klotz, 1950); Adolf von Harnack, *Das Wesen des Christentums: Mit einem Geleitwort von Wolfgang Trillhaas* (Gütersloher Taschenbücher and Siebenstern 227; Gütersloh: Gütersloher Verlagshaus Mohn, 1985); Adolf Harnack, *Das Wesen des Christentums: Herausgegeben und kommentiert von Trutz Rendtorff* (Gütersloh: Kaiser and Gütersloher Verlagshaus, 1999) 33 (1900), 40 (1985), and 87 (1999). ET: *What Is Christianity* (London, Edinburgh, Oxford: Williams and Norgate, and New York: Putnam, 1901, 3rd rev. ed. [quoted here] 1904) 52.

> can and does unite with Him – shows us that the Gospel is in no wise a positive religion like the rest; that it contains no statutory or particularistic elements; *that it is, therefore, religion itself.*[65]

But Wellhausen understood Q much more in analogy to Wrede's Mark. For, in his view, Q was later than Mark, hence hardly more reliable:

> What is most important for the comparison is what appears to be only a superficial difference: the source [Q], which in Mark is narrowly contained, in Matthew and Luke trickles through on all sides. This is enough to prove the priority of Mark, also prior to Q.[66]

Harnack's reconstruction of Q complete with commentary was in large measure intended as a refutation of Wellhausen:

> I, on the contrary, believe that I can show in the following pages that Wellhausen in his characteristic of Q has unconsciously allowed himself to be influenced by the tendencies of St. Matthew and St. Luke, that he has attributed to Q what belongs to these gospels, and that in not a few passages he has preferred St. Mark on insufficient grounds. The conclusions at which I have arrived stand therefore in strong opposition to the results of his criticism.[67]

Yet he nonetheless retained the assumption of a hypothetical Aramaic origin. For this was involved in ascribing apostolic Matthean authorship to Q, which in turn justified Harnack in according ultimate authority to Q:

> Seeing that our St. Matthew cannot have been composed by an Apostle, and that the tradition: Ματθαῖος Ἑβραΐδι διαλέκτῳ τὰ λόγια συνετάξατο ["Matthew collected in the Hebrew=Aramaic language the sayings/oracles"], already dates from about A. D. 100, there is a strong balance of probability that Q is a work of St. Matthew; but more cannot be said.... But whoever the author, or rather the redactor, of Q may have been, he was a man deserving of the highest respect. To his reverence and faithfulness, to his simple-minded common-sense, we owe this priceless compilation of the sayings of Jesus. ...
>
> On the one hand St. Mark – wherein page by page the student is reduced to despair by the inconsistencies, the discrepancies, and the incredibilities of the narrative – and yet without this gospel we should be deprived of every thread of consistent and concrete historical information concerning the life of Jesus; and on the other hand, this compilation of sayings, which alone affords us a really exact and profound conception of the teaching of Jesus, and is free from bias, apologetic or otherwise, and yet gives us no history. ...

[65] Harnack, *Das Wesen des Christentums*, 41 (1900), 47 (1985), and 96 (1999). ET: *What Is Christianity*, 65.

[66] Wellhausen, *Einleitung in die drei ersten Evangelien*, [1]1905: 84, n. 1; [2]1911: 75, n. 2.

[67] Harnack, *Sprüche und Reden Jesu*, 136. ET: *The Sayings of Jesus*, 194.

> Which is the more valuable? Eighteen centuries of Christianity have answered this question, and their answer is true. *The portrait of Jesus as given in the sayings of Q has remained in the foreground. … The collection of sayings and St. Mark must remain in power, but the former takes precedence.* Above all, the tendency to exaggerate the apocalyptic and eschatological element in our Lord's message, and to subordinate to this the purely religious and ethical elements, will ever find its refutation in Q. This source is the authority for that which formed the central theme of the message of our Lord – that is, the revelation of the knowledge of God, and the moral call to repent and to believe, to renounce the world and to gain heaven – this and nothing else.[68]

Wellhausen then published in 1911 a second edition in which he repeated, indeed strengthened, his earlier position.[69]

Between the two World Wars, the form critics Rudolf Bultmann[70] and Martin Dibelius[71] both assumed the existence of Q, though their point of departure was more nearly that of Wellhausen than that of Harnack. For it was Wellhausen[72] who had anticipated the new kerygmatic orientation:

68 Harnack, *Sprüche und Reden Jesu*, 172-73. ET: *The Sayings of Jesus*, 248-51.

69 Wellhausen, *Einleitung in die drei ersten Evangelien*, [2]1911, 170-76: In an appended "Corrolarium" he refuted the argument of Kirsopp Lake, "The Date of Q," that Q was written no later than 50 C. E.

70 Rudolf Bultmann's only essay on Q, written before World War I, only two years after Wellhausen's second edition, built explicitly on him rather than on Harnack: "Was lässt die Spruchquelle über die Urgemeinde erkennen?" *Oldenburgisches Kirchenblatt* 19 (1913) 35-37, 41-44: 35. ET: "What the Sayings Source Reveals about the Early Church," *The Shape of Q: Signal Essays on the Sayings Gospel* (ed. John S. Kloppenborg; Minneapolis: Fortress, 1994) 23-34: 23, n. 1:

> The following explication presupposes a definite solution to the Synoptic problem, which obviously I cannot pursue in more detail here. I refer the reader to B. Weiss 1908; Jülicher 1904; and Wellhausen 1905, 1911.

Bultmann, *Jesus*, 18 (reprint 1951, 16): "The translation of the Gospel texts often follows that of J. Wellhausen."

71 Martin Dibelius, *Die Formgeschichte des Evangeliums* (Tübingen: Mohr-Siebeck, 1919, revised [2]1933, [5]1966 ed. Günther Bornkamm) 236, n. 1; ET: *From Tradition to Gospel*, tr. Bertram Lee Woolf (New York: Scribners, n.d.), 235, n. 1, appeals to Wellhausen, *Einleitung in die drei ersten Evangelien*, [1]1905, 66-67, for his own skepticism (quoted below, p. 40) regarding Q.

72 Martin Hengel, in his "Einleitung" to *Evangelienkommentare*, vi-vii:

> He ends with a harsh criticism of the nineteenth century's research into the life of Jesus, which goes much beyond that of A. Schweitzer, with whom he debates critically, and which in many regards has contact with Martin Kähler and the early dialectic theology of K. Barth and R. Bultmann. In the critical research on the Gospels between the two world wars which he thereby fructified, the effect of the New Testament scholar Wellhausen is most readily visible.

> It is as the crucified, resurrected and returning one that Jesus is the Christian Messiah, not as religious teacher. The apostolic gospel, which preaches faith in the Christ, is the real one, and not the gospel of Jesus which prescribes to the church its moral. ... And the expression purportedly committed by Harnack, "not the Son, but only the Father belongs in the Gospel," is basically false, if it is intended to claim a fact and not merely expresses a postulate.[73]

Harnack had indeed said: "*The Gospel, as Jesus proclaimed it, has to do with the Father only and not with the Son.*"[74] Wellhausen, apparently quoting from hearsay, left out the decisive "*as Jesus proclaimed it.*"[75] The "Gospel" that Wellhausen had in view was of course that of the church, i.e. the kerygma, which became more nearly what one could refer to as "the essence of Christianity" down through history, e.g. in the form of the *Apostolicum* and subsequent creeds, whereas Jesus' message was largely overlooked, though occasionally rediscovered, as by Francis of Assisi.

6.2 *The Heart of the Gospel or of the Law Adolf von Harnack vs. Karl Barth*

The debate between Wellhausen and Harnack was to a remarkable extent repeated in 1923 in a debate between von Harnack and Karl Barth. Here it is quite clear that dialectic theology created a theological climate in which Wellhausen's position regarding the relative unimportance, not to say illegitimacy, of Q would have the ascendancy.[76]

[73] Wellhausen, *Einleitung in die drei ersten Evangelien*, [2]1911, 153, also quoted by Hengel in his "Einleitung," *Evangelienkommentare*, vii. The quotation is not in the first edition at all.

[74] Harnack, *Das Wesen des Christentums*, 91 (1900), 90 (1985), and 154 (1999). ET: *What Is Christianity*, 147.

[75] Harnack, *Das Wesen des Christentums*, in the endnotes added to the 1908 edition (56th to 60th thousand), drew attention to this omission distorting his position (on p. 183 of the 1950 edition and p. 154-55, n. 22, of the 1999 edition).

[76] This exchange was published in *Die christliche Welt*, 1923, as follows: Harnack: "Fünfzehn Fragen an die Verächter der wissenschaftlichen Theologie unter den Theologen," 6-8; Barth: "Fünfzehn Antworten an Herrn Professor von Harnack," 89-91; Harnack: "Offener Brief an Herrn Professor K. Barth," 142-44; "Antwort auf Herrn Professor von Harnacks offenen Brief," 244-52; and Harnack: "Nachwort zu meinem offenen Brief an Herrn Professor Karl Barth," 305-6. This debate has been republished in Barth's *Gesammelte Vorträge*, vol. 3: *Theologische Fragen und Antworten* (Zollikon: Evangelischer Verlag, 1957) 7-31: 7-9, 9-13, 13-17, 18-30, 30-31. ET in *The Beginnings of Dialectic Theology*, Vol. 1 (ed. James M. Robinson; Richmond, Va.: John Knox, 1968): Harnack: "Fifteen Questions to Those Among the Theologians Who

Harnack spoke of "the close connection, even equating, of love for God and love for one's neighbor which constitutes the heart of the gospel,"[77] to which Barth replied: "Does anything show more clearly than this 'heart' (not of the gospel, but of the law), that God does not make alive unless he first slays?"[78] Thus the central sayings of Jesus (Mark 12:28-34 parr.) that Harnack hailed as "gospel" were for Barth "law," over against which he appealed to the "gospel" of God granting life only after death, i.e. in a dialectic relation with death. The implication of the history-of-religions classification of Jesus as Jew by Wellhausen[79] and Bultmann[80] was heard theologically as the dialectic of law and gospel, in which sense Q is by definition not gospel, but law.

Whereas Q refers to its sayings as "the poor are evangelized" (Q 7:22), Paul makes clear that any other gospel than his kerygma, even if it come from an angel, is anathema (Gal 1:8-9). This tension persists down to the present, as the theological background of the discussion as to whether Sayings Gospels such as Q and the *Gospel of Thomas* should be called Gospels at all.[81]

Are Contemptuous of the Scientific Theology," 165-66; Barth: "Fifteen Answers to Professor von Harnack," 167-70; Harnack: "An Open Letter to Professor Karl Barth," 171-74; Barth: "An Answer to Professor von Harnack's Open Letter," 175-85; and Harnack: "Postscript to My Open Letter to Professor Karl Barth," 186-87.

77 Harnack, "Fünfzehn Fragen," 8. ET: "Fifteen Questions," 165.

78 Barth, "Fünfzehn Antworten," 11. ET: "Fifteen Answers," 168.

79 Julius Wellhausen, *Einleitung in die drei ersten Evangelien*, [1]1905, 113, [2]1911, 102: "Jesus was no Christian, but rather a Jew."

80 Rudolf Bultmann, "Das Verhältnis der urchristlichen Christusbotschaft zum historischen Jesus," SHAW.PH, Jg. 1960, Abh. 3 (Heidelberg: Winter, 1960, [3]1962) 8. ET: "The Primitive Christian Kerygma and the Historical Jesus," in *The Historical Jesus and the Kerygmatic Christ* (ed. Carl E. Braaten and Roy A. Harrisville; Nashville: Abingdon, 1964) 15-42: 19:

> I am further attacked because in my book *Primitive Christianity* I have not described Jesus' preaching in the chapter on 'Primitive Christianity,' but rather in the chapter on 'Judaism,' and hence have conceived of Jesus as a Jew. Similarly, the objection has been raised that in my *Theology of the New Testament* I have stated that Jesus' preaching belongs to the presuppositions of New Testament theology. Over against the reproach that I conceive of Jesus as a Jew and assign him to the sphere of Judaism I must first of all simply ask: Was Jesus – the historical Jesus! – a Christian? Certainly not, if Christian faith is faith in him as the Christ. And even if he should have known that he was the Christ ("Messiah") and should actually have demanded faith in himself as the Christ, then he would still not have been a Christian and ought not to be described as the subject of Christian faith, though he is nevertheless its object.

81 For the resultant discussion about the legitimacy of calling Q a "Sayings Gospel," see Frans Neirynck, "Q: From Source to Gospel," *ETL* 71 (1995) 421-34; reprinted in *Evangelica* III, 419-31. Kloppenborg Verbin, *Excavating Q*, "Q as a 'Gospel': What's in a Name," 398-408.

7 Form Criticism

7.1 *Q as a Stratum*
Martin Dibelius

In other regards as well, the form critics played down the importance of Q. For the focus of attention had shifted to the oral transmission of traditions under the influence of their social settings, rather than remaining on written sources incorporated in later texts. Therefore whether Q was a single written Greek document, conceivably subject to reconstruction in a critical edition, was not relevant.

Dibelius abandoned the hypothetical Aramaic Q behind the Greek Q, but nonetheless was very skeptical about Q being a tangible Greek document:

> The text used by Matthew and Luke was Greek, otherwise there would have been no such agreement. All the genuine sayings of Jesus were once translated. But it seems possible to conceive this process in such a way that even in bilingual Churches it was handed on in Greek, and that these Greek sayings were brought together in a Greek-speaking region. This is much more probable than the other case, that the Aramaic words were first assembled and then translated as a connected writing. For in this case we shall have to assume even for the earliest Christian generation a certain literary activity – and that is out of the question. …
>
> But the greatest doubts arise when we consider the literary category of Q, for we have not the slightest idea whether and in what way this writing, deduced piecemeal, can have constituted a book. … In these, as in other questions, we must be careful not to speak with too great self-confidence of Q as a definitely ascertained entity.
>
> As long as we leave this fact out of sight we run the danger of reckoning with as much certainty upon the source which we do not know as upon Mark which we can see in front of us. We tend to forget that we are dealing with a hypothetical entity. …
>
> By such a systematic self-limitation, we abandon the possibility of reconstructing the source in its fullness. For even in the case of sections which can be reconstructed, we must earnestly ask the question whether they all really belonged to the same "writing." This may appear doubtful and has, in fact, been doubted. The present position of research into the source Q warrants our speaking rather of a stratum than of a document. We clearly recognize the effort of the churches to gather together words of Jesus in the manner of Q, but we do not know whether the result of these efforts was one or more books or indeed any books at all.[82]

[82] Dibelius, *Die Formgeschichte des Evangeliums*, 234-36. ET: *From Tradition to Gospel*, 233-35. (The misleading translation of "einmal" as "at the same time" is here corrected to "once.")

The nature of this "stratum" is for Dibelius the paraenesis prevalent in the first generation of Christianity, prior to a christological rearrangement of the sayings into a more biographical cast:

> Hence we can say that at an early date, viz. already in the time of Paul, words of Jesus had been collected for hortatory purposes. …
>
> In the whole of the Q material recognizable by us there is no reference to the story of the Passion. If the tendency of our source was toward narrative, we ought surely to expect a Passion story. … Thus the Q material which we have received shows in its essential content no narrative inference. We must infer as this source little else than speeches, mostly indeed isolated, i.e. sayings without context. …
>
> Thus the total content of the groups of material which we deal with in Q still shows clearly the original tendency of such collections. Their purpose is not to deal with the life of Jesus, but to give His words in order that they may be followed and in order that they may instruct.[83]

7.2 *Q as a Variously Translated Document*
Rudolf Bultmann

Bultmann retained Wellhausen's hypothesis of an Aramaic Q, though he gave up the idea of a single Greek translation:

> We have to conclude that Q, which originally appeared in an Aramaic version, was variously translated into Greek, because it obviously was known to Matthew and Luke in different versions.[84]

Bultmann, for his part, in distinction from Dibelius, apparently conceived of Q as more than a stratum, but rather as a single document with ascertainable beginning and conclusion:

> Q … is prefaced by the eschatological preaching of John the Baptist; the beatitudes, full of eschatological consciousness, follow; the close is constituted by sayings dealing with the parousia.[85]

[83] Dibelius, *Die Formgeschichte des Evangeliums,* 244-45. ET: *From Tradition to Gospel*, 243-45.

[84] Bultmann, *Die Geschichte der synoptischen Tradition* (FRLANT.NF 12; 1921, [2]1931 revised), 354. ET: *The History of the Synoptic Tradition* (New York and Evanston: Harper and Row, 1963, [2]1968 [the heavily corrected translation of the second edition is quoted here]) 328. In a footnote Bultmann refers not only to Wellhausen, *Einleitung in die drei ersten Evangelien*, [2]1911, 59-60, but, in first place, to Adolf Jülicher, *Einleitung in das Neue Testament* (ed. Erich Fascher; Tübingen: Mohr-Siebeck, [7]1904), 340-41. The relevance of the dependence on Jülicher and Fascher is made evident by Günther Bornkamm, "Evangelien, synoptische," *RGG*, 3rd ed., 2 (1958), 753-66: 755-56, 758-60: 756.

[85] Rudolf Bultmann, *Theologie des Neuen Testaments* (Tübingen: Mohr-Siebeck, 1. Lieferung 1948, 43; [1]1958, [5]1965, 44). ET: *Theology of the New Testament* (New York: Scribners, 2 volumes, 1951, 1955), 1. 42.

In either case, the result is that during the period of form criticism there was no single Greek archetype that one might hope to reconstruct. For since Dibelius thought Q might be actually an indeterminate number of separate texts,[86] rather than a single text, and hence better conceived of as a stratum than as a written text, and Bultmann considered Q to be an Aramaic text variously translated into Greek, the possibility of reconstructing a critical text of Q seemed precluded.

8 Q in Lukan Sequence

8.1 *The Standard Assumption of Lukan Sequence* *Burnett Hillman Streeter and T. W. Manson*

The English tradition, on the other hand, was largely uninvolved in form criticism at the time, and hence continued by and large its high level of assurance as to the existence of a reliable Q document, the position which Hawkins had reached by the turn of the century.[87] For this approach was carried forward by Burnett Hillman Streeter,[88] and reached its standard form and widest dissemination in T. W. Manson's "The Sayings of Jesus," which included a commentary on Q.[89] Yet Manson's commentary is not based on a critical text of Q, but only on the text of Matthew and Luke printed in parallel columns, somewhere behind which Q must lurk.

With regard to the sequence of Q, there was high confidence that the order of Luke was that of Q. For there had been a traditional lack of confidence in Matthew's sequence, based on the then-current perception of

[86] This conjecture was carried through by W. L. Knox, *The Sources of the Synoptic Gospels*, volume 2, *St. Luke and St. Matthew* (Cambridge: Cambridge University Press, 1957).

[87] Hawkins, *Horae Synopticae* ([1]1899, [2]1909) and "Probabilities as to the So-called Double Tradition of St. Matthew and St. Luke" (1911).

[88] Burnett Hillman Streeter, "On the Original Order of Q," and "The Original Extent of Q," both in *Studies in the Synoptic Problem*, 141-64, 185-208; and *The Four Gospels* (London: Macmillan, 1924, reprint 1951).

[89] Major, Manson, and Wright, *The Mission and Message of Jesus*. Manson's "The Sayings of Jesus" is Book II, 301-639: "3. The Sources: (a) The Document Q," 307-12; "Text and Commentary: I. – The Document Q," 331-440. Manson's contribution to the volume was published as a separate volume, *The Sayings of Jesus as recorded in the Gospels according to St. Matthew and St. Luke arranged with introduction and commentary* (London: SCM, 1949; reprint 1971): "3. The Sources: (a) The Document Q," 15-21; "Text and Commentary: I. – The Document Q," 39-148.

[90] This view of the sequence was the working hypothesis and conclusion of the basic study by Streeter, "On the Original Order of Q," 145-47.

Matthew's use of Mark.[90] Quite apart from dated presuppositions, such as was reflected in describing Mark as relating events "in their historical sequence" and Q being "a loose collection of sayings," the precedent of Matthew's use of Mark ("entirely rearranged the order of practically every section in the first six chapters of Mark"), on which the working hypothesis was based, is inadequately presented. For Matt 12-28 follows Markan order with hardly any exceptions, at least as faithfully as does Luke. It is Matt 3-11 which does not (hence the Matthean rearrangement of Mark 1-6). For in this first major redactional unit within Matthew, his attention is not directed to Mark so much as to Q, into which Markan material (as well as much subsequent Q material, cf. Matt 5-7; 10) is imbedded when useful to carry forward Q's agenda.[91]

8.2 *The "Proof" of Lukan Sequence*
Vincent Taylor

Vincent Taylor carried the argument for Lukan order one step further, by providing what he considered compelling new evidence that it was that of Q, with the objective of putting the Q hypothesis on a sound foundation.[92] He argued that Matthew, when composing his five discourses (and indeed when composing the "Rest of Matthew"), each time went through Q in the Q sequence, presumably to extract sayings that fitted the topic of the given discourse (though in many cases the relation to a unifying "topic" is hard to detect). For, as Taylor's thesis ran, the Q material in each discourse is used in the Lukan sequence, which thus is validated as the Q sequence.

Yet the overwhelming quantity of exceptions to such a straightforward thesis renders such a schematism highly unreliable, in spite of a second essay intended to provide detailed support.[93] When his rule does not in many instances actually apply, even if one grants that Matthew could have gone through Q several times in composing a single discourse, Taylor explains the divergences of sequence in various ways: The preference

[91] James M. Robinson, "The Matthean Trajectory from Q to Mark," in *Ancient and Modern Perspectives on the Bible and Culture: Essays in Honor of Hans Dieter Betz* (ed. Adela Yarbro Collins; Atlanta: Scholars, 1998 [1999]) 122-54.

[92] Vincent Taylor, "The Order of Q," *JTS*, n. s. 4 (1953) 27-31, reprinted in Vincent Taylor, *New Testament Essays* (Grand Rapids, MI: Eerdmans, 1972) 90-94.

[93] Vincent Taylor, "The Original Order of Q," in *New Testament Essays: Studies in Memory of T. W. Manson, 1893-1958* (ed. A. J. B. Higgins; Manchester: Manchester University Press, 1959) 246-69, reprinted in Taylor, *New Testament Essays*, 95-118.

for the Markan position; or the preference for the position of M (thought to be a written source and hence with a fixed sequence); or the omission of sayings already used in a previous discourse; or simply Matthean interpretation. Though some of these are no doubt correct explanations of exceptions to his rule, they cumulatively become special pleading.

Today the point of departure continues to be the Lukan sequence, but without a prejudice in its favor; the sequence is an open question that must in each case be tested."[94] "Q Texts in Matthean Order" and "Divergences from the Lukan Sequence" are given above, pp. 5-7, 9-10.

9 Proclamation and Redaction

9.1 *The Revival of Q Studies*
Martin Dibelius and Günther Bornkamm

The revival of the study of Q after World War II took place primarily in Heidelberg, under the leadership of Dibelius' successor, and a student of Bultmann, Günther Bornkamm. He was one of the founders of the distinctively post-war innovation, redaction criticism, initiated by his redaction critical analysis of the Stilling of the Storm in Matt 8:23-27:

> This characterization of the story of the stilling of the storm as a "nature miracle" does not, however, exhaust its meaning for Matthew. By inserting it into a definite context and by his own presentation of it, he gives it a new meaning which it does not yet have with the other evangelists. ...
>
> Matthew is not only a hander-on of the narrative, but also its oldest exegete, and in fact the first to interpret the journey of the disciples with Jesus in the storm and the stilling of the storm with reference to discipleship, and that means with reference to the little ship of the Church.[95]

[94] James M. Robinson, "The Sequence of Q: The Lament over Jerusalem," in *Von Jesus zum Christus: Christologische Studien. Festgabe für Paul Hoffmann zum 65. Geburtstag* (ed. Rudolf Hoppe and Ulrich Busse; BZNW 93; Berlin and New York: Walter de Gruyter, 1998) 225-60.

[95] Günther Bornkamm, "Die Sturmstillung im Matthäusevangelium," *Wort und Dienst*: Jahrbuch der Theologischen Schule Bethel, NF 1 (1948) 49-54, reprinted in Günther Bornkamm, Gerhard Barth and Heinz Joachim Held, *Überlieferung und Auslegung im Matthäusevangelium* (WMANT 1; Neukirchen: Neukirchener Verlag, 1960), 48-53: 49, 51. ET: *Tradition and Interpretation in Matthew* (London: SCM, and Philadelphia: Westminster, 1963), 52-57: 53, 55.

The approach of redaction criticism made it methodologically more possible to reconstruct the critical text of Q, by making use of distinctive Matthean and Lukan traits of syntax, vocabulary, and theology (broadly understood), identified by studying their redaction of Mark, and then using these traits as objective criteria for identifying their redactional alterations in Q. These Matthean and Lukan "fingerprints" on the Q sayings facilitate the reconstruction of the Q text, in that one is often able thereby to identify and peel off the Matthean and Lukan redaction. This serves to bring to the surface the critical text of Q itself.

Martin Dibelius had already anticipated redaction criticism in the case of Q, by distinguishing between the bulk of early Q material and later accretions added by the Q redaction:

> Nevertheless it may be granted that the collection used by Matthew and Luke already shows traces of a more advanced development.
>
> Thus passages appear to have been included which, though of totally different origin, have still the same office in this connection, viz. the handing down of the sayings of Jesus, to show and to prove who He was whose word had been gathered in the churches. ...
>
> All this is naturally conceived not in a historical, or biographical, but in a practical interest. But this particular practical interest outweighs the one which brought about the gathering of the sayings of Jesus as already discussed. The immediate object was to obtain from the words of Jesus not only solutions of problems or rules for one's own life, but also to derive from them some indications about the nature of the Person who had uttered them. ... It is even not altogether out of the question that these special features of the source Q came into being under the influence of the Gospel of Mark. Granted, we cannot say anything certain about the matter, because the date of Q, and especially the chronology for its development, is altogether unknown to us.[96]

Dibelius had in fact shared the then-prevalent placing of Q materials around the middle of the century, or even earlier:

> Probably there was more than one collection of sayings; at all events the existence of collections such as that contained in our alleged document Q is entirely probable, even at the time when Paul was receiving his missionary training from those who were believers before him, i.e., in the thirties or at the beginning of the forties of the first century A.D.[97]

[96] Dibelius, *Die Formgeschichte des Evangeliums*, 245-47. ET: *From Tradition to Gospel*, 245-46.

[97] Martin Dibelius, "Die Bergpredigt," in *Botschaft und Geschichte: Gesammelte Aufsätze*, Vol. 1: *Zur Evangelienforschung* (ed. Günther Bornkamm; Tübingen: Mohr-Siebeck, 1953) 79-174: 97-98. ET: *The Sermon on the Mount* (New York: Scribners, 1940) 28-29.

But by dating collections contained in Q even earlier than 50 C.E. and the redaction of Q possibly even later than Mark, i.e. to 70 C.E. or even later (thus, in a way, doing justice both to Harnack and to Wellhausen), Dibelius invited the effort to distinguish the tendency at work in the late redaction from that at work in the early original collections. The redaction criticism of Q had become inevitable.

9.2 *The Q Group's Distinctive Message*
Heinz Eduard Tödt

Heinz Eduard Tödt's Heidelberg dissertation of 1956 focused attention on the problem that Q lacked sayings about Jesus' death and resurrection:

> Harnack rightly stresses again and again that the concept of Jesus' passion which is present in the Gospel of Mark as his so-called Paulinism is absent in Q. How is this absence comprehensible in material which was transmitted by a community which after all must have been acquainted with Jesus' passion?[98]

Tödt recognized that the logical inference for the form critics would be to emphasize the kerygma's centrality and hence to play down the importance of the sayings of Jesus, and as a result to classify Q as secondary:

> The masters of the method of form-criticism, Bultmann and Dibelius, both established, each in his own specific way, the theological priority of the community's kerygma of the passion over the Q material.
>
> The faith of the first Christians was that the passion and resurrection meant the beginning of the new era. Accordingly they were living in expectation of an imminent end. The point from which they took the direction of their life was exclusively what God had done at the cross and the resurrection. Only after it had become evident that the end had been delayed did the Christians realize that they needed valid moral instructions for the regulation of their life in the world. So the sayings were compiled at this later stage as a secondary supplement to the unique central core, the kerygma of the passion.[99]

[98] Heinz Eduard Tödt, *Der Menschensohn in der synoptischen Überlieferung* (Gütersloh: Gütersloher Verlagshaus Mohn, 1959) 217. ET: *The Son of Man in the Synoptic Tradition* (London: SCM, and Philadelphia: Westminster, 1965) 237.

[99] Tödt, *Der Menschensohn in der synoptischen Tradition*, 218. ET: *The Son of Man in the Synoptic Tradition*, 238.

Such a later stage for Q, over against the kerygma, would not necessitate a dating as late as that of Wellhausen, but was primarily a logical, i.e. theological, position of being secondary to the kerygma. For if Dibelius had emphasized the presence of such paraenetic collections even in Paul's experience, Bultmann also ascribed Q to the primitive community: "It seems to me that the sayings source (*Spruchquelle*) employed by Matthew and Luke is the nearest to the primitive community."[100] Furthermore Tödt sensed that Bultmann had by implication postulated a Q community, by conceding that, from the very beginning, the primitive community had used Jesus' sayings as the actual content of their proclamation:

> A momentous step towards an appropriate understanding of this Q material was taken by Bultmann. He realized that the primitive community gathered up Jesus' proclamation and continued to proclaim it. And, in fact, there are many passages the preservation and collection of which can easily be understood as being due to an urge to do this. Of course this idea upsets the prevailing notion that the earliest and central message of the proclamation was the passion kerygma alone. Instead this idea assumes that there was a community which accepted as its central commission the passing on of Jesus' message.[101]

But Tödt himself was the first to draw out the implications of this recognition that Q was not just the paraenetic material of a monolithic primitive church, and thus subservient to its standard kerygma,[102] but rather presented the central message of a distinct Q community, whose "kerygma" was itself the sayings of Jesus:

> There are two spheres of tradition, distinguished both by their concepts and by their history. The centre of the one sphere is the passion kerygma; the centre of the other sphere is the intention to take up again the proclamation of Jesus' message. The Q material belongs to the second sphere. ... The concepts of the passion kerygma remained

[100] Bultmann, "Was läßt die Spruchquelle über die Urgemeinde erkennen?" 35. ET: "What the Sayings Source Reveals about the Early Church," 23.

[101] Tödt, *Der Menschensohn in der synoptischen Tradition*, 225-26. ET: *The Son of Man in the Synoptic Tradition,* 247. (The translation here has been edited to make it more literal. For the English-language preference for the idiom "teachings of Jesus," completely absent from the German original, obscures Tödt's point: The message of Jesus is a kind of proclamation in its own right, not just ethical teaching for catechumens who had been baptized on the basis of faith in the kerygma of cross and resurrection.)

[102] For this standard view cf. e.g. Manson, *The Mission and Message of Jesus*, 308:

> The most probable explanation is that there is no Passion-story because none is required, Q being a book of instruction for people who are already Christian and know the story of the Cross by heart.

> outside this sphere. Thus the Q material proved to be an independent source of Christological cognition.[103]

Ever since Tödt, the study of Q has had a sociological concomitant, the Q group, the previously overlooked outcome of the impact of Jesus on his hearers and beneficiaries in Galilee.

9.3 *The Sapiential Myth in Q*
Ulrich Wilckens

Ulrich Wilckens' Heidelberg dissertation, also of 1956, emphasized the distinctively sapiential orientation of much of Q:

> The motif that Wisdom abandons the earth is also found in a Q saying, Jesus' threat against Jerusalem: Matt 23:37-39 par. Luke 13:34-35. In Matthew this saying follows upon another threat against "this generation," Matt 23:34-36 par. Luke 11:49-51, where Matthew has retained from Q the sequence of both sayings and Luke the introduction to this last threat (διὰ τοῦτο καὶ ἡ σοφία τοῦ θεοῦ εἶπεν ["Therefore also the Wisdom of God said:"]). Hence the saying Matt 23:37ff was in Q originally a saying of Wisdom that Matthew put on Jesus' tongue. ... Here an echo of the myth 1 Enoch 42 becomes clear: In resignation, Wisdom withdraws back into heaven. She wanted to collect to herself the children of Jerusalem as her children, but they did not want it. Now she withdraws from them and will leave them to themselves until the parousia of the Messiah.[104]
>
> The situation is similar for the saying Matt 11:16-19 (Luke 7:31-35). ... These "children of Wisdom" are precisely hers, who in contrast to the *massa perditionis* of "this generation" have turned to her. With them, Wisdom has found recognition, whereas she otherwise was rejected on all sides. But how can "Wisdom" be introduced here, where, after all, the talk is about John and Jesus? Well, John and Jesus are her messengers who represent her and through whom she speaks,

[103] Tödt, *Der Menschensohn in der synoptischen Tradition*, 244-45. ET: *The Son of Man in the Synoptic Tradition*, 268-69. (The translation of "Verkündigung der Botschaft" as "teaching of what Jesus had taught" again obscures Tödt's emphasis, to the effect that it was Jesus' proclamation that continued to be proclaimed, as an alternative to, rather than an ethical, catechetical application of, the proclamation of the Easter kerygma. The translation has again been edited to make it more literal and thus to make this point more clear.)

[104] Ulrich Wilckens, *Weisheit und Torheit: Eine exegetisch-religionsgeschichtliche Untersuchung zu 1. Kor. 1 und 2* (BHT 26; Tübingen: Mohr-Siebeck, 1959) 163-64. See also his article σόφια, *TWNT* 7 (1964) 465-529, especially "Die Logienquelle," 515-18. ET: *TDNT* 7 (1971) 465-526, especially "The Logia," 515-17.

> just as in Wis 7:27 Wisdom "passes from generation to generation into holy souls and equips them as friends of God and prophets."[105]

It is quite similar in the case of Matt 11:25-27 = Q 10:21-22:

> ... Jesus speaks as revealer, as does Wisdom. ... The pericope thus stands in very close proximity to the Wisdom speculations in Sirach and Wisdom. ... Matt 11:25ff can without further ado be fitted into this development. In our context it is only interesting that here the person of Jesus is merged with the figure of Wisdom.[106]

Hence I, participating in this Heidelberg discussion while on sabbatic leave in Heidelberg 1959-60, suggested that the literary *genre* of Q might be sapiential.[107]

9.4 *The Deuteronomistic View of History in Q* *Odil Hannes Steck*

Odil Hannes Steck, in his 1965 dissertation in Heidelberg (where he was also an assistant), traced throughout the Bible the deuteronomistic view of history, which served to vindicate God with regard to disasters that fell upon Israel, especially the fall of Jerusalem in 586 B.C.E., as the inevitable result of Israel having killed the prophets God had sent. This deuteronomistic view of history cropped up in Judaism, especially in sapiential texts taken over into primitive Christianity, where it is found primarily in Q 6:23c; 11:49-51; 13:34-35:

> Luke 6:22-23, Matt 23:29-31 [Q 13:34-35], and Luke 11:49-51 do show that this relation is not limited to the isolated element of the violent fate of the prophets. In Matt 23:29-31 the conceptual relation of this element to Late[108] Judaism's tradition of the deuteronomistic view of history is taken over; in Luke 6:22-23 the coherence of the concepts of the suffering of the righteous and the deuteronomistic statements about prophets points to the conceptual content of this area of

[105] Wilckens, *Weisheit und Torheit*, 197-98.

[106] Wilckens, *Weisheit und Torheit*, 198-200. (Wilckens includes here Matt 11:28-30, though, since absent from Luke, it was apparently not in Q).

[107] James M. Robinson, "Basic Shifts in German Theology," *Interpretation* 16 (1962) 76-97: 82-86, and "LOGOI SOPHON: On the Gattung of Q," in *Trajectories through Early Christianity*, 71-113.

[108] The idiom "Late Judaism" was until recently carried over inappropriately to refer to Judaism contemporary with "Late Antiquity" as itself "Late." (See already in the case of Albert Schweitzer above, p. 30.) But in fact during the period of Late Antiquity one had to do with Early Judaism.

> tradition; and in Luke 11:49-51 even a firmly formulated unit of tradition is derived from it.[109]

Whereas Q 11:49 is actually introduced as a saying of Wisdom, and her sending of emissaries beginning with the foundation of the world would not fit a human speaker, not even Jesus, it is actually Q 13:34-35 whose language most clearly presupposes personified Wisdom. Steck found its roots, as in the case of Q 11:49-51, to lie in Jewish wisdom literature:

> Thus, after all, it seems most likely to me, along with many scholars, that personified Wisdom was the original subject of the saying. ... *The subject of the Jerusalem saying is hence the Wisdom of Sir 24 residing in Jerusalem, which has received from God Israel as its abode, and is identical with the law*! Hence Luke 13:34-35 shows how, going beyond 11:49-50, now also this element of the concept of Wisdom has been connected with the tradition of the deuteronomistic view of history. If already in Sir 24 the myth of Wisdom plays a role, in that Wisdom, despised by the nations, has found precisely in Israel its place, then again in Luke 13:35bα ["you will not see me ..."], to the extent that, after all, in the background stands the concept of the ascent of Wisdom, resigning herself. Thus in the Jerusalem saying there is present a further development of the tradition of Sir 24, more radical than which one can hardly imagine: It is precisely the Wisdom which has no abode among the nations, but has found its dwelling in Israel, which will now also abandon Israel![110]

Such a drastic application of the deuteronomistic view of history can, in Steck's view, only fit the siege of Jerusalem, a time when other Jewish sources reported similar forebodings:

> But is such a horrendous word of judgment conceivable at all in Jewish tradition? The difficulties in explaining the saying as a Christian creation, but also the outcome of our analysis in terms of the history of traditions, according to which there is a connection of sapiential and deuteronomistic tradition, each in its Late Jewish formulation, without a single specifically Christian element emerging, point after all in this direction. This Jewish word of judgment, which takes away any future for one's own people, is more understandable if one reflects that it must have been spoken under the unmediated impression of the impending catastrophe of Jerusalem. ...
>
> Accordingly, everything does speak for the view that the Jerusalem saying is a Jewish word of judgment spoken between C.E. 66 and 70

[109] Odil Hannes Steck, *Israel und das gewaltsame Geschick der Propheten: Untersuchungen zur Überlieferung des deuteronomistischen Geschichtsbildes im Alten Testament, Spätjudentum und Urchristentum* (WMANT 23; Neukirchen-Vluyn: Neukirchener Verlag, 1967) 286.

[110] Steck, *Israel und das gewaltsame Geschick der Propheten*, 230-32.

> in or near Jerusalem. If one looks at the listed parallels, then the assumption that a *vaticinium ex eventu* is at hand is quite unnecessary, it even has obvious historical facts against it. If one looks at the various factions in Jerusalem at the time of the Jewish war, then the author of the Jerusalem saying can be sought neither among the Zealots, nor generally among the war party; he must rather have belonged to the peace party, which saw in the resistance movement the reason for their fear of God's judgment in the capture and destruction of the city. The situation in terms of the history of traditions suggests that Luke 13:34-35 arose in the same circles, led by wisdom teachers, as did the admittedly older judgment saying Luke 11:49-50.[111]

This led Steck to the somewhat awkward conclusion that Matt 23:37-39 par. Luke 13:34-35, in spite of such a high degree of verbal identity between Matthew and Luke that this text would otherwise be ascribed with certainty to Q, nonetheless cannot have belonged to Q, since Q was traditionally dated much earlier:

> Here we bracket out the Jerusalem saying, since, in spite of the extensive agreement of the Matthean and Lukan formulations, its relation to the sayings source is not clear.... The motive for taking the saying up into Christian tradition may have been the expectation of the fall of Jerusalem also among Palestinian Christians, who take the saying over and ascribe it to Jesus.[112]

Still, the revival of the deuteronomistic view of history at the time leading up to the siege of Jerusalem provided Steck with the key to understanding Q:

> The deuteronomistic view of history, in its Late Jewish formulation, is admittedly not presented thematically as such in Q. As is indeed also the case in Late Jewish tradition, it can stand, as the known, only in the background of the presentation, and nevertheless be presupposed as the comprehensive conceptual framework in which the individual statements stand and to whose conceptual structure they are related.[113]

9.5 *The Redaction of Q*
Dieter Lührmann

Whereas Steck did not carry through an analysis of other Q texts on the basis of this working hypothesis (with the exception of Q 6:23c[114]),

[111] Steck, *Israel und das gewaltsame Geschick der Propheten*, 237-39.
[112] Steck, *Israel und das gewaltsame Geschick der Propheten*, 283, n. 1.
[113] Steck, *Israel und das gewaltsame Geschick der Propheten*, 286.
[114] Steck, *Israel und das gewaltsame Geschick der Propheten*, 257-60.

Dieter Lührmann (assistant in Heidelberg from 1965-1968), in his habilitation of 1968 dedicated to Bornkamm, did elevate Steck's thesis into the tendency characteristic of the whole redaction of Q.[115] Lührmann realized that Steck's exclusion of Matt 23:37-39 par. Luke 13:34-35 from Q was not defensible, given their high verbal identity. "His reasons (absence of a context, late dating) say nothing about whether it belongs to Q."[116] Rather one would have to adjust the standard mid-century or even earlier date of Q[117] into a later time frame. But even Lührmann could only move gingerly, though of necessity, in that direction: "All these observations point to the fact that the redaction of Q is not to be put all too early, but rather in the Hellenistic congregation of about the 50s or 60s."[118]

The gradual shift that has taken place over the last generation for the assumed dating of Q from around 50 C.E. to around 70 C.E. has in a subtle way produced a new weighting for some of the perennial issues of Q research. If Q were not composed a generation prior to Mark, but is contemporary with Mark, then Mark's use of Q is correspondingly less probable.[119] Furthermore, such a late dating for the redaction of Q made it all the more necessary to assume that earlier compositions were imbedded in Q, as Dibelius had argued.

This intensive period of research on Q reached its preliminary conclusion in 1972 with the Q monograph of Siegfried Schulz.[120] He regarded Q as a written, Greek text, making it reasonable to weigh the probability of Matthean versus Lukan redaction of Q in the case of each divergence of vocabulary:

> The striking agreements in wording within the Q material permit one to infer a source collection composed in Greek, just as the sequence

[115] Dieter Lührmann, *Die Redaktion der Logienquelle* (WMANT 33; Neukirchen-Vluyn: Neukirchener Verlag, 1969).

[116] Lührmann, *Die Redaktion der Logienquelle*, 44, n. 5.

[117] Representative of the many that could be listed is Manson, *The Mission and Message of Jesus*, 312: "about the middle of the first century, probably rather before than after A. D. 50." See also Dibelius, cited above, p. 45.

[118] Lührmann, *Die Redaktion der Logienquelle*, 88.

[119] The most thorough recent presentation of the case for Mark's use of Q is that of Harry T. Fleddermann, *Mark and Q: A Study of the Overlap Texts* (BETL 122; Leuven: University Press and Peeters, 1995). But the "Assessment" by Frans Neirynck, published in the same volume, 261-307 (reprinted in *Evangelica* III, 505-45), and the review article by Joseph Verheyden, "Mark and Q," *ETL* 72 (1996) 408-17, refute the details with sufficient cogency to leave this theory still a minority view.

[120] Siegfried Schulz, *Q: Die Spruchquelle der Evangelisten*, 5, reported that his work was based on Q seminars he had conducted, beginning in 1960.

> and doublets lead one to think of a written source which Matthew and Luke had before them. Which of the two Evangelists has preserved the original Q text, whether Matthew or Luke, can in no case be known in advance, but must be verified from case to case, in fact primarily with the help of an investigation of word statistics.[121]

Unfortunately he did not follow through with a reconstruction of the text of Q itself.[122]

9.6 *The Introduction of Roman Catholic Q Scholarship Athanasius Polag and Paul Hoffmann*

By this time, a revival of interest in Q was documented on all sides. But it is especially in Roman Catholic scholarship where this is prominent, once the encyclical *Divino afflante Spiritu*, issued in 1943, followed in 1965 by Vatican II's "*Constitutio dogmatica de divina revelatione 'Dei Verbum'*," had opened the door to scholarship presupposing the existence of Q.[123] Athanasius Polag, working on Q, produced in Trier a licentiate in 1966, and a doctorate in 1968.[124] Paul Hoffmann's Münster habilitation in 1968 worked through the theological dimensions of Q even more systematically.[125]

Of the impressive number of beginning Q scholars who published from the late '50s to the early '70s, Hoffmann is the only one who has consistently continued Q research down to the present, and whose views have as a result kept in step with ongoing Q research. He was initially hesitant about the feasibility of a redactional theory, since he presupposed the early dating of Q, in terms of which there is not only less time,

[121] Schulz, *Q: Die Spruchquelle der Evangelisten*, 41.

[122] Siegfried Schulz, *Griechisch-deutsche Synopse der Q-Überlieferungen* (Zürich: Theologischer Verlag, 1972), is a booklet printed separately to accompany the monograph. But it merely prints out the parallel Matthean and Lukan texts, as had Manson before him.

[123] To be sure, there had been precursors, such as Josef Schmid, *Matthäus und Lukas: Eine Untersuchung des Verhältnisses ihrer Evangelien* (BibS[F] 23: 2-4; Freiburg im Breisgau: Herder, 1930).

[124] Athanasius Polag, "Der Umfang der Logienquelle" (typescript 1966), and "Die Christologie der Logienquelle" (typescript 1968); *Die Christologie der Logienquelle* (WMANT 45; Neukirchen-Vluyn: Neukirchener Verlag, 1977); and finally *Fragmenta Q: Textheft zur Logienquelle*. Much of *Fragmenta Q* is translated in Ivan Havener, Q: *The Sayings of Jesus, With a Reconstruction of Q by Athanasius Polag*.

[125] Paul Hoffmann, *Studien zur Theologie der Logienquelle* (NTAbh.NF 8; Münster: Aschendorff, [1]1972, [2]1975, [3]1982).

but indeed less need, for a redaction distinct from the ongoing informal collecting of sayings into smaller clusters of tradition.[126] But he has come to advocate Lührmann's redactional theory, along with his later dating:

> My present occupation with redactional history is at the same time an attempt to repair a deficit in my Habilitationsschrift, *Studien zur Theologie der Logienquelle*. ...
>
> I would, however, depart from my discussion in the *Studien* in seeing as correct the reference to the situation in the Jewish-Roman war, which Steck expounds. ...
>
> The question of the age and origins of the genuine SM [Son of man] sayings, as assembled especially in Q 17, is in need of further investigation in this context. In doing so, we should take final leave from the often too "self-evident" assumption that in the SM sayings we are dealing with the oldest Christian or even dominical tradition. In this respect I wish expressly to correct my own position.[127]

The result is a new understanding of Q's theology in that late setting:

> The saying [Q 13:34-35] looks back to the vain efforts on Israel's behalf and reflects the imminently expected, or perhaps already completed (?), destruction of Jerusalem in the framework of the deuteronomistic view of history as the consequence of the rejection of the envoys. ...
>
> If we assume this to be QR's [Q redaction's] situation, various characteristics of QR find a plausible explanation. I would mention first of all the intensification of imminent expectation. ... It seems more plausible to relate them to the final phase of the Jewish-Roman war. In the situation of political crisis in Jewish, especially Zealot circles, but also in the Christian groups, as the re-worked Palestinian piece of tradition in Mk 13 shows, that phase brought about the expectation of the imminent in-breaking of the end times. ... The reception of the partly traditional statements in Q that are characterized by the imminent expectation is then less the legacy of an eschatological fervour that has been going on for decades, but rather an indication of a renaissance of the

[126] This was the criticism of Hoffmann by Lührmann, *Die Redaktion der Logienquelle*, 8.

[127] Paul Hoffmann, "QR und der Menschensohn: Eine vorläufige Skizze," in *The Four Gospels 1992: Festschrift Frans Neirync*k (eds. F. Van Segbroeck, C. M. Tuckett, G. Van Belle, J. Verheyden; BETL 100; 3 vols.; Leuven: University Press and Peeters, 1992) 1: 421-56: 421, 451, n. 50, 452, n. 56. This is reprinted in his collected essays, *Tradition und Situation: Studien zur Jesusüberlieferung in der Logienquelle und den synoptischen Evangelien* (NTAbh.NF 28; Münster: Aschendorff, 1995) 243-78: 243, 273, n. 51, 274-75, n. 57. ET: "The Redaction of Q and the Son of Man: A Preliminary Sketch," in *The Gospel Behind the Gospels: Current Studies on Q*, 159-198: 159, 191-92, n. 50, 193, n. 56.

> early Christian imminent expectation in response to the challenge of the general socio-political situation of crisis in the late 60s. This would also correspond better with the general sociology-of-religions insight that apocalyptic expectations generally appear in waves and are reactions to concrete crisis situations.
>
> The Palestinian tradition from the time of the Jewish-Roman war, preserved in Mk 13, which – apart from Q – represents the earliest evidence of the Christian reception of the SM [Son of man] expectation of Dan 7 (though already transformed in its own way), now also sheds light on the appearance of the SM sayings in Q. ... Nonetheless, the parallel appearance of this expectation in Mk 13 and QR could indicate that the SM concept gained special significance for Christian circles during this late phase in the transmission of Q, i.e. in the period around 70 CE, and that it was then that there took place its reception and theological integration into the traditional Q material that was not previously characterized by it. ...
>
> The "late dating" of QR proposed here would, finally, provide an explanation for the currency of the SM concept in Christian circles in the second half of the first century. ...
>
> The above considerations presuppose a fair proximity, in both space and time, to the Gospel of Matthew. If we suppose the period around 70 for QR and the 80s for MtR [Matthean redaction], we are dealing with a span of ten or at most twenty years. It thus becomes clear again, that QR indeed represents only an "intermediate stage" in the process of early Christian tradition from the Jesus of history through to the Gospel of Matthew. Perhaps this is also one of the reasons why Q has not survived as an independent document but only in its reception by the great evangelists.[128]

Lührmann's definition of Q's redaction has by now gained general acceptance among Q scholars, and functions as the presupposition for the next step in the history of Q research.[129]

[128] Hoffmann, "QR und der Menschensohn: Eine vorläufige Skizze," 451-53, 456 (*Tradition und Situation* 273-74, 276, 278). ET: "The Redaction of Q and the Son of Man: A Preliminary Sketch," 192-93, 195, 197. The view that the Q redaction took place after the Jewish War, at about 75 C.E., has been advocated by Burton L. Mack, *The Lost Gospel: The Book of Q and Christian Origins* (San Francisco: HarperSanFrancisco, 1993) 177, and Matti Myllykoski, "The Social History of Q and the Jewish War," *Symbols and Strata: Essays on the Sayings Gospel Q* (ed. Risto Uro; SESJ 65; Helsinki: The Finnish Exegetical Society, and Göttingen: Vandenhoeck und Ruprecht, 1996) 144-99: 199.

[129] John S. Kloppenborg, "The Sayings Gospel Q and the Quest of the Historical Jesus," *HTR* 89 (1996) 307-44: 321, n. 66, has given an impressive list of those accepting Lührmann's redactional thesis. It includes most of the important Q scholars of today.

10 Sapiential Origins of Q and Thomas

10.1 *A Sapiential Sayings Gospel behind Q and Thomas* *Helmut Koester*

Helmut Koester, a pupil of Bultmann,[130] became Bornkamm's Heidelberg assistant from 1954-56, where he completed his habilitation in 1956 and continued as Dozent until 1959, by which time he had moved to Harvard, already as a visiting professor in 1958, bringing with him the Heidelberg Q tradition:

> The predecessor of the Christian collection and transmission of one particular aspect of Jesus' sayings was the Gattung *logoi sophon*, primarily developed in the Jewish wisdom movement. This existing form served as a focus of crystallization for the preservation of one particular aspect of Jesus' historical appearance and work: his teachings. It is not possible to discuss here the complex questions regarding historical and primitive sayings or groups of sayings in these early pre-Q and pregospel collections. It is highly probable, however, that such collections were dominated by wisdom sayings, legal statements (critique of old conduct and pronouncements regarding new conduct), prophetic sayings (including some I-words, beatitudes, and woes), and parables, just as in Jesus' own teaching. As is partly evident from Q, sayings predicting Jesus' suffering, death, and resurrection, and the material reflecting the development of a christological evaluation of the person of Jesus, were still absent; detailed apocalyptic predictions, such as those contained in Mark 13, were not part of such primitive collections; specific regulations for the life of the church (*Gemeinderegeln*) were equally absent.
>
> What was the theological tendency of such collections of *logoi*? The answer to this depends entirely upon the christological post-Easter frame to which they were subjected. Q domesticated the *logoi* through a kind of apocalypticism which identified Jesus with the future Son of man. Mark (and subsequently Matthew and Luke) were able to incorporate the *logoi* in the "gospel" developed on the basis of the early Hellenistic (Pauline) kerygma. Neither of these developments seems to have touched the *logoi* tradition that found its way into the *Gospel of Thomas*. The criterion controlling Thomas's *logoi* is apparently closely connected with the internal principle of this Gattung as it gave focus to the transmission of Jesus' sayings: the authority of the word of wisdom as such, which rests in the assumption that Wisdom is present in the teacher of the word.[131]

[130] Koester's Marburg dissertation of 1954 already focussed attention on the non-canonical sayings tradition: *Synoptische Überlieferung bei den apostolischen Vätern* (TU 65; Berlin: Akademie-Verlag, 1957).

[131] Helmut Koester, "GNOMAI DIAPHOROI: The Origin and Nature of Diversification in the History of Early Christianity," *HTR* 58 (1965) 279-318: 300-301. German

Building on Philipp Vielhauer's view that the apocalyptic Son of man sayings do not go back to Jesus himself,[132] Koester argued that they are late in the Q trajectory (and completely absent from the *Gospel of Thomas)*, and only serve to obscure the earlier sapiential focus of Q:

> The basis of the *Gospel of Thomas* is a sayings collection which is more primitive than the canonical gospels, even though its basic principle is not related to the creed of the passion and resurrection. Its principle is nonetheless theological. Faith is understood as belief in Jesus' words, a belief which makes what Jesus proclaimed present and real for the believer. The catalyst which has caused the crystallization of these sayings into a "gospel" is the view that the kingdom is uniquely present in Jesus' eschatological preaching and that eternal wisdom about man's true self is disclosed in his words. ...
>
> The relation of this "sayings gospel," from which the *Gospel of Thomas* is derived, to the synoptic sayings source Q, is an open question. Without doubt, most of its materials are Q sayings (including some sayings which appear occasionally in Mark). But it must have been a version of Q in which the apocalyptic expectation of the Son of man was missing, and in which Jesus' radicalized eschatology of the kingdom and his revelation of divine wisdom in his own words were dominant motifs.[133]

publication: "GNOMAI DIAPHOROI: Ursprung und Wesen der Mannigfaltigkeit in der Geschichte des frühen Christentums," *ZTK* 65 (1968) 160-203: 184-85. The German text was republished in *Entwicklungslinien durch die Welt des Frühchristentums*, 107-46: 129-30. The English text was republished in *Trajectories through Early Christianity*, 114-57: 137-39, quoted here. (The last sentence is edited to make it more literal.)

[132] Koester, "GNOMAI DIAPHOROI," 138, n. 66:

> Whether any apocalyptic Son of man sayings were existent at this stage is very doubtful. Cf. Philipp Vielhauer, "Gottesreich und Menschensohn in der Verkündigung Jesu," in *Festschrift für Günther Dehn*, 1957, pp. 51-79; idem, "Jesus und der Menschensohn," *ZThK* 60 (1963): 133-77; both articles are reprinted in his *Aufsätze zum Neuen Testament*, Theologische Bücherei, 31, 1965, pp. 55-91, 92-140. Cf. also Norman Perrin, *Rediscovering the Teaching of Jesus* [(New York: Harper & Row, 1967)], passim.

[133] Koester, "One Jesus and Four Primitive Gospels," *HTR* 61 (1968) 203-47: 229-30, reprinted in *Trajectories through Early Christianity* [quoted here] 158-204: 186. The German text was published in Koester and Robinson, *Entwicklungslinien durch die Welt des Frühchristentums*, 147-90: 172-73. In his more recent book, *Ancient Christian Gospels: Their History and Development* (London: SCM, and Philadelphia: Trinity Press International, 1990), Koester worked out in more detail the relation between "Thomas and the Synoptic Sayings Source (Q)" (86-95), to conclude (95):

> Thus, the *Gospel of Thomas* is either dependent upon the earliest version of Q or, more likely, shares with the author of Q one or several very early collections of Jesus' sayings.

A critique is provided by Christopher M. Tuckett, "Q and Thomas: Evidence of a Primitive 'Wisdom Gospel'? A Response to H. Koester," *ETL* 67 (1991) 346-60. A

10.2 *Two Editions of Q*
John S. Kloppenborg

This primarily German revival of Q studies more than a generation ago, once transplanted to America, came into focus largely through the synthesis produced by John S. Kloppenborg in his Toronto dissertation of 1984.[134] He built upon Lührmann's identification of the Q redactor, my identification of the sapiential *genre*, and Koester's focus on sources behind Q and *Thomas*. Indeed, the later one is obliged to place the redaction of Q, down to the time around 70 C.E., the more some explanation is required to account for what would seem to be early, pre-redactional (non-deuteronomistic) collections of sapiential material.[135] Lührmann himself had, in passing, called attention to such archaic collections:

> Collecting of this sort is found in other parts of the Synoptic tradition as well as in Q, for example, in the programmatic speech that forms the basis of the Lukan Sermon on the Plain and the Matthaean Sermon on the Mount (Luke 6:20-49 // Matt 5:1-7:29), in Q 12:22-32, 33-34, in Q 12:2-7, or in Luke 11:33, 34-36.... Examples of this kind could be multiplied.
>
> The presence of such collections suggests that Q is already the (provisional) result of a long process of tradition and that, correspondingly, the content of Q is not homogeneous. Rather, just as is the case elsewhere in the Synoptic tradition, Q reflects various stages in the assimilation of the preaching of Jesus by the early church.[136]

But Lührmann, building on Steck, placed the sapiential orientation of Q nearest to the final redaction, where Wisdom is personified in terms of the Wisdom myth:

> One set of sayings that are clearly influenced by late Jewish wisdom turns out to be the latest stratum, and therefore the stratum that is

supportive exposition of Koester's position is provided by Stephen J. Patterson, "Wisdom in Q and Thomas," in *In Search of Wisdom: Essays in Memory of John J. G. Gammie* (ed. L. G. Purdue, B. B. Scott, and W. J. Wisemann; Louisville, Ky: Westminster/John Knox, 1993) 187-221. See also the argument summarized below for a pre-Q text of Q 12:22b-31 (Free from Anxiety like Ravens and Lilies).

[134] John S. Kloppenborg, *The Formation of Q: Trajectories in Ancient Wisdom Collections*.

[135] For the resultant tension between the archaic collections and the redaction that calls for substantive criticism, see James M. Robinson, "The Critical Edition of Q and the Study of Jesus," in *The Sayings Source Q and the Historical Jesus* (ed. Andreas Lindemann; BETL 158; Leuven: University Press and Peeters, 2001) 27-52.

[136] Lührmann, *Die Redaktion der Logienquelle*, 84. ET: "Q in the History of Early Christianity," in *The Shape of Q: Signal Essays on the Sayings Gospel*, 59-73: 59.

> chronologically, although not necessarily tradition-historically, nearest the redaction of Q. That datum may not at first glance be surprising, since the influence of this current on the preaching of Jesus is recognizable elsewhere in the Synoptic tradition. But the frequency and the special character of these sayings and the patterning of Q as a whole on a *genre* deriving from sapiential literature indicate that this influence had considerable importance in the transmission of Q.[137]

Kloppenborg, on the other hand, identified, as an early formative stage in the emergence of Q, rather than personified Wisdom, six "sapiential speeches," which he argued came together into an early written layer of Q, since it is into them that the later material reflecting the deuteronomistic redaction was interpolated, not vice versa:

> Alongside the large complexes which evince the motifs of judgment and polemic there are substantial units whose primary redactional intent is paraenetic, hortatory and instructional, and indeed compare favorably in their structure with the "instruction," a widely attested genre of wisdom literature. They include:
> 1. Q 6:20b-23b, 27-35, 36-45, 46-49,
> 2. Q 9:57-60, (61-62); 10:2-11, 16,
> 3. Q 11:2-4, 9-13,
> 4. Q 12:2-7, 11-12,
> 5. Q 12:22b-31, 33-34 and probably
> 6. Q 13:24; 14:26-27; 17:33; 14:34-35.
>
> Since some of these blocks contain secondary interpolations that express the perspective of the polemical redaction, it is reasonable to assume that the hortatory instructions were literarily antecedent to the polemical materials and that at some point in the development of Q the instructional material was edited in accordance with the later perspective.[138]

It has been pointed out[139] that Kloppenborg's thesis is one of several alternate and independent expressions of a rather widespread recognition that the clusters he identified are indeed early clusters, composed before the final redaction:

> Three of these are among the early pre-redactional "collections" listed by Lührmann.[140]

[137] Lührmann, *Die Redaktion der Logienquelle*, 97-98. ET: "Q in the History of Early Christianity," 69.

[138] John S. Kloppenborg, "The Sayings Gospel Q: Literary and Stratigraphic Problems," in *Symbols and Strata: Essays on the Sayings Gospel Q*, 1-66: 48.

[139] James M. Robinson, "The Q Trajectory: Between John and Matthew via Jesus," in *The Future of Early Christianity: Essays in Honor of Helmut Koester* (ed. Birger A. Pearson; Minneapolis: Fortress, 1991) 173-94: 185-89.

[140] Lührmann, *Die Redaktion der Logienquelle*, 84: units 1, 4 (only Q 12:2-7) and 5.

> Five are listed by Siegfried Schulz as going back to "the kerygma of the oldest Q congregations of the Palestinian-Syrian border areas."[141]
> Five are included by Dieter Zeller in his list of "six larger groups of sayings that may have grown up around a kernel of admonition."[142]
> Four are among the pre-Q collections of aphoristic sayings, each displaying a similar structure, presented by Ronald A. Piper in his London dissertation.[143]
> Four are in the Sermon on the Mount dated to around 50 C.E. as a result of the Jerusalem Council by Hans Dieter Betz.[144]

It is striking that such very divergent studies, in method and orientation, tend to agree to such a large extent about there having been such sapiential clusters at an early stage of the development. Indeed the two that are most relevant, Q 6:20-49 (the Inaugural Sermon) and Q 12:22b-31 (Free from Anxiety Like Ravens and Lilies), are actually on each of these lists.

Kloppenborg has welcomed such drawing of "attention to the convergence of the results obtained by Zeller, Kloppenborg, and Piper,"[145] and himself has added Heinz Schürmann to the list:

> It might also be noted that Schürmann, while hesitant to follow the stratigraphical model of Kloppenborg, has now recognized the importance of the six topically organized instructional speeches in the composition of Q and acknowledges that such "speeches" were already "finished" units prior to the final redaction of Q.[146]

[141] Schulz, *Q: Die Spruchquelle der Evangelisten*, 57-175: units 1 (except Q 6:43-49), 3, 4 (only Q 12:4-9), 5 and 6 (only Q 16:17-18).

[142] Dieter Zeller, *Die weisheitlichen Mahnsprüche bei den Synoptikern* (FzB 17; Würzburg: Echter Verlag, 1977) 191: units 1 (except Q 6:34-35a, 37b-38a, 39-40), 2 (except Q 9:57-62; 10:8b, 11b, but with Q 10:12), 3 (except Q 11:9-13), 4 (except Q 12:11-12, but with Q 12:9-10), 5. However Zeller has not appropriated Kloppenborg's theory of a first, sapiential edition of Q. See Zeller, "Redaktionsprozesse und wechselnder 'Sitz im Leben' beim Q-Material," in *Logia – Les paroles de Jésus – The Sayings of Jesus: Mémorial Joseph Coppens* (ed. J. Delobel; BETL 59; Leuven: Peeters and Leuven University Press, 1982) 395-409; Zeller, "Eine weisheitliche Grundschrift in der Logienquelle?" in *The Four Gospels 1992: Festschrift Frans Neirynck*, 1: 389-401.

[143] Ronald A. Piper, *Wisdom in the Q-Tradition: The Aphoristic Teaching of Jesus*: units 1 (except Q 6:20b-23b, 46-49), 3 (except Q 11:2-4), 4 (adding Q 12:8-9), 5 (except Q 12:33-34).

[144] Hans Dieter Betz, *The Sermon on the Mount* (ed. Adela Yarbro Collins; Hermeneia; Minneapolis: Fortress, 1995): units 1, 3, 5 and 6 (only Q 13:24-27).

[145] Kloppenborg, "The Sayings Gospel Q: Literary and Stratigraphic Problems," 52.

[146] Kloppenborg, "The Sayings Gospel Q: Literary and Stratigraphic Problems," 53-54. He refers to Heinz Schürmann, "Zur Kompositionsgeschichte der Redenquelle: Beobachtungen an der lukanischen Q-Vorlage," in *Der Treue Gottes trauen: Beiträge zum Werk des Lukas: Für Gerhard Schneider* (ed. C. Bussmann and W. Radl; Freiburg: Herder, 1991) 326-42: 327-28, 332.

To this list of advocates of early sapiential clusters can also be added Migaku Sato, though also a rather unwilling supporter:

> Here, more as a concession, precisely those sayings collections are named that Zeller and Kloppenborg had worked out as the sapiential collections 1, 2, 3 and 5 of the first edition of Q.[147]

Kloppenborg went on to argue that these sapiential collections had been assembled into what amounted to a first edition of Q prior to the deuteronomistic redaction:

> Given the techniques of interpolation and insertion, it is reasonable to assume that the "wisdom speeches" were *already in a written form* when they were glossed. Otherwise one would expect a greater degree of homogeneity and fewer abrupt transitions.[148]

This is the dimension of Kloppenborg's thesis that has met with the most resistance, which at times has even obscured the nigh-consensus as to the existence of such early sapiential collections. This is partly due to the widespread view that the first period was dominated by apocalypticism, with the inference that it was only the delay of the parousia mitigating that apocalyptic "enthusiasm" which made it necessary, in a second phase, to come to grips with the ongoing realities of normal life.[149]

This kind of banal every-day advice is what one has, in the case of Q all too uncritically, associated with the term "sapiential."[150] But that concept of sapiential, in the time frame in question, has been superceded by John G. Gammie's studies of the trajectories in Jewish wisdom literature,[151] from which Kloppenborg draws the conclusion:

[147] James M. Robinson, "Die Logienquelle: Weisheit oder Prophetie? Anfragen an Migaku Sato, Q und Prophetie," *EvT* 53 (1993) 367-89: 385. See Martin Ebner, *Jesus – ein Weisheitslehrer? Synoptische Weisheitslogien im Traditionsprozess* (HBS 15; Freiburg: Herder, 1998) 32:

> In addition, Robinson succeeded in showing that Sato – without letting it come to expression in his overall conception –, in the case of the sapiential compositions, which he fully recognizes as preliminary stages of his prophetic book, comes rather close to the six "sapiential speeches" that, according to Kloppenborg – incidentally already thus separated out by Zeller 1977 –, comprise the oldest basic contents of Q: Programmatic Discourse (Q 6), Mission Discourse (Q 10), Instruction on Prayer (Q 11), Call for Freedom from Anxiety (Q 12), and finally Concluding Exhortations (Q 13-14).

[148] Kloppenborg, *The Formation of Q*, 244.

[149] One may note the criticism of this view expressed by Tödt and Hoffmann.

[150] For a summary of scholarly literature correcting that inference and documenting the sapiential sayings in Q see Robinson, "Die Logienquelle: Weisheit oder Prophetie?" 374-77.

[151] John G. Gammie, "The Sage in Sirach" and "From Prudentialism to Apocalypticism: The Houses of the Sages Amid the Varying Forms of Wisdom," both in *The Sage in*

> Although some of the *literary forms* – the instruction, for example – adopted by sages demonstrate remarkable stability over a millennium or more, the *content* of the wisdom tradition is itself remarkably diverse and adaptable. …
>
> To characterize Q as "sapiential" is not, therefore, to imply a depiction of Jesus as a teacher of this-worldly, prudential wisdom, still less to imply an intellectual world that was hermetically sealed against eschatology, prophetic traditions, and the epic traditions of Israel.[152]

Quite apart from how one assesses the very obscure beginning of the Q community, Kloppenborg goes on to make clear that his analysis is literary, without necessarily involving historical inferences or presuppositions:

> To say that the wisdom components were formative for Q and that the prophetic judgment oracles and apophthegms describing Jesus' conflict with "this generation" are secondary is not to imply anything about the ultimate tradition-historical provenance of any of the sayings. It is indeed possible, indeed probable, that some of the materials from the secondary compositional phase are dominical or at least very old, and that some of the formative elements are, from the standpoint of authenticity or tradition-history, relatively young. Tradition-history is not convertible with *literary history*, and it is the latter which we are treating here.[153]

Kloppenborg has concluded his recent detailed report on Q research as follows:

> It may not be too bold to suggest that in addition to the existing consensus, initiated by Lührmann's study, that the polemic against "this generation" and the announcement of judgment provide organizing motifs at one level of the redaction of the Sayings Gospel, a second consensus point has emerged: Key to the understanding of the formation of Q is the recognition of the presence of large blocks of topically organized "sapiential" sayings, each exhibiting a similar structure, and Sitz im Leben, rhetorical intention.[154]

Israel and the Ancient Near East (ed. John G. Gammie and Leo G. Perdue; Winona Lake: Eisenbrauns, 1990) 355-72, 479-97, and "Paraenetic Literature: Toward the Morphology of a Secondary Genre" [within wisdom literature], in *Paraenesis: Act and Form* [= *Semeia* 50], 1990, 41-77.

152 Kloppenborg Verbin, *Excavating Q*, 385, 388.

153 Kloppenborg, *The Formation of Q*, 245.

154 Kloppenborg, "The Sayings Gospel Q: Literary and Stratigraphic Problems," 55.

10.3 *A Scribal Error Behind Q*
T. C. Skeat, James M. Robinson and Christoph Heil

One sapiential collection shared by all those listed above, Free from Anxiety like Ravens and Lilies (Q 12:22b-31), has been traced back to a written Greek text that antedates the archetype of the Q text used by Matthew and Luke.[155] It is found in the *Gospel of Thomas* 36, as preserved in *P. Oxy.* 655, which is a very early form of this small sayings collection. For the fragmentary papyrus attests a reading o]ὐ ξα[ί]νει, "not card," which is free of a scribal error found in the canonical texts: Matthew 6:28: αὐξάνουσιν par. Luke 12:27: αὐξάνει, "grow." The correct reading is otherwise attested only in the original hand of Codex Sinaiticus at Matt 6:28 (οὐ ξένουσιν, itacism for οὐ ξαίνουσιν[156]), which was erased by the first corrector in favor of the standard Matthean reading αὐξάνουσιν (i. e., "not card" was "corrected" into "grow").[157]

On closer examination, it turns out that Saying 36 of the *Gospel of Thomas* in *P. Oxy.* 655 does not yet display other traits that critical scholarship throughout the twentieth century (but without consulting *P. Oxy.* 655) has rightly identified as secondary intrusions into that very old pre-Q collection:[158]

155 T. C. Skeat, "The Lilies of the Field," *ZNW* 37 (1938) 211-14.

156 T. C. Skeat, in a letter of April, 1999, pointed out why the shift from -αι- to -ε- in the case of οὐ ξένουσιν is to be considered a normal oral fluctuation, whereas the shifts from οὐ to αὐ- and from -αί- to -ά- in the case of οὐ ξαίνει becoming αὐξάνει are copyists' mistakes in writing:

> Vowels were certainly not 'carelessly interchanged' but were written to reflect current pronunciation. In the case of αὐξάνει for οὐ ξαίνει, αυ and ου were certainly not pronounced identically, nor were αι and α. αι and ε, however, were certainly pronounced identically, as in Modern Greek, and this explains the scribe of Sinaiticus writing ξενουσι for ξαινουσι.

157 James M. Robinson and Christoph Heil, "Zeugnisse eines schriftlichen, griechischen vorkanonischen Textes: Mt 6,28b א*, P.Oxy. 655 I,1-17 (EvT 36) und Q 12,27," *ZNW* 89 (1998) 30-44. To the criticicsm of this essay by Jens Schröter, "Vorsynoptische Überlieferung auf P.Oxy. 655? Kritische Bemerkungen zu einer erneuerten These," *ZNW* 90 (1999) 265-72, see the reply by Robinson and Heil, "Noch einmal: Der Schreibfehler in Q 12,27," *ZNW* 92 (2001) 113-22.

158 James M. Robinson, "The Pre-Q Text of the (Ravens and) Lilies: Q 12:22b-31 and P.Oxy. 655 (*Gos. Thom.* 36)," in *Text und Geschichte: Facetten theologischen Arbeitens aus dem Freundes- und Schülerkreis. Dieter Lührmann zum 60. Geburtstag* (ed. Stefan Maser and Egbert Schlarb; MTSt NF 50; Marburg: Elwert, 1999) 143-180; for a more readable summary see James M. Robinson, "A Written Greek Sayings Cluster Older than Q: A Vestige," *HTR* 92 (1999) 61-77. See further the endpapers and the "Excursus on the Scribal Error in Q 12:27" in *The Critical Edition of Q*, xcix-ci. as well as Robinson and Heil, "The Lilies of the Field: Saying 36 of the *Gospel of Thomas* and Secondary Accretions in Q 12.22b-31," *NTS* 47 (2001) 1-25.

1. In Q 12:22b, food and clothing will be provided by God, as the ravens (Q 12:24) and lilies (Q 12:27) exemplify. But Q 12:23 interrupts this expected flow of thought in the little collection, by degrading food and clothing in favor of higher values, "soul"/"life" and "body" (ψυχή and σῶμα), a spiritual value structure in no way exemplified by ravens and lilies. Hence Q 12:23, and the references to ψυχή and σῶμα in Q 12:22b, have seemed to be secondary intrusions, and indeed turn out to be missing from Saying 36 in *P. Oxy*. 655!

2. Q 12:25, expressing morose resignation as to one's inability to raise oneself by one's own bootstraps (literally: to increase one's stature or life-span), not only separates off the lilies (Q 12:27) from the ravens (Q 12:24) in the sequence of Q, making it necessary to recreate the original context by inserting the redactional verse Q 12:26, but also stands in sharp contrast to the glowing trust in God's caring that is characteristic of the collection as a whole. But in *P. Oxy*. 655 Saying 36 continues the theme of trust in God: "Who might add to your stature? That one will give you your clothing!"

3. The original climax, that your Father will surely provide the basic necessities of food, drink, and clothing (Q 12:29, 30b), thereby returned appropriately as an *inclusio* to the point of departure in Q 12:22b. But this is then followed in Q 12:31 by a second climax, bringing for the first time a reference to the kingdom of God into the collection, which hence has been considered secondary. This anti-climactic reference to the kingdom is also absent from *P. Oxy*. 655!

11 The Critical Edition of Q

11.1 *The Minimal Q Text* *Pap. Q*

What has made a critical edition of Q seem at least a possibility is the emergence of Q as a text originally written in Greek, whose Matthean and Lukan redaction can often be detected and discounted by applying the methods and results of redaction criticism in identifying Matthean and Lukan redactional traits in their treatment of Mark. Yet that undertaking itself, modeled after papyrology and textual criticism, has sought to maintain its objectivity to the particular *status quaestionis* of Q interpretation at the time it was first undertaken by the International Q Project, in order that *The Critical Edition of Q* and *The Sayings Gospel Q* be usable for scholars of all opinions,[159] so as to function as a standard tool in our discipline.[160] Hence its method has neither presupposed a view as to the layering of the text of Q, nor a view as to what extent or in what way Q reflects the sayings of Jesus and/or of the Q community. The only presupposition is the general outcome of the history of Q research that has rendered the undertaking possible at all, namely the conclusion that there was a written Greek text of Q which functioned as an archetype, copies of which were available to the Matthean and Lukan communities and used by their Evangelists. It is that archetype which *The Critical Edition of Q* has sought to reconstitute and *The Sayings Gospel Q* seeks to make more readily available to scholarship, as does *The Sayings of Jesus* to an even wider audience.

This undertaking began as a research project entitled "Q: A Lost Collection of Jesus' Sayings," launched at the Institute for Antiquity and Christianity in 1983,[161] and at the Annual Meetings of the Society of Biblical Literature as "Study of Q Consultations" (1983-1984). One of its initial policies has now become standard usage in Q research, namely the use of Lukan chapter and verse references when quoting Q.[162] The

159 Current opinion is of course widely divided: "Der Entwurf von J. M. Robinson und H. Köster und die darauf aufbauende amerikanische Position" is the title of a sub-section, and a main focus in the polemic, of Jens Schröter, *Erinnerung an Jesu Worte: Studien zur Rezeption der Logienüberlieferung in Markus, Q und Thomas* (WMANT 76; Neukirchen: Neukirchener Verlag, 1997) 132-36. A position somewhat similar to that of Schröter is that of Richard A. Horsley with Jonathan A. Draper, *Whoever Hears You Hears Me: Prophets, Performance, and Tradition in Q* (Harrisburg, Penn.: Trinity Press International, 1999). The converse position is that of Thomas Zöckler, *Jesu Lehren im Thomasevangelium* (NHMS 47; Leiden: Brill, 1999) 2, n. 4: "To be sure, Schröter handles only a part of the Thomas sayings, but he discusses intensively the history of research on Thomas and Q and in this connection carries out at times sharp criticism of the research proposals of Koester and Robinson, and it is to the latter that the present work is decisively oriented." According to Martin Ebner, *Jesus – ein Weisheitslehrer? Synoptische Weisheitslogien im Traditionsprozess*, 31, "the assumption of a sapiential kernel of Q seems to be the solution that is more plausible and that does more justice to the text."

160 Those who deny the existence of Q as a whole will of course not be satisfied: Michael Goulder, "Is Q a Juggernaut?" *JBL* 115 (1996) 667-81; Goulder, "Self-Contradiction in the IQP," *JBL* 118 (1999) 506-17. The IQP has indeed refrained from entering into the never-ending discussion over the existence of Q, and has preferred to concentrate its energy (Goulder: "enormous industry," 506) on seeking to reconstruct the text of Q, on the assumption that this may in the end be a more compelling and useful argument for its existence. See the response by Robert A. Derrenbacker, Jr. and John S. Kloppenborg Verbin, "Self-Contradiction in the IQP? A Reply to Michael Goulder," *JBL* 120 (2001) 57-76.

161 "New Project Launched," *Bulletin of the Institute for Antiquity and Christianity* 10.4 (1983) 6.

162 James M. Robinson, "The Sermon on the Mount/Plain: Work Sheets for the Reconstruction of Q," SBL.SP 22 (1983) 451-54: 451-52:

consultations developed into a Q Seminar (1985-1989), which in turn was given the status of the International Q Project by the Research and Publications Committee of the Society of Biblical Literature in 1989.[163]

With the help of Leif Vaage and Jon Daniels, at the time Research Associates of the Q Project of the Institute for Antiquity and Christianity, a brochure (entitled *Pap. Q*) was prepared to inaugurate the Project at the Annual Meeting of SBL in Anaheim, Calif., in November, 1985. It contained the text shared by Matthew and Luke, letter by letter (though in transliteration, since Greek was not yet readily available on word processors), with sigla identifying the lacunae caused by divergences due to Matthean and/or Lukan redaction. A brief introduction explained:

> The following pages present a modern simulation of the quire of a tattered papyrus, with the surviving letters enmeshed within a *lacunae*-ridden web of fibre-like *sigla*. This printout, like a unique papyrus, contains the only extant vestiges of the otherwise lost collection of Jesus' sayings familiarly known as Q.
>
> Reworked by Matthew and Luke as they incorporated it in differing ways into their Gospels, the text of Q was in the process "corrupted" by the "moth" of Luke and the "rust" of Matthew. For when Luke or Matthew made a change in it, we are left with an awkward situation: At places where the two Gospels are so alike that a shared dependence on Q is to be assumed, but where Luke and Matthew nonetheless diverge in some details of wording or order, it is unclear which has altered and which has retained Q. Hence both readings become suspect, resulting in a fragmented text like a tattered papyrus shot through with *lacunae*. By the painstaking process of analyzing the

> We might adopt the policy of citing Q as follows: Q 6:20 (rather than Lk 6:20 par., or Luke 6:20 //, or Mt 5:3 // Lk 6:20). This practice would mean that one regards something in Lk 6:20 as coming from Q (though not necessarily implying that Luke, rather than Matthew or some wording or sequence diverging in part from both, preserves the wording or sequence of Q). This would be a crisp way of referring to Q as an entity in its own right, without the problem of numbering the Q sayings in a different numbering system than that of Luke (e.g., like the numeration of the 114 sayings in the *Gospel of Thomas*). Thus we could refer to a specific verse without prematurely settling upon a numeration system that would soon become antiquated, or without the problem of constantly renumbering (both of which problems have emerged in the case of the *Gospel of Thomas*).

In fact none of the various numbering systems that have been proposed for Q have gained general acceptance other than the one based on Luke proposed here.

[163] For further details concerning the beginning of the project see James M. Robinson, "The Sayings of Jesus: Q," *The Drew Gateway*, 54.1 (1983 [1985]) 26-38: 35-37; Robinson, "A Critical Text of the Sayings Gospel Q," *RHPR* 72 (1992) 15-22 (a paper presented at the SNTS meeting of 1991); and Frans Neirynck, "The International Q Project," *ETL* 69 (1993) 221-25, reprinted in his *Q-Synopsis: The Double Tradition Passages in Greek*, Revised Edition with Appendix (Leuven: University Press and Peeters, 1995) 75-79.

> syntax, vocabulary, and theology of the canonical Gospels Luke and Matthew and the pre-canonical Gospel Q, one may seek to fill the *lacunae*, as one would seek to edit a papyrus.[164]

This "minimal Q" text was considered the point of departure for the work ahead:

> It is to be hoped that this printout of Pap. Q can be replaced by succeeding drafts of Q, as the work moves from its point of departure at the level of a tattered papyrus, toward a critical text constantly being improved.[165]

However, from its inception, this narrowly focused exercise was cast in a much broader and more important context. For it provided new access to Jesus and his first followers:

> The resultant critical text of Q is (at least) one step removed from Jesus himself, in that the sayings it ascribes to Jesus (and to John) are actually those proclaimed in Jesus' name by his Galilean successors. This critical text will however be (at least) one step nearer to Jesus than are Luke and Matthew, to the extent that most of the sayings they ascribe to Jesus are their reworkings of the Q text. A critical text of Q is thus indispensable for advances in our understanding of Jesus, of his immediate followers, and of the Gospels of Luke and Matthew. Thus the all-but-impossible critical task is thoroughly matched by its unrivaled importance: Quite frankly, the "shock" of the Jesus movement is less blunted when not imbedded in the cushioning provided by the next generation.[166]

11.2 *The Critical Edition of Q*
The International Q Project

A Q Section in SBL's Annual Program itself has continued without interruption, and is intended for a wider public, while the members of the International Q Project, co-chaired by James M. Robinson and John S. Kloppenborg, have met annually just prior to the Annual Meeting of SBL for one or two days of concentrated work (1989-1996),[167] as well as

164 James M. Robinson, Leif Vaage and Jon Daniels, *Pap. Q* (Claremont, Calif.: The Institute for Antiquity and Christianity, 1985). The Introduction (pp. 1-2) was composed by Robinson, the transcription of the *lacunae*-laden minimal Q text (pp. 3-20) by Vaage and Daniels. The quotation is the opening of the Introduction, 1.

165 *Pap Q*, 2.

166 *Pap Q*, 1.

167 The meeting at Anaheim 17 xi 1989 was attended by 21 members, that at New Orleans 16 xi 1990 by 23 members, that at Kansas City 22 xi 1991 by 24 members, that at San Francisco 20 xi 1992 by 24 members, that at Washington, D.C. 18-19 xi 1993 by

once or twice each summer at one of the Project's centers (1991-1994).[168] The General Editors have met regularly (1995-1999)[169] to revise and edit the critical text of Q.

In 1992 Paul Hoffmann had proposed a German branch of the International Q Project to be located at the University of Bamberg. Ever since the first organizational meeting held there (21-25 vi 1993), the Bamberg members have participated in the work and attended the meetings of the International Q Project.

In 1994 Peeters Press offered to publish the Databases, Evaluations and resultant Critical Text developed by the International Q Project. A contract to this effect was signed in Bamberg in 1995. This series, which is entitled Documenta Q: Reconstructions of Q Through Two Centuries of Gospel Research Excerpted, Sorted, and Evaluated, has thus far published six volumes,[170] and further volumes will continue to appear.

The work on *The Critical Edition of Q*, *The Sayings Gospel Q*, and *The Sayings of Jesus* has been structured in such a way as to minimize subjectivity and attain a degree of overall objectivity. A check-and-balance protection against the subjectivity of an individual scholar has been provided by the collaboration of more than forty scholars in establishing the first draft,[171] followed by the joint work of the three General Editors in refining that into the text published in full detail in *The Critical Edition of Q* and here in simplified format as *The Sayings Gospel Q*. The

29 members, that at Chicago 17-18 xi 1994 by 26 members, that at Philadelphia 16 xi 1995 by 23 members, and that at New Orleans 23 xi 1996 by 25 members.

[168] The meeting at Claremont 12-14 vii 1991 was attended by 15 members, that at Claremont 31 vii-2 viii 1992 by 15 members, that at Toronto 6-8 viii 1993 by 19 members, that at Claremont 23-27 v 1994 by 15 members, and that at Rattenbach, Germany 22-26 viii 1994 by 16 members.

[169] The General Editors met 1-10 vi 1995 (Bamberg), 16 xi 1995 (Philadelphia), 11-21 viii 1996 (Bamberg), 22 xi 1996 (New Orleans), 20-25 vii 1998 (Bamberg), and 27-31 vii 1999 (Bamberg).

[170] *Q 11:2b-4* [The Lord's Prayer] 1996; *Q 4:1-13, 16: The Temptations of Jesus – Nazara*, 1996; *Q 12:49-59: Children against Parents – Judging the Time – Settling out of Court*, 1997; *Q 12:8-12: Confessing and Denying – Speaking against the Holy Spirit – Hearings before Synagogues*, 1997; *Q 22:28, 30: You Will Judge the Twelve Tribes of Israel*, 1998; *Q 6:20-21: The Beatitudes for the Poor, Hungry, and Mourning*, 2001.

[171] The International Q Project has published in the October issue of *JBL* almost each year from 1990-1997 the sayings whose critical text was established the previous year: 109 (1990) 499-501; 110 (1991) 494-98; 111 (1992) 500-08; 112 (1993) 500-06; 113 (1994) 495-99; 114 (1995) 475-85; 116 (1997) 521-25. These reports did not contain the sayings in a reconstructed Q sequence, but rather in the order in which the Databases and Evaluations were prepared, discussed, and voted on. Hence, though decisions as to sequence were indeed involved in the process, when Matthew and Luke disagree on the positioning, they were not included in the annual reports.

critical text also has the advantage of being somewhat less the product of a given generation, in that the Database, stretching back to the discovery of Q in 1838, provides a certain balance to the inherent danger of overemphasizing the present.

Whereas in previous generations the trend has been to leave open the exact wording, and refer only to the verses "behind" which a Q saying lurks, there has been, during the time when the International Q Project has been doing its work, a striking escalation of efforts, even outside that context, to reconstruct the actual wording of Q.

11.3 *The English Translation*
James M. Robinson

The style of the translation is intended to reflect the style of the text of Q itself. To be avoided is the improvement of the Q text's style, begun already by Matthew and Luke and continuing in the liturgical cadence of most translations. For it is Q itself that is being translated. Conversely, what may have been intended by Jesus, John, or those involved in oral transmission is not what determines the translation (e.g. Q 3:16b, see below). Rather, the translation seeks to reflect the saying as the redactor of Q might have understood it.

What is offered is a fresh translation, seeking to avoid language that is so familiar (at times so offensive) that one no longer listens to what the text has to say, but also seeking to avoid language that is so bold that it would distract from what the text has to say and instead attract attention to itself.[172] Thus it seeks to facilitate the intention of the text itself: "Everyone hearing my words *and acting on them* ..." (Q 6:47).

Inclusive language is preferred, again in such a way as not to attract attention to the language itself, and so as to respect the cultural limitations of the text as given. It is not assumed that Jesus or the Q movement

[172] By way of illustration: *The Complete Gospels: Annotated Scholars Version* (ed. Robert J. Miller; Santa Rosa, Calif.: Polebridge, 1992; revised and expanded edition, third edition = first Harper Collins paperback edition, San Francisco: HarperSanFrancisco, 1994), contains a "Cameo Essay" (p. 448) explaining the policy of translating μακάριος and οὐαί with "Congratulations" and "Damn": It is "performative language" that should be translated with the modern equivalent rather than the traditional language that is "archaic language and now nearly empty of meaning." But since, at least in this case, the dominant focus of attention and discussion has unfortunately become the bold new language itself, thereby actually distracting from the meaning the text seeks to convey, such potentially provocative and thus distracting translations tend to be avoided.

transcended intellectually their culture in such regards.[173] Hence, patriarchal references to God as a benevolent Father are left as such (Q 6:35c, 36; 10:21 *bis*, 22 *tris*; 11:2b, 13; 12:6, 30), rather than, for example, opening the Lord's Prayer with a politically more correct form of address: "Mother-Father," or "Parent."

Designations for Jesus pose their own problems. The perhaps all-too-familiar translation "Son of man" is not retained (Q 6:22; 7:34; 9:58; 11:30; 12:8, 10, 40; 17:24, 26, 30), but the somewhat more inclusive and still recognizable "son of humanity" is preferred, rather than the freer translation, "human," which would obscure the Semitic idiom as such. "Son of Humanity" is capitalized only when the saying in question suggests a superhuman person (Q 12:40; 17:24, 26, 30), in analogy to the capitalization of "God" and "Father."

"Son" is also retained in references to God's Son (Q 3:22; 4:3, 9; 10:22 *tris*). When used of God-like humans in general, "son" is used (Q 6:35c), rather than the familiar modulation "child." For "child," while more inclusive, obscures the continuity in terminology from God-like humans to Jesus.

Similarly in the case of κύριος one normally has the standard Jewish (LXX) usage referring to God as "Lord" (Q 4:12, 8; 10:2, 21; 13:35; 16:13), whereas in other instances it is a matter of a human "master," as the householder or slave-owner (Q 12:42, 43, 46; 13:25; 14:21; 19:16, 18, 20), or as the teacher (Q 6:46; 9:59), though such human designations no doubt acquired progressively an indeterminate degree of theologizing of a christological kind.

"Spirit" poses similar problems: If Q 3:16b is old Baptist tradition, ἐν πνεύματι ἁγίῳ καὶ πυρί, referring to God's apocalyptic action, could have meant "in holy wind and fire," i.e. with devastating hurricanes and bolts of lightning, as acts of God in judgment. But since Q interpreted the prediction of Q 3:16b to be referring to Jesus as the one

[173] Luise Schottroff, *Itinerant Prophetesses: A Feminist Analysis of the Sayings Source Q* (Occasional Papers 21; Claremont, Calif.: Institute for Antiquity and Christianity, 1991); Schottroff, "Wanderprophetinnen: Eine feministische Analyse der Logienquelle," *EvT* 51 (1991) 332-44. Helga Melzer-Keller, *Jesus und die Frauen: Eine Verhältnisbestimmung nach den synoptischen Überlieferungen* (HBS 14; Herder: Freiburg, 1997), Teil 4: "Jesus und die Frauen in der Logienquelle," 330-53; Melzer-Keller, "Frauen in der Logienquelle und ihrem Trägerkreis: Ist Q das Zeugnis einer patriarchatskritischen, egalitären Bewegung?" in *Wenn Drei das Gleiche sagen ... Studien zu den ersten drei Evangelien* (ed. Stefan H. Brandenburger and Thomas Hieke; Theologie 14; Münster: Lit, 1998) 37-62; Melzer-Keller, "Wie frauenfreundlich ist die Logienquelle?" *BK* 54 (1999) 89-92.

to come (Q 7:19, 22), ἐν πνεύματι would refer to the Spirit present with Jesus and his followers (Q 4:1; 12:10, 12). But this in turn is not yet as advanced as the trinitarian associations suggested by "the Holy Spirit." Hence an intermediate translation is used: "in holy Spirit" and "the holy Spirit." Capital letters are not used for other superhuman forces, such as evil spirits (Q 11:24, 26), demons (Q 7:33; 11:14 *bis*, 15 *bis*, 19, 20), or angels (Q 4:10; 12:8, 9).

11.4 *The Sayings Gospel Q in Greek and English Ongoing Scholarship*

It is not to be assumed that the present volume, *The Sayings Gospel Q in Greek and English with Parallels from the Gospels of Mark and Thomas*, is a last word. Technological advances in the use of the computer make the assimilation of a mass of diverse data increasingly attainable, from which methodological advances are emerging.[174] Many serious differences of opinion have characterized efforts to reconstruct the text of Q in the past, as has been made quite clear from the two centuries of Gospel research that has been excerpted, sorted and evaluated by members of the International Q Project, as well as from the critical apparatus in *The Critical Edition of Q* itself. Such diversity will no doubt continue in the Q studies of the future, though advances that gain general acceptance should also result.

The Sayings Gospel Q, as well as *The Critical Edition of Q*, and *The Sayings of Jesus: The Sayings Gospel Q in English*, are intended in their layout to facilitate the study of Q, and thus to stimulate this ongoing process. Similarly the series Documenta Q, publishing the Databases and Evaluations, will make clear how the decisions presupposed in

[174] Computer-engendered tools are already being published: *Synoptic Concordance: A Greek Concordance to the First Three Gospels in Synoptic Arrangement, statistically evaluated, including occurrences in Acts; Griechische Konkordanz zu den ersten drei Evangelien in synoptischer Darstellung, statistisch ausgewertet, mit Berücksichtigung der Apostelgeschichte* (ed. Paul Hoffmann, Thomas Hieke, Ulrich Bauer; Berlin and New York: de Gruyter, 4 volumes, 1999-2000). See the reviews by Frans Neirynck, *ETL* 75 (1999) 407-18 and 76 (2000) 481-83. Conversely, the dissertation of Thomas Bergemann, *Q auf dem Prüfstein: Die Zuordnung des Mt/Lk-Stoffes zu Q am Beispiel der Bergpredigt* (FRLANT 158; Göttingen: Vandenhoeck und Ruprecht, 1993), limited to word statistics, is not to be regarded as a methodological advance, in spite of its appeal to recent computer technology. See Adelbert Denaux, "Criteria for Identifying Q-Passages: A Critical Review of a Recent Work by T. Bergemann," *NovT* 37 (1995) 105-129; further, the book reviews by Thomas Hieke, *BK* 54 (1999) 95-96, and Kloppenborg Verbin, *Excavating Q*, 62-66.

The Sayings Gospel Q were reached, as well as making a mass of relevant material scattered over two centuries, in three or more languages, and often in inaccessible journals and out-of-print books, more readily available. It is thus to be hoped that the refinement of the text of Q will continue unabated, in the ongoing series Documenta Q and elsewhere, indeed at an accelerated tempo, so as to make an electronic and/or printed revision of the present work from time to time desirable.

SIGLA

The complex battery of sigla in *The Critical Edition of Q* is indispensable in discussing the establishment of the critical text itself. But for those whose interest is focused instead on the text of Q thus established, rather than upon the process leading to that outcome, the critical text of Q is printed here as a continuous text, without such sigla.

The only sigla used here are those indicating the degree of certainty ascribed to the text, since this is important for every user of the text of Q:

⟦ ⟧ Double square brackets are used surrounding verse numbers, and, if a whole section is involved, its title, as well as individual Greek and English words, to indicate a degree of uncertainty of {C} in a descending scale from {A} to {D} (with {U} as indeterminate).

« » Double angle brackets are used in the Greek and English texts to indicate that a Q text is only in one Gospel, and hence that a critical text cannot be established by the usual comparison of both Gospels. This is the case in Q 6: ⟦29↔30/Matt 5:41⟧; 7:⟦29⟧; 10:7, ⟦8⟧; 12:33, ⟦49⟧; 14:21; 15:⟦8-10⟧; 17:⟦20⟧, ⟦21⟧. In the English translation, double angle brackets also embrace a gist or flow of thought, or the most probable terms, which may well be rather clear, even though the Greek text could not be reconstructed. This is the case in Q 4:2; 6:37, 42; 7:⟦30⟧; 10:21; 11:⟦21-22⟧, 48; 12:⟦54⟧, 58; 14:18, ?19?, 21; 15:4; 17:⟦21⟧. Further, these sigla identify words needed for a smooth rendering in English, even though there is no explicit equivalent in the Greek text behind the translation. This is the case in Q 3:8, 17; 6:20, 21, 23, 30, 34, 40, 45; 7:26, 28, 34; 11:14, 19, 25, 26, 34, 35, 46b, 52, 47, 48, 49, 50, 51; 12:3, 6, ⟦55⟧, ⟦56⟧; 13:26, 27, 34, 35; 16:16; 17:1, 34, 35; 19:21, 24.

… Three dots indicate that there is some text that cannot be reconstituted, where not even a gist is suggested.

.. Two dots indicate that there may be some text here that cannot be reconstituted, though even this remains uncertain.

?? In such cases where even the existence of any text at all is in doubt, the verse numbers and, if a whole section is involved, its title, are put between question marks, to call attention to the high degree of uncertainty, for example, Q 11:?27-28??Hearing and Keeping God's Word?

< > Angle brackets embrace an emendation in the text.

↔ A line pointing in both directions is used to indicate the location of a Q saying that is not in Luke, and hence cannot be identified in terms of Lukan chapter and verse numeration. Instead, the Q verses just before (Q 6:29) and just after (Q 6:30) are listed to identify the location, and the Matthean reference is added to identify the text: Q 6:29↔30/Matt 5:41.

Parallel texts from the Gospels of Mark and *Thomas* have been put beneath each section of Q. The English translation of Markan parallels is that of the New Revised Standard Version. But in both Mark and *Thomas* the language is adapted to fit the translation of Q, so that the same Greek is translated the same, and divergent Greek is translated differently. This makes it easier to compare accurately Q, Mark, and *Thomas* in their English translations.

The Greek fragments of the *Gospel of Thomas* that are extant in *P. Oxy*. 1, 654, and 655 are here presented in their original Greek text. The usual sigla for editing papyri at times occur:

[ ] In lacunae, restored lettering is put in square brackets.

. A dot is put under a letter that is not visually unambiguous.

( ) Parentheses surround lettering abbreviated in the Greek original but spelled out in the transcription, such as in the case of *nomina sacra,* e.g. Ἰ(ησοῦ)ς in the standard quotation formula.

< > Angle brackets indicate the editor's correction of a scribal omission or error: *Gos. Thom.* 33.1 (P. Oxy. 1) at Q 12:3.

In the English translation, material not actually present in the Coptic or Greek text, but needed for a smooth formulation in English, is inserted in parentheses.

The complete text of the *Gospel of Thomas* is preserved almost intact in the Coptic translation from Nag Hammadi Codex II, Tractate 2. The Greek text presented here is the retroversion by the Berliner Arbeitskreis für koptisch-gnostische Schriften.

Abbreviations in references to scholarly literature are those found in *The SBL Handbook of Style: For Ancient Near Eastern, Biblical, and Early Christian Studies* (ed. Patrick H. Alexander et al.; Peabody, Mass.: Hendrickson, 1999), supplemented when necessary by *IATG*[2].

THE TEXT OF Q
IN GREEK AND ENGLISH

THE TEXT OF Q IN GREEK

with Parallels from the Gospels of Mark and Thomas

Q 3:⟦0⟧
⟦Incipit⟧

Matt 3:0 | Luke 3:0

⟦<… Ἰησου…>⟧

Q 3:2b-3a
The Introduction of John

Matt 3:1, 5 | Luke 3:2b-3a

2b <…> Ἰωάννη…
3a <…> πᾶσα..η.. περίχωρο… τοῦ Ἰορδάνου <…>.

Mark 1:4-5a

4 ἐγένετο Ἰωάννης ὁ βαπτίζων ἐν τῇ ἐρήμῳ καὶ κηρύσσων βάπτισμα
μετανοίας εἰς ἄφεσιν ἁμαρτιῶν.
5a καὶ ἐξεπορεύετο πρὸς αὐτὸν πᾶσα ἡ Ἰουδαία χώρα

Q 3:7-9
John's Announcement of Judgment

Matt 3:7-10 | Luke 3:7-9

7 ⟦εἶπεν⟧ τοῖς ⟦ἐρχ⟧ομένο<ι>ς ⟦ὄχλοις⟧ βαπτισ⟦θῆναι⟧· γεννήματα
ἐχιδνῶν, τίς ὑπέδειξεν ὑμῖν φυγεῖν ἀπὸ τῆς μελλούσης ὀργῆς;
8 ποιήσατε οὖν καρπὸν ἄξιον τῆς μετανοίας καὶ μὴ δόξητε λέγειν
ἐν ἑαυτοῖς· πατέρα ἔχομεν τὸν Ἀβραάμ. λέγω γὰρ ὑμῖν ὅτι δύναται ὁ θεὸς ἐκ τῶν λίθων τούτων ἐγεῖραι τέκνα τῷ Ἀβραάμ.
9 ἤδη δὲ ἡ ἀξίνη πρὸς τὴν ῥίζαν τῶν δένδρων κεῖται· πᾶν οὖν δένδρον μὴ ποιοῦν καρπὸν καλὸν ἐκκόπτεται καὶ εἰς πῦρ βάλλεται.

Mark 1:5

καὶ ἐξεπορεύετο πρὸς αὐτὸν πᾶσα ἡ Ἰουδαία χώρα καὶ οἱ Ἱεροσολυμῖται πάντες, καὶ ἐβαπτίζοντο ὑπ᾽ αὐτοῦ ἐν τῷ Ἰορδάνῃ ποταμῷ ἐξομολογούμενοι τὰς ἁμαρτίας αὐτῶν.

THE TEXT OF Q IN ENGLISH

with Parallels from the Gospels of Mark and Thomas

Q 3:⟦0⟧
⟦Incipit⟧

Matt 3:0 | Luke 3:0

⟦<… Jesus …>⟧

Q 3:2b-3a
The Introduction of John

Matt 3:1, 5 | Luke 3:2b-3a

2b <…> John
3a <…> all the region of the Jordan <…>.

Mark 1:4-5a

4 John the baptizer appeared in the wilderness, proclaiming a baptism of repentance for the forgiveness of sins.
5a And people from the whole Judean region

Q 3:7-9
John's Announcement of Judgment

Matt 3:7-10 | Luke 3:7-9

7 He said to the ⟦crowds coming to be⟧ bapti⟦zed⟧: Snakes' litter! Who warned you to run from the impending rage?
8 So bear fruit worthy of repentance, and do not presume to tell yourselves: We have as «fore»father Abraham! For I tell you: God can produce children for Abraham right out of these rocks!
9 And the ax already lies at the root of the trees. So every tree not bearing healthy fruit is to be chopped down and thrown on the fire.

Mark 1:5

And people from the whole Judean region and all the people of Jerusalem were going out to him, and were baptized by him in the river Jordan, confessing their sins.

Q 3:16b-17
John and the One to Come

Matt 3:11-12 Luke 3:16b-17

16b ἐγὼ μὲν ὑμᾶς βαπτίζω ⟦ἐν⟧ ὕδατι, ὁ δὲ ὀπίσω μου ἐρχόμενος ἰσχυρότερός μού ἐστιν, οὗ οὐκ εἰμὶ ἱκανὸς τ⟦ὰ⟧ ὑποδήματ⟦α⟧ ⟦βαστά⟧σαι· αὐτὸς ὑμᾶς βαπτίσει ἐν πνεύματι ⟦ἁγίῳ⟧ καὶ πυρί·
17 οὗ τὸ πτύον ἐν τῇ χειρὶ αὐτοῦ καὶ διακαθαριεῖ τὴν ἅλωνα αὐτοῦ καὶ συνάξει τὸν σῖτον εἰς τὴν ἀποθήκην αὐτοῦ, τὸ δὲ ἄχυρον κατακαύσει πυρὶ ἀσβέστῳ.

Mark 1:7-8

7 Καὶ ἐκήρυσσεν λέγων· ἔρχεται ὁ ἰσχυρότερός μου ὀπίσω μου, οὗ οὐκ εἰμὶ ἱκανὸς κύψας λῦσαι τὸν ἱμάντα τῶν ὑποδημάτων αὐτοῦ.
8 ἐγὼ ἐβάπτισα ὑμᾶς ὕδατι, αὐτὸς δὲ βαπτίσει ὑμᾶς ἐν πνεύματι ἁγίῳ.

Q 3:⟦21b-22⟧
⟦The Baptism of Jesus⟧

Matt 3:16-17 Luke 3:21b-22

⟦**21**⟧ ⟦.. Ἰησου.. βαπτισθε…νεῳχθη…ο… οὐρανο…,⟧
⟦**22**⟧ ⟦καὶ .. τὸ πνεῦμα … ἐπ᾽ αὐτόν· … υἱ… .⟧

Mark 1:9-11

9 Καὶ ἐγένετο ἐν ἐκείναις ταῖς ἡμέραις ἦλθεν Ἰησοῦς ἀπὸ Ναζαρὲτ τῆς Γαλιλαίας καὶ ἐβαπτίσθη εἰς τὸν Ἰορδάνην ὑπὸ Ἰωάννου.
10 καὶ εὐθὺς ἀναβαίνων ἐκ τοῦ ὕδατος εἶδεν σχιζομένους τοὺς οὐρανοὺς καὶ τὸ πνεῦμα ὡς περιστερὰν καταβαῖνον εἰς αὐτόν·
11 καὶ φωνὴ ἐγένετο ἐκ τῶν οὐρανῶν· σὺ εἶ ὁ υἱός μου ὁ ἀγαπητός, ἐν σοὶ εὐδόκησα.

Q 4:1-4, 9-12, 5-8, 13
The Temptations of Jesus

Matt 4:1-11 Luke 4:1-13

1 ⟦ὁ⟧ δὲ Ἰησοῦς ⟦ἀν⟧ή⟦χθη⟧ ⟦εἰς⟧ τὴ⟦ν⟧ ἔρημ⟦ον ὑπὸ⟧ τ⟦οῦ⟧ πνεύμα⟦τος⟧
2 πειρα⟦σθῆναι⟧ ὑπὸ τοῦ διαβόλου. καὶ … ἡμέρας τεσσεράκοντα, .. ἐπείνασεν.
3 καὶ εἶπεν αὐτῷ ὁ διάβολος· εἰ υἱὸς εἶ τοῦ θεοῦ, εἰπὲ ἵνα οἱ λίθοι οὗτοι ἄρτοι γένωνται.

Q 3:16b-17
John and the One to Come

Matt 3:11-12 Luke 3:16b-17

16b I baptize you ⟦in⟧ water, but the one to come after me is more powerful than I, whose sandals I am not fit to ⟦take off⟧. He will baptize you in ⟦holy⟧ Spirit and fire.
17 His pitchfork «is» in his hand, and he will clear his threshing floor and gather the wheat into his granary, but the chaff he will burn on a fire that can never be put out.

Mark 1:7-8

7 And he preached, saying: The one who is more powerful than I is coming after me; I am not fit to stoop down and untie the thong of his sandals.
8 I have baptized you in water; but he will baptize you in the Holy Spirit.

Q 3:⟦21b-22⟧
⟦The Baptism of Jesus⟧

Matt 3:16-17 Luke 3:21b-22

⟦**21**⟧ ⟦.. Jesus … baptized, heaven opened ..,⟧
⟦**22**⟧ ⟦and .. the Spirit … upon him … Son … .⟧

Mark 1:9-11

9 In those days Jesus came from Nazareth of Galilee and was baptized by John in the Jordan.
10 And just as he was coming up out of the water, he saw the heavens torn apart and the Spirit descending like a dove upon him.
11 And a voice came from heaven: You are my Son, the Beloved; with you I am well pleased.

Q 4:1-4, 9-12, 5-8, 13
The Temptations of Jesus

Matt 4:1-11 Luke 4:1-13

1 And Jesus was led ⟦into⟧ the wilderness by the Spirit

2 ⟦to be⟧ tempted by the devil. And «he ate nothing» for forty days, .. he became hungry.
3 And the devil told him: If you are God's Son, order that these stones become loaves.

4 καὶ ἀπεκρίθη ⟦αὐτ<ῷ>⟧ ὁ Ἰησοῦς· γέγραπται ὅτι οὐκ ἐπ' ἄρτῳ
μόνῳ ζήσεται ὁ ἄνθρωπος.
9 παραλαμβάνει αὐτὸν ⟦ὁ διάβολος⟧ εἰς Ἰερουσαλὴμ καὶ ἔστησεν
αὐτὸν ἐπὶ τὸ πτερύγιον τοῦ ἱεροῦ καὶ εἶπεν αὐτῷ· εἰ υἱὸς εἶ τοῦ
θεοῦ, βάλε σεαυτὸν κάτω·
10 γέγραπται γὰρ ὅτι τοῖς ἀγγέλοις αὐτοῦ ἐντελεῖται περὶ σοῦ
11 καὶ ἐπὶ χειρῶν ἀροῦσίν σε, μήποτε προσκόψῃς πρὸς λίθον τὸν
πόδα σου.
12 καὶ ⟦ἀποκριθεὶς⟧ εἶπεν αὐτῷ ὁ Ἰησοῦς· γέγραπται· οὐκ
ἐκπειράσεις κύριον τὸν θεόν σου.
5 καὶ παραλαμβάνει αὐτὸν ὁ διάβολος εἰς ὅρος ⟦ὑψηλὸν λίαν⟧ καὶ
δείκνυσιν αὐτῷ πάσας τὰς βασιλείας τοῦ κόσμου καὶ τὴν δόξαν
αὐτῶν
6 καὶ εἶπεν αὐτῷ· ταῦτά σοι πάντα δώσω,
7 ἐὰν προσκυνήσῃς μοι.
8 καὶ ⟦ἀποκριθεὶς⟧ ὁ Ἰησοῦς εἶπεν αὐτῷ· γέγραπται· κύριον τὸν
θεόν σου προσκυνήσεις καὶ αὐτῷ μόνῳ λατρεύσεις.
13 καὶ ὁ διάβολος ἀφίησιν αὐτόν.

Mark 1:12-13

12 Καὶ εὐθὺς τὸ πνεῦμα αὐτὸν ἐκβάλλει εἰς τὴν ἔρημον.
13 καὶ ἦν ἐν τῇ ἐρήμῳ τεσσεράκοντα ἡμέρας πειραζόμενος ὑπὸ τοῦ
σατανᾶ, καὶ ἦν μετὰ τῶν θηρίων, καὶ οἱ ἄγγελοι διηκόνουν αὐτῷ.

Q 4:16
Nazara

Matt 4:13 Luke 4:16

<…> Ναζαρά <…>.

Mark 6:1

Καὶ ἐξῆλθεν ἐκεῖθεν καὶ ἔρχεται εἰς τὴν πατρίδα αὐτοῦ, καὶ ἀκολουθοῦσιν αὐτῷ οἱ μαθηταὶ αὐτοῦ.

Q 6:20-21
Beatitudes for the Poor, Hungry, and Mourning

Matt 5:1-4, 6 Luke 6:20-21

20 <…> καὶ ⟦ἐπάρ⟧ας το⟦ὺς ὀφθαλμοὺς⟧ αὐτοῦ ⟦εἰς τοὺς⟧ μαθ-
ητὰ⟦ς⟧ αὐτοῦ ..λέγ…· μακάριοι οἱ πτωχοί, ὅτι ⟦ὑμετέρα⟧ ἐστὶν ἡ
βασιλεία τοῦ θεοῦ.

4 And Jesus answered ⟦him⟧: It is written: A person is not to live only
from bread.
9 ⟦The devil⟧ took him along to Jerusalem and put him on the tip of the
temple and told him: If you are God's Son, throw yourself down.

10 For it is written: He will command his angels about you,
11 and on their hands they will bear you, so that you do not strike your
foot against a stone.
12 And Jesus ⟦in reply⟧ told him: It is written: Do not put to the test the
Lord your God.
5 And the devil took him along to a ⟦very high⟧ mountain and showed
him all the kingdoms of the world and their splendor,

6 and told him: All these I will give you,
7 if you bow down before me.
8 And ⟦in reply⟧ Jesus told him: It is written: Bow down to the Lord
your God, and serve only him.
13 And the devil left him.

Mark 1:12-13

12 And the Spirit immediately drove him out into the wilderness.
13 He was in the wilderness forty days, tempted by Satan; and he was with the
wild beasts; and the angels waited on him.

Q 4:16
Nazara

Matt 4:13 | Luke 4:16

<…> Nazara <…>.

Mark 6:1

He left that place and came to his hometown, and his disciples followed him.

Q 6:20-21
Beatitudes for the Poor, Hungry, and Mourning

Matt 5:1-4, 6 | Luke 6:20-21

20 <…> And ⟦rais⟧ing his ⟦eyes to⟧ his disciples he said: Blessed are
⟦«you»⟧ poor, for God's reign is for ⟦you⟧.

21 μακάριοι οἱ πεινῶντες, ὅτι χορτασθήσ⟦εσθε⟧. μακάριοι οἱ ⟦πενθ⟧ο⟦ῦ⟧ντες, ὅτι ⟦παρακληθήσ<εσθε>⟧.

Gos. Thom. 54 (Nag Hammadi II 2)

Λέγει Ἰησοῦς· μακάριοι οἱ πτωχοί, ὅτι ὑμετέρα ἐστὶν ἡ βασιλεία τῶν οὐρανῶν.

Gos. Thom. 69.2 (Nag Hammadi II 2)

μακάριοι οἱ πεινῶντες, ἵνα χορτασθῇ ἡ κοιλία τοῦ θέλοντος.

Q 6:22-23
The Beatitude for the Persecuted

Matt 5:11-12 Luke 6:22-23

22 μακάριοί ἐστε ὅταν ὀνειδίσωσιν ὑμᾶς καὶ ⟦διώξ⟧ωσιν καὶ ⟦εἴπ⟧ωσιν ⟦πᾶν⟧ πονηρὸν ⟦καθ'⟧ ὑμῶν ἕνεκεν τοῦ υἱοῦ τοῦ ἀνθρώπου.
23 χαίρετε καὶ ⟦ἀγαλλιᾶσθε⟧, ὅτι ὁ μισθὸς ὑμῶν πολὺς ἐν τῷ οὐρανῷ· οὕτως γὰρ ⟦ἐδίωξαν⟧ τοὺς προφήτας τοὺς πρὸ ὑμῶν.

Gos. Thom. 69.1a (Nag Hammadi II 2)

Λέγει Ἰησοῦς· μακάριοι οἱ δεδιωγμένοι ἐν τῇ καρδίᾳ αὐτῶν.

Gos. Thom. 68.1 (Nag Hammadi II 2)

Λέγει Ἰησοῦς· μακάριοί ἐστε ὅταν μισήσωσιν ὑμᾶς καὶ διώξωσιν ὑμᾶς.

Q 6:27-28, 35c-d
Love Your Enemies

Matt 5:44-45 Luke 6:27-28, 35c-d

27 ἀγαπᾶτε τοὺς ἐχθροὺς ὑμῶν
28 ⟦καὶ⟧ προσεύχεσθε ὑπὲρ τῶν ⟦διωκ⟧όντων ὑμᾶς,
35c-d ὅπως γένησθε υἱοὶ τοῦ πατρὸς ὑμῶν, ὅτι τὸν ἥλιον αὐτοῦ ἀνατέλλει ἐπὶ πονηροὺς καὶ ⟦ἀγαθοὺς καὶ βρέχει ἐπὶ δικαίους καὶ ἀδίκους⟧.

21 Blessed are ⟦«you»⟧ who hunger, for ⟦you⟧ will eat ⟦your⟧ fill. Blessed are ⟦«you»⟧ who ⟦mourn⟧, for ⟦<you> will be consoled⟧.

Gos. Thom. 54 (Nag Hammadi II 2)

Jesus says: Blessed are (you) poor, for heaven's reign is for you.

Gos. Thom. 69.2 (Nag Hammadi II 2)

Blessed are those who hunger in order that the stomach of the one who craves for (it) may eat its fill.

Q 6:22-23
The Beatitude for the Persecuted

Matt 5:11-12 Luke 6:22-23

22 Blessed are you when they insult and ⟦persecute⟧ you, and ⟦say every kind of⟧ evil ⟦against⟧ you because of the son of humanity.

23 Be glad and ⟦exult⟧, for vast is your reward in heaven. For this is how they ⟦persecuted⟧ the prophets who «were» before you.

Gos. Thom. 69.1a (Nag Hammadi II 2)

Jesus says: Blessed are those who have been persecuted in their heart.

Gos. Thom. 68.1 (Nag Hammadi II 2)

Jesus says: Blessed are you when they hate you and persecute you.

Q 6:27-28, 35c-d
Love Your Enemies

Matt 5:44-45 Luke 6:27-28, 35c-d

27 Love your enemies
28 ⟦and⟧ pray for those ⟦persecuting⟧ you,
35c-d so that you may become sons of your Father, for he raises his sun on bad and ⟦good and rains on the just and unjust⟧.

Q 6:29, ⟦29↔30/Matt 5:41⟧, 30
Renouncing One's Own Rights

Matt 5:39b-42 Luke 6:29-30

29 ⟦ὅστις⟧ σε ⟦ῥαπίζει⟧ εἰς τὴν σιαγόνα, στρέψον ⟦αὐτῷ⟧ καὶ τὴν
ἄλλην· καὶ ⟦τῷ θέλοντί σοι κριθῆναι καὶ⟧ τὸν χιτῶνά σου ⟦λαβεῖν,
ἄφες αὐτῷ⟧ καὶ τὸ ἱμάτιον.
⟦**29↔30/Matt 5:41**⟧ ⟦«καὶ ὅστις σε ἀγγαρεύσει μίλιον ἕν, ὕπαγε
μετ' αὐτοῦ δύο.»⟧
30 τῷ αἰτοῦντί σε δός, καὶ ⟦ἀπὸ⟧ τ⟦οῦ δανι<ζομένου> τὰ⟧ σ⟦ὰ⟧ μὴ
ἀπ⟦αίτει⟧.

Gos. Thom. 95 (Nag Hammadi II 2)

(1) [Λέγει Ἰησοῦς]· ἐὰν ἔχητε ἀργύριον, μὴ δανείζετε,
(2) ἀλλὰ δίδοτε [αὐτὸ] παρ' οὗ οὐκ ἀπολήμψεσθε αὐτά.

Q 6:31
The Golden Rule

Matt 7:12 Luke 6:31

καὶ καθὼς θέλετε ἵνα ποιῶσιν ὑμῖν οἱ ἄνθρωποι, οὕτως ποιεῖτε αὐτοῖς.

Gos. Thom. 6.3 (P. Oxy. 654)

[καὶ ὅ τι μισ]εῖτε μὴ ποιεῖτ[ε·]

Gos. Thom. 6.3 (Nag Hammadi II 2)

καὶ ὅ τι μισεῖτε μὴ ποιεῖτε.

Q 6:32, 34
Impartial Love

Matt 5:46, 47 Luke 6:32, 34

32 .. ε⟦ἰ⟧ .. ἀγαπ⟦ᾶ⟧τε τοὺς ἀγαπῶντας ὑμᾶς, τίνα μισθὸν ἔχετε;
οὐχὶ καὶ οἱ τελῶναι τὸ αὐτὸ ποιοῦσιν;
34 καὶ ἐὰν ⟦δανίσητε παρ' ὧν ἐλπίζετε λαβεῖν, τί<να μισθὸν
ἔχε>τε⟧; οὐχὶ καὶ ⟦οἱ ἐθνικ⟧οὶ τὸ αὐτὸ ποιοῦσιν;

Gos. Thom. 95 (Nag Hammadi II 2)

(1) [Λέγει Ἰησοῦς]· ἐὰν ἔχητε ἀργύριον, μὴ δανείζετε,
(2) ἀλλὰ δίδοτε [αὐτὸ] παρ' οὗ οὐκ ἀπολήμψεσθε αὐτά.

Q 6:29, ⟦29↔30/Matt 5:41⟧, 30
Renouncing One's Own Rights

Matt 5:39b-42 Luke 6:29-30

29 ⟦The one who slaps⟧ you on the cheek, offer ⟦him⟧ the other as well; and ⟦to the person wanting to take you to court and get⟧ your shirt, ⟦turn over to him⟧ the coat as well.
⟦29↔30/Matt 5:41⟧ ⟦«And the one who conscripts you for one mile, go with him a second.»⟧
30 To the one who asks of you, give; and ⟦from the one who borrows⟧, do not ⟦ask⟧ back ⟦«what is»⟧ yours.

Gos. Thom. 95 (Nag Hammadi II 2)

(1) [Jesus says:] If you have money, do not lend out at interest.
(2) Rather, give [it] to the one from whom you will not get it (back).

Q 6:31
The Golden Rule

Matt 7:12 Luke 6:31

And the way you want people to treat you, that is how you treat them.

Gos. Thom. 6.3 (P. Oxy. 654)

[and] do not do [what] you [hate].

Gos. Thom. 6.3 (Nag Hammadi II 2)

And do not do what you hate.

Q 6:32, 34
Impartial Love

Matt 5:46, 47 Luke 6:32, 34

32 .. If you love those loving you, what reward do you have? Do not even tax collectors do the same?
34 And if you ⟦lend «to those» from whom you hope to receive, what <reward do> you < have>?⟧ Do not even ⟦the Gentiles⟧ do the same?

Gos. Thom. 95 (Nag Hammadi II 2)

(1) [Jesus says:] If you have money, do not lend out at interest.
(2) Rather, give [it] to the one from whom you will not get it (back).

Q 6:36
Being Full of Pity like Your Father

Matt 5:48 Luke 6:36

⟦γίν⟧εσθε οἰκτίρμονες ὡς .. ὁ πατὴρ ὑμῶν οἰκτίρμων ἐστίν.

Q 6:37-38
Not Judging

Matt 7:1-2 Luke 6:37-38

37 .. μὴ κρίνετε, ... μὴ κριθῆτε· ⟦ἐν ᾧ γὰρ κρίματι κρίνετε κριθήσεσθε,⟧
38 ⟦καὶ⟧ ἐν ᾧ μέτρῳ μετρεῖτε μετρηθήσεται ὑμῖν.

Mark 4:24b-e

βλέπετε τί ἀκούετε. ἐν ᾧ μέτρῳ μετρεῖτε μετρηθήσεται ὑμῖν καὶ προστεθήσεται ὑμῖν.

Q 6:39
The Blind Leading the Blind

Matt 15:14 Luke 6:39

μήτι δύναται τυφλὸς τυφλὸν ὁδηγεῖν; οὐχὶ ἀμφότεροι εἰς βόθυνον πεσοῦνται;

Gos. Thom. 34 (Nag Hammadi II 2)

Λέγει Ἰησοῦς· τυφλὸς ἐὰν προάγῃ τυφλόν, ἀμφότεροι πίπτουσιν εἰς βόθυνον.

Q 6:40
The Disciple and the Teacher

Matt 10:24-25a Luke 6:40

οὐκ ἔστιν μαθητὴς ὑπὲρ τὸν διδάσκαλον· ⟦ἀρκετὸν τῷ μαθητῇ ἵνα γένη⟧ται ὡς ὁ διδάσκαλος αὐτοῦ.

Q 6:36
Being Full of Pity like Your Father

Matt 5:48 Luke 6:36

Be full of pity, just as your Father .. is full of pity.

Q 6:37-38
Not Judging

Matt 7:1-2 Luke 6:37-38

37 .. Do not pass judgment, «so» you are not judged. ⟦For with what judgment you pass judgment, you will be judged.⟧
38 ⟦And⟧ with the measurement you use to measure out, it will be measured out to you.

Mark 4:24b-e

Pay attention to what you hear; with the measurement you use to measure out, it will be measured out to you, and still more will be given you.

Q 6:39
The Blind Leading the Blind

Matt 15:14 Luke 6:39

Can a blind person show the way to a blind person? Will not both fall into a pit?

Gos. Thom. 34 (Nag Hammadi II 2)

Jesus says: If a blind person leads a blind person, both fall into a pit.

Q 6:40
The Disciple and the Teacher

Matt 10:24-25a Luke 6:40

A disciple is not superior to the teacher. ⟦It is enough for the disciple that he become⟧ like his teacher.

Q 6:41-42
The Speck and the Beam

Matt 7:3-5 Luke 6:41-42

41 τί δὲ βλέπεις τὸ κάρφος τὸ ἐν τῷ ὀφθαλμῷ τοῦ ἀδελφοῦ σου,
τὴν δὲ ἐν τῷ σῷ ὀφθαλμῷ δοκὸν οὐ κατανοεῖς;
42 πῶς … τῷ ἀδελφῷ σου· ἄφες ἐκβάλω τὸ κάρφος ⟦ἐκ⟧ τ⟦οῦ⟧
ὀφθαλμ⟦οῦ⟧ σου, καὶ ἰδοὺ ἡ δοκὸς ἐν τῷ ὀφθαλμῷ σου; ὑποκριτά,
ἔκβαλε πρῶτον ἐκ τοῦ ὀφθαλμοῦ σου τὴν δοκόν, καὶ τότε διαβλέψεις ἐκβαλεῖν τὸ κάρφος … τ… ὀφθαλμ… τοῦ ἀδελφοῦ σου.

Gos. Thom. 26.2 (P. Oxy. 1)

[…] καὶ τότε διαβλέψεις ἐκβαλεῖν τὸ κάρφος τὸ ἐν τῷ ὀφθαλμῷ τοῦ ἀδελφοῦ σου.

Gos. Thom. 26.1-2 (Nag Hammadi II 2)

(1) Λέγει Ἰησοῦς· τὸ κάρφος τὸ ἐν τῷ ὀφθαλμῷ τοῦ ἀδελφοῦ σου βλέπεις, τὴν δὲ δοκὸν τὴν ἐν τῷ ὀφθαλμῷ σου οὐ βλέπεις.
(2) ὅταν ἐκβάλῃς τὴν δοκὸν ἐκ τοῦ ὀφθαλμοῦ σου, τότε διαβλέψεις ἐκβαλεῖν τὸ κάρφος ἐκ τοῦ ὀφθαλμοῦ τοῦ ἀδελφοῦ σου.

Q 6:43-45
The Tree Is Known by its Fruit

Matt 7:16b, 18; 12:33b-35 Luke 6:43-45

43 .. οὔ<κ> ἔστιν δένδρον καλὸν ποιοῦν καρπὸν σαπρόν, οὐδὲ
⟦πάλιν⟧ δένδρον σαπρὸν ποιοῦν καρπὸν καλόν.
44 ἐκ γὰρ τοῦ καρποῦ τὸ δένδρον γινώσκεται. μήτι συλλέγουσιν
ἐξ ἀκανθῶν σῦκα ἢ ἐκ τριβόλων σταφυλ⟦άς⟧;
45 ὁ ἀγαθὸς ἄνθρωπος ἐκ τοῦ ἀγαθοῦ θησαυροῦ ἐκβάλλει ἀγαθά,
καὶ ὁ πονηρὸς ⟦ἄνθρωπος⟧ ἐκ τοῦ πονηροῦ ⟦θησαυροῦ⟧ ἐκβάλλει
πονηρά· ἐκ γὰρ περισσεύματος καρδίας λαλεῖ τὸ στόμα ⟦αὐτοῦ⟧.

Gos. Thom. 45.1-4 (Nag Hammadi II 2)

(1) Λέγει Ἰησοῦς· οὐ τρυγῶσιν ἐξ ἀκανθῶν σταφυλὰς οὐδὲ συλλέγουσιν σῦκα ἀπὸ τριβόλων· οὐ γὰρ διδόασιν καρπόν.
(2) ἀγαθὸς ἄνθρωπος προφέρει ἀγαθόν τι ἐκ τοῦ θησαυροῦ αὐτοῦ.
(3) κακ[ὸς] ἄνθρωπος προφέρει πονηρὰ ἐκ τοῦ θησαυροῦ αὐτοῦ τοῦ κακοῦ, ὅς (ἐστιν) ἐν τῇ καρδίᾳ αὐτοῦ, καὶ λαλεῖ πονηρά.
(4) ἐκ γὰρ τοῦ περισσεύματος τῆς καρδίας προφέρει πονηρά.

Q 6:41-42
The Speck and the Beam

Matt 7:3-5 Luke 6:41-42

41 And why do you see the speck in your brother's eye, but the beam in your own eye you overlook?
42 How «can you» say to your brother: Let me throw out the speck ⟦from⟧ your eye, and just look at the beam in your own eye? Hypocrite, first throw out from your own eye the beam, and then you will see clearly to throw out the speck «in» your brother's eye.

Gos. Thom. 26.2 (P. Oxy. 1)

[…] and then you will see clearly to throw out the speck in your brother's eye.

Gos. Thom. 26.1-2 (Nag Hammadi II 2)

(1) Jesus says: The speck in your brother's eye you see, but the beam in your own eye you do not see.
(2) When you throw out the beam from your own eye, then you will see clearly to throw out the speck from your brother's eye.

Q 6:43-45
The Tree Is Known by its Fruit

Matt 7:16b, 18; 12:33b-35 Luke 6:43-45

43 .. No healthy tree bears rotten fruit, nor ⟦on the other hand⟧ does a decayed tree bear healthy fruit.
44 For from the fruit the tree is known. Are figs picked from thorns, or grape⟦s⟧ from thistles?
45 The good person from «one's» good treasure casts up good things, and the evil ⟦person⟧ from the evil ⟦treasure⟧ casts up evil things. For from exuberance of heart ⟦one's⟧ mouth speaks.

Gos. Thom. 45.1-4 (Nag Hammadi II 2)

(1) Jesus says: Grapes are not harvested from thorns, nor are figs picked from thistles, for they do not produce fruit.
(2) A good person brings forth good from one's treasure.
(3) A bad person brings forth evil things from the bad treasure that is in one's heart, and (in fact) one speaks evil things.
(4) For out of the exuberance of the heart one brings forth evil things.

Q 6:46
Not Just Saying Master, Master

Matt 7:21 Luke 6:46

τί .. με καλεῖτε· κύριε κύριε, καὶ οὐ ποιεῖτε ἃ λέγω;

Mark 3:35a

ὃς γὰρ ἂν ποιήσῃ τὸ θέλημα τοῦ θεοῦ,

Q 6:47-49
Houses Built on Rock or Sand

Matt 7:24-27 Luke 6:47-49

47 πᾶς ὁ ἀκούων μου τ… λόγ… καὶ ποιῶν αὐτούς,
48 ὅμοιός ἐστιν ἀνθρώπῳ, ὃς ᾠκοδόμησεν ⟦αὐτοῦ τὴν⟧ οἰκίαν ἐπὶ
τὴν πέτραν· καὶ κατέβη ἡ βροχὴ καὶ ἦλθον οἱ ποταμοὶ ⟦καὶ ἔπνευσαν οἱ ἄνεμοι⟧ καὶ προσέπεσαν τῇ οἰκίᾳ ἐκείνῃ, καὶ οὐκ ἔπεσεν,
τεθεμελίωτο γὰρ ἐπὶ τὴν πέτραν.
49 καὶ ⟦πᾶς⟧ ὁ ἀκούων ⟦μου τοὺς λόγους⟧ καὶ μὴ ποιῶν ⟦αὐτοὺς⟧
ὅμοιός ἐστιν ἀνθρώπῳ ὃς ᾠκοδόμησεν ⟦αὐτοῦ τὴν⟧ οἰκὶαν ἐπὶ τὴν
ἄμμον· καὶ κατέβη ἡ βροχὴ καὶ ἦλθον οἱ ποταμοὶ ⟦καὶ ἔπνευσαν
οἱ ἄνεμοι⟧ καὶ προσέκοψαν τῇ οἰκίᾳ ἐκείνῃ, καὶ εὐθὺς ἔπεσεν καὶ
ἦν ⟦ἡ πτῶσις⟧ αὐτῆς μεγά⟦λη⟧.

Q 7:1, 3, 6b-9, ?10?
The Centurion's Faith in Jesus' Word

Matt 7:28a; 8:5-10, 13 Luke 7:1, 3, 6b-10

1 ⟦καὶ ἐγένετο ὅτε⟧ ἐ⟦πλήρω⟧σεν .. τοὺς λόγους τούτους, εἰσῆλθεν
εἰς Καφαρναούμ.
3 <>ἦλθεν αὐτῷ ἑκατόνταρχ⟦ο⟧ς παρακαλῶν αὐτὸν ⟦καὶ λέγων·⟧ ὁ
παῖς ⟦μου κακῶς ἔχ<ει>. καὶ λέγει αὐτῷ· ἐγὼ⟧ ἐλθὼν θεραπεύσ⟦ω⟧
αὐτόν;
6b-c καὶ ἀποκριθεὶς ὁ ἑκατόνταρχος ἔφη· κύριε, οὐκ εἰμὶ ἱκανὸς
ἵνα μου ὑπὸ τὴν στέγην εἰσέλθῃς,
7 ἀλλὰ εἰπὲ λόγῳ, καὶ ἰαθή⟦τω⟧ ὁ παῖς μου.
8 καὶ γὰρ ἐγὼ ἄνθρωπός εἰμι ὑπὸ ἐξουσίαν, ἔχων ὑπ᾽ ἐμαυτὸν
στρατιώτας, καὶ λέγω τούτῳ· πορεύθητι, καὶ πορεύεται, καὶ ἄλλῳ·
ἔρχου, καὶ ἔρχεται, καὶ τῷ δούλῳ μου· ποίησον τοῦτο, καὶ ποιεῖ.

Q 6:46
Not Just Saying Master, Master

Matt 7:21 Luke 6:46

.. Why do you call me: Master, Master, and do not do what I say?

Mark 3:35a

Whoever does the will of God

Q 6:47-49
Houses Built on Rock or Sand

Matt 7:24-27 Luke 6:47-49

47 Everyone hearing my sayings and acting on them
48 is like a person who built ⟦one's⟧ house on bedrock; and the rain poured down and the flash-floods came, ⟦and the winds blew⟧ and pounded that house, and it did not collapse, for it was founded on bedrock.
49 And ⟦everyone⟧ who hears ⟦my sayings⟧ and does not act on ⟦them⟧ is like a person who built ⟦one's⟧ house on the sand; and the rain poured down and the flash-floods came, ⟦and the winds blew⟧ and battered that house, and promptly it collapsed, and its ⟦fall⟧ was devastating.

Q 7:1, 3, 6b-9, ?10?
The Centurion's Faith in Jesus' Word

Matt 7:28a; 8:5-10, 13 Luke 7:1, 3, 6b-10

1 ⟦And it came to pass when⟧ he .. ended these sayings, he entered Capernaum.
3 There came to him a centurion exhorting him ⟦and saying: My⟧ boy ⟦<is> doing badly. And he said to him: Am I⟧, by coming, to heal him?

6b-c And in reply the centurion said: Master, I am not worthy for you to come under my roof;
7 but say a word, and ⟦let⟧ my boy ⟦be⟧ healed.
8 For I too am a person under authority, with soldiers under me, and I say to one: Go, and he goes, and to another: Come, and he comes, and to my slave: Do this, and he does «it».

9 ἀκούσας δὲ ὁ Ἰησοῦς ἐθαύμασεν καὶ εἶπεν τοῖς ἀκολουθοῦσιν·
λέγω ὑμῖν, οὐδὲ ἐν τῷ Ἰσραὴλ τοσαύτην πίστιν εὗρον.
?10? <..>

Mark 2:1

Καὶ εἰσελθὼν πάλιν εἰς Καφαρναοὺμ δι' ἡμερῶν ἠκούσθη ὅτι ἐν οἴκῳ
ἐστίν.

Q 7:18-19, 22-23
John's Inquiry about the One to Come

Matt 11:2-6 Luke 7:18-19, 22-23

18 .. ὁ .. Ἰωάννης ⟦ἀκούσας περὶ πάντων τούτων⟧ πέμψ⟦ας⟧ διὰ τῶν
μαθητῶν αὐτοῦ
19 ⟦εἶπεν⟧ αὐτῷ· σὺ εἶ ὁ ἐρχόμενος ἢ ⟦ἕτερ⟧ον προσδοκῶμεν;

22 καὶ ἀποκριθεὶς εἶπεν αὐτοῖς· πορευθέντες ἀπαγγείλατε Ἰωάννῃ
ἃ ἀκούετε καὶ βλέπετε· τυφλοὶ ἀναβλέπουσιν καὶ χωλοὶ περιπα-
τοῦσιν, λεπροὶ καθαρίζονται καὶ κωφοὶ ἀκούουσιν, καὶ νεκροὶ
ἐγείρονται καὶ πτωχοὶ εὐαγγελίζονται·
23 καὶ μακάριός ἐστιν ὃς ἐὰν μὴ σκανδαλισθῇ ἐν ἐμοί.

Q 7:24-28
John – More than a Prophet

Matt 11:7-11 Luke 7:24-28

24 τούτων δὲ ἀπελθόντων ἤρξατο λέγειν τοῖς ὄχλοις περὶ Ἰωάν-
νου· τί ἐξήλθατε εἰς τὴν ἔρημον θεάσασθαι; κάλαμον ὑπὸ ἀνέμου
σαλευόμενον;
25 ἀλλὰ τί ἐξήλθατε ἰδεῖν; ἄνθρωπον ἐν μαλακοῖς ἠμφιεσμένον;
ἰδοὺ οἱ τὰ μαλακὰ φοροῦντες ἐν τοῖς οἴκοις τῶν βασιλέων εἰσίν.
26 ἀλλὰ τί ἐξήλθατε ἰδεῖν; προφήτην; ναὶ λέγω ὑμῖν, καὶ περ-
ισσότερον προφήτου.
27 οὗτός ἐστιν περὶ οὗ γέγραπται· ἰδοὺ ⟦ἐγὼ⟧ ἀποστέλλω τὸν
ἄγγελόν μου πρὸ προσώπου σου, ὃς κατασκευάσει τὴν ὁδόν σου
ἔμπροσθέν σου.
28 λέγω ὑμῖν· οὐκ ἐγήγερται ἐν γεννητοῖς γυναικῶν μείζων Ἰωάν-
νου· ὁ δὲ μικρότερος ἐν τῇ βασιλείᾳ τοῦ θεοῦ μείζων αὐτοῦ ἐστιν.

9 But Jesus, on hearing, was amazed, and said to those who followed: I tell you: Not even in Israel have I found such faith.
?10? <..>

Mark 2:1

And entering again into Capernaum after some days, it was reported that he was at home.

Q 7:18-19, 22-23
John's Inquiry about the One to Come

Matt 11:2-6 Luke 7:18-19, 22-23

18 And John, ⟦on hearing about all these things⟧, send⟦ing⟧ through his disciples,
19 ⟦said⟧ to him: Are you the one to come, or are we to expect someone else?
22 And in reply he said to them: Go report to John what you hear and see: The blind regain their sight and the lame walk around, the skin-diseased are cleansed and the deaf hear, and the dead are raised, and the poor are evangelized.
23 And blessed is whoever is not offended by me.

Q 7:24-28
John – More than a Prophet

Matt 11:7-11 Luke 7:24-28

24 And when they had left, he began to talk to the crowds about John: What did you go out into the wilderness to look at? A reed shaken by the wind?
25 If not, what *did* you go out to see? A person arrayed in finery? Look, those wearing finery are in kings' houses.
26 But «then» what did you go out to see? A prophet? Yes, I tell you: Even more than a prophet!
27 This is the one about whom it has been written: Look, I am sending my messenger ahead of you, who will prepare your path in front of you.

28 I tell you: There has not arisen among women's offspring «anyone» who surpasses John. Yet the least significant in God's kingdom is more than he.

Mark 1:2

Καθὼς γέγραπται ἐν τῷ Ἠσαΐᾳ τῷ προφήτῃ· ἰδοὺ ἀποστέλλω τὸν ἄγγελόν μου πρὸ προσώπου σου, ὃς κατασκευάσει τὴν ὁδόν σου·

Gos. Thom. 78.1-3 (Nag Hammadi II 2)

(1) Λέγει Ἰησοῦς· (διὰ) τί ἐξήλθατε εἰς τὸν ἀγρόν; θεάσασθαι κάλαμον σαλευόμενον ὑπὸ τοῦ ἀνέμου;
(2) καὶ θεάσασθαι ἄνθρωπον μαλακὰ ἱμάτια ἔχοντα [ὡς οἱ] βασιλεῖς [ὑμῶν] καὶ οἱ μεγιστάνοι ὑμῶν;
(3) οὗτοι ἔχουσιν τὰ ἱμάτια τὰ μαλακὰ καὶ οὐ δυνήσονται γνῶναι τὴν ἀλήθειαν.

Gos. Thom. 46 (Nag Hammadi II 2)

(1) Λέγει Ἰησοῦς· ἀπὸ Ἀδὰμ μέχρι Ἰωάννου τοῦ βαπτιστοῦ ἐν γεννητοῖς γυναικῶν μείζων Ἰωάννου τοῦ βαπτιστοῦ οὐδείς ἐστιν, ἵνα μὴ ... οἱ ὀφθαλμοὶ αὐτοῦ.
(2) εἶπον δέ· ὅστις μικρὸς γενήσεται ἐν ὑμῖν τὴν βασιλείαν γνώσεται καὶ μείζων Ἰωάννου ἔσται.

Q 7:⟦29-30⟧
⟦For and Against John⟧

Matt 21:32 Luke 7:29-30

⟦29⟧ ⟦«ἦλθεν γὰρ Ἰωάννης πρὸς ὑμᾶς», .. οἱ .. τελῶναι καὶ ... ἐ...σαν ...⟧
⟦30⟧ ⟦... δὲ ... αὐτ... .⟧

Q 7:31-35
This Generation and the Children of Wisdom

Matt 11:16-19 Luke 7:31-35

31 τίνι .. ὁμοιώσω τὴν γενεὰν ταύτην καὶ τίνι ἐ<στ>ὶν ὁμοί<α>;
32 ὁμοία ἐστὶν παιδίοις καθημένοις ἐν ⟦ταῖς⟧ ἀγορ⟦αῖς⟧ ἃ προσφω-
νοῦντα ⟦τοῖς ἑτέρ⟧οις λέγουσιν· ηὐλήσαμεν ὑμῖν καὶ οὐκ ὠρχή-
σασθε, ἐθρηνήσαμεν καὶ οὐκ ἐκλαύσατε.
33 ἦλθεν γὰρ Ἰωάννης μὴ.. ἐσθίων μήτε πίνων, καὶ λέγετε· δαιμόνιον ἔχει.
34 ἦλθεν ὁ υἱὸς τοῦ ἀνθρώπου ἐσθίων καὶ πίνων, καὶ λέγετε· ἰδοὺ
ἄνθρωπος φάγος καὶ οἰνοπότης, τελωνῶν φίλος καὶ ἁμαρτωλῶν.

35 καὶ ἐδικαιώθη ἡ σοφία ἀπὸ τῶν τέκνων αὐτῆς.

Mark 1:2

As it is written in the prophet Isaiah: Look, I am sending my messenger ahead of you, who will prepare your path;

Gos. Thom. 78.1-3 (Nag Hammadi II 2)

(1) Jesus says: Why did you go out to the countryside? To look at a reed shaken by the wind,
(2) and to see a person dressed in soft clothing [like your] kings and your great persons?
(3) They are dressed in soft clothing and will not be able to recognize the truth.

Gos. Thom. 46 (Nag Hammadi II 2)

(1) Jesus says: From Adam to John the Baptist, among women's offspring there is no one who surpasses John the Baptist so that his (i.e. John's) eyes need not be downcast.
(2) But I have (also) said: Whoever among you becomes little will know the kingdom and will surpass John.

Q 7:⟦29-30⟧
⟦For and Against John⟧

Matt 21:32 | Luke 7:29-30

⟦29⟧ ⟦«For John came to you», … the tax collectors and … «responded positively»,⟧
⟦30⟧ ⟦but «the religious authorities rejected» him.⟧

Q 7:31-35
This Generation and the Children of Wisdom

Matt 11:16-19 | Luke 7:31-35

31 .. To what am I to compare this generation and what <is it> like?
32 It is like children seated in ⟦the⟧ market-place⟦s⟧, who, addressing ⟦the others⟧, say: We fluted for you, but you would not dance; we wailed, but you would not cry.
33 For John came, neither eating nor drinking, and you say: He has a demon!
34 The son of humanity came, eating and drinking, and you say: Look! A person «who is» a glutton and drunkard, a chum of tax collectors and sinners!
35 But Wisdom was vindicated by her children.

Q 9:57-60
Confronting Potential Followers

Matt 8:19-22 Luke 9:57-60

57 καὶ εἶπέν τις αὐτῷ· ἀκολουθήσω σοι ὅπου ἐὰν ἀπέρχῃ.
58 καὶ εἶπεν αὐτῷ ὁ Ἰησοῦς· αἱ ἀλώπεκες φωλεοὺς ἔχουσιν καὶ τὰ
πετεινὰ τοῦ οὐρανοῦ κατασκηνώσεις, ὁ δὲ υἱὸς τοῦ ἀνθρώπου οὐκ
ἔχει ποῦ τὴν κεφαλὴν κλίνῃ.
59 ἕτερος δὲ εἶπεν αὐτῷ· κύριε, ἐπίτρεψόν μοι πρῶτον ἀπελθεῖν
καὶ θάψαι τὸν πατέρα μου.
60 εἶπεν δὲ αὐτῷ· ἀκολούθει μοι καὶ ἄφες τοὺς νεκροὺς θάψαι τοὺς
ἑαυτῶν νεκρούς.

Gos. Thom. 86 (Nag Hammadi II 2)

(1) Λέγει Ἰησοῦς· [αἱ ἀλώπεκες ἔχου]σιν τοὺς [φωλεοὺς αὐτῶν] καὶ τὰ πετεινὰ ἔχει [τὴν] κατασκήνωσιν αὐτῶν,
(2) ὁ δὲ υἱὸς τοῦ ἀνθρώπου οὐκ ἔχει ποῦ τὴν κεφαλὴν αὐτοῦ κλίνῃ καὶ ἀναπαύσηται.

Q 10:2
Workers for the Harvest

Matt 9:37-38 Luke 10:2

..λεγε... τοῖς μαθηταῖς αὐτοῦ· ὁ μὲν θερισμὸς πολύς, οἱ δὲ ἐργάται ὀλίγοι· δεήθητε οὖν τοῦ κυρίου τοῦ θερισμοῦ ὅπως ἐκβάλῃ ἐργάτας εἰς τὸν θερισμὸν αὐτοῦ.

Gos. Thom. 73 (Nag Hammadi II 2)

Λέγει Ἰησοῦς· ὁ μὲν θερισμὸς πολύς, οἱ δὲ ἐργάται ὀλίγοι· δεήθητε δὲ τοῦ κυρίου ἵνα ἐκβάλῃ ἐργάτας εἰς τὸν θερισμόν.

Q 10:3
Sheep among Wolves

Matt 10:16 Luke 10:3

ὑπάγετε· ἰδοὺ ἀποστέλλω ὑμᾶς ὡς πρόβατα ἐν μέσῳ λύκων.

Q 9:57-60
Confronting Potential Followers

Matt 8:19-22 Luke 9:57-60

57 And someone said to him: I will follow you wherever you go.
58 And Jesus said to him: Foxes have holes, and birds of the sky have
nests; but the son of humanity does not have anywhere he can lay his
head.
59 But another said to him: Master, permit me first to go and bury my
father.
60 But he said to him: Follow me, and leave the dead to bury their own
dead.

Gos. Thom. 86 (Nag Hammadi II 2)

(1) Jesus says: [Foxes have their holes] and birds have their nest.

(2) But the son of humanity does not have anywhere he can lay down his head (and) rest.

Q 10:2
Workers for the Harvest

Matt 9:37-38 Luke 10:2

He said to his disciples: The harvest is plentiful, but the workers are few. So ask the Lord of the harvest to dispatch workers into his harvest.

Gos. Thom. 73 (Nag Hammadi II 2)

Jesus says: The harvest is plentiful, but the workers are few. But ask the Lord that he may dispatch workers into the harvest.

Q 10:3
Sheep among Wolves

Matt 10:16 Luke 10:3

Be on your way! Look, I send you like sheep in the midst of wolves.

Q 10:4
No Provisions

Matt 10:9-10a | Luke 10:4

μὴ βαστάζετε ⟦βαλλάντιον⟧, μὴ πήραν, μὴ ὑποδήματα, μηδὲ ῥάβ-δον· καὶ μηδένα κατὰ τὴν ὁδὸν ἀσπάσησθε.

Mark 6:8-9

8 καὶ παρήγγειλεν αὐτοῖς ἵνα μηδὲν αἴρωσιν εἰς ὁδὸν εἰ μὴ ῥάβδον μόνον, μὴ ἄρτον, μὴ πήραν, μὴ εἰς τὴν ζώνην χαλκόν,
9 ἀλλὰ ὑποδεδεμένους σανδάλια, καὶ μὴ ἐνδύσησθε δύο χιτῶνας.

Q 10:5-9
What to Do in Houses and Towns

Matt 10:7-8, 10b-13 | Luke 10:5-9

5 εἰς ἣν δ' ἂν εἰσέλθητε οἰκίαν, ⟦πρῶτον⟧ λέγετε· εἰρήνη ⟦τῷ οἴκῳ τούτῳ⟧.
6 καὶ ἐὰν μὲν ἐκεῖ ᾖ υἱὸς εἰρήνης, ἐλθάτω ἡ εἰρήνη ὑμῶν ἐπ' αὐτόν· ε⟦ἰ⟧ δὲ μή, ἡ εἰρήνη ὑμῶν ⟦ἐφ'⟧ ὑμᾶς ⟦ἐπιστραφήτω⟧.
7 ⟦ἐν αὐτῇ δὲ τῇ οἰκίᾳ⟧ μέν⟦ε⟧τε «ἐσθίοντες καὶ πίνοντες τὰ παρ' αὐτῶν»· ἄξιος γὰρ ὁ ἐργάτης τοῦ μισθοῦ αὐτοῦ. ⟦μὴ μεταβαίνετε ἐξ οἰκίας εἰς οἰκίαν.⟧
8 καὶ εἰς ἣν ἂν πόλιν εἰσ⟦έρχησθε⟧ καὶ δέχωνται ὑμᾶς, ⟦«ἐσθίετε τὰ παρατιθέμενα ὑμῖν»⟧
9 καὶ θεραπεύετε τοὺς ἐν αὐτῇ ἀσθεν⟦οῦντας⟧ καὶ λέγετε ⟦αὐτοῖς⟧· .. ἤγγικεν ἐφ' ὑμᾶς ἡ βασιλεία τοῦ θεοῦ.

Mark 6:10b-c, 12-13

10b-c ὅπου ἐὰν εἰσέλθητε εἰς οἰκίαν, ἐκεῖ μένετε ἕως ἂν ἐξέλθητε ἐκεῖθεν.
12 Καὶ ἐξελθόντες ἐκήρυξαν ἵνα μετανοῶσιν,
13 καὶ δαιμόνια πολλὰ ἐξέβαλλον, καὶ ἤλειφον ἐλαίῳ πολλοὺς ἀρρώσ-τους καὶ ἐθεράπευον.

Gos. Thom. 14.4a-c

(4a) καὶ ὅταν εἰσέρχησθε εἰς πᾶσαν γῆν καὶ περιπατῆτε ἐν ταῖς χώραις,
(4b) ὅταν παραδέχωνται ὑμᾶς, ἐσθίετε τὸ παρατιθέμενον ὑμῖν
(4c) (καὶ) θεραπεύετε τοὺς ἀσθενεῖς ἐν αὐτοῖς.

Q 10:4
No Provisions

Matt 10:9-10a | Luke 10:4

Carry no ⟦purse⟧, nor knapsack, nor shoes, nor stick, and greet no one on the road.

Mark 6:8-9

8 He ordered them to take nothing on the road except a stick; no bread, no knapsack, no money in their belts;
9 but to wear sandals and not to put on two tunics.

Q 10:5-9
What to Do in Houses and Towns

Matt 10:7-8, 10b-13 | Luke 10:5-9

5 Into whatever house you enter, ⟦first⟧ say: Peace ⟦to this house⟧!

6 And if a son of peace be there, let your peace come upon him; but if
not, ⟦let⟧ your peace ⟦return upon⟧ you.
7 ⟦And at that house⟧ remain, «eating and drinking whatever they provide», for the worker is worthy of one's reward. ⟦Do not move around
from house to house.⟧
8 And whatever town you enter and they take you in, ⟦«eat what is set
before you»⟧,
9 and cure the sick there, and say ⟦to them⟧: God's reign has reached
unto you.

Mark 6:10b-c, 12-13

10b-c Wherever you enter a house, remain there until you leave the place.

12 So they went out and proclaimed that all should repent.
13 They cast out many demons, and anointed with oil many who were ill and
cured them.

Gos. Thom. 14.4a-c

(4a) And if you enter into any land and wander from place to place,
(4b) (and) if they take you in, (then) eat what is set before you.
(4c) Cure the sick among them!

Q 10:10-12
Response to a Town's Rejection

Matt 10:14-15 Luke 10:10-12

10 εἰς ἣν δ' ἂν πόλιν εἰσέλθητε καὶ μὴ δέχωνται ὑμᾶς, ἐξ⟦ερχόμε-
νοι ἔξω⟧ τ⟦ῆς πόλεως ἐκείνης⟧
11 ἐκτινάξατε τὸν κονιορτὸν τῶν ποδῶν ὑμῶν.
12 λέγω ὑμῖν ⟦ὅτι⟧ Σοδόμοις ἀνεκτότερον ἔσται ἐν τῇ ἡμέρᾳ
ἐκείνῃ ἢ τῇ πόλει ἐκείνῃ.

Mark 6:11

καὶ ὃς ἂν τόπος μὴ δέξηται ὑμᾶς μηδὲ ἀκούσωσιν ὑμῶν, ἐκπορευόμενοι ἐκεῖθεν ἐκτινάξατε τὸν χοῦν τὸν ὑποκάτω τῶν ποδῶν ὑμῶν εἰς μαρτύριον αὐτοῖς.

Q 10:13-15
Woes against Galilean Towns

Matt 11:21-24 Luke 10:13-15

13 οὐαί σοι, Χοραζίν· οὐαί σοι, Βηθσαϊδά· ὅτι εἰ ἐν Τύρῳ καὶ
Σιδῶνι ἐγενήθησαν αἱ δυνάμεις αἱ γενόμεναι ἐν ὑμῖν, πάλαι ἂν ἐν
σάκκῳ καὶ σποδῷ μετενόησαν.
14 πλὴν Τύρῳ καὶ Σιδῶνι ἀνεκτότερον ἔσται ἐν τῇ κρίσει ἢ ὑμῖν.

15 καὶ σύ, Καφαρναούμ, μὴ ἕως οὐρανοῦ ὑψωθήσῃ; ἕως τοῦ ᾅδου
καταβήσῃ.

Q 10:16
Whoever Takes You in Takes Me in

Matt 10:40 Luke 10:16

ὁ δεχόμενος ὑμᾶς ἐμὲ δέχεται, ⟦καὶ⟧ ὁ ἐμὲ δεχόμενος δέχεται τὸν ἀποστείλαντά με.

Mark 9:37

ὃς ἂν ἓν τῶν τοιούτων παιδίων δέξηται ἐπὶ τῷ ὀνόματί μου, ἐμὲ δέχεται· καὶ ὃς ἂν ἐμὲ δέχηται, οὐκ ἐμὲ δέχεται ἀλλὰ τὸν ἀποστείλαντά με.

Q 10:10-12
Response to a Town's Rejection

Matt 10:14-15 Luke 10:10-12

10 But into whatever town you enter and they do not take you in, on going out ⟦from that town⟧,
11 shake off the dust from your feet.
12 I tell you: For Sodom it shall be more bearable on that day than for that town.

Mark 6:11

If any place does not take you in and they refuse to hear you, as you leave there, shake off the soil from beneath your feet as a testimony against them.

Q 10:13-15
Woes against Galilean Towns

Matt 11:21-24 Luke 10:13-15

13 Woe to you, Chorazin! Woe to you, Bethsaida! For if the wonders performed in you had taken place in Tyre and Sidon, they would have repented long ago, in sackcloth and ashes.
14 Yet for Tyre and Sidon it shall be more bearable at the judgment than for you.
15 And you, Capernaum, up to heaven will you be exalted? Into Hades shall you come down!

Q 10:16
Whoever Takes You in Takes Me in

Matt 10:40 Luke 10:16

Whoever takes you in takes me in, ⟦and⟧ whoever takes me in takes in the one who sent me.

Mark 9:37

Whoever takes in one such child in my name takes me in, and whoever takes me in takes in not me but the one who sent me.

Q 10:21
Thanksgiving that God Reveals Only to Children

Matt 11:25-26 Luke 10:21

ἐν … εἶπεν· ἐξομολογοῦμαί σοι, πάτερ, κύριε τοῦ οὐρανοῦ καὶ τῆς γῆς, ὅτι ἔκρυψας ταῦτα ἀπὸ σοφῶν καὶ συνετῶν καὶ ἀπεκάλυψας αὐτὰ νηπίοις· ναὶ ὁ πατήρ, ὅτι οὕτως εὐδοκία ἐγένετο ἔμπροσθέν σου.

Q 10:22
Knowing the Father through the Son

Matt 11:27 Luke 10:22

πάντα μοι παρεδόθη ὑπὸ τοῦ πατρός μου, καὶ οὐδεὶς γινώσκει τὸν υἱὸν εἰ μὴ ὁ πατήρ, οὐδὲ τὸν πατέρα ⟦τις γινώσκει⟧ εἰ μὴ ὁ υἱὸς καὶ ᾧ ἐὰν βούληται ὁ υἱὸς ἀποκαλύψαι.

Gos. Thom. 61.3b (Nag Hammadi II 2)

παρεδόθη μοι ἐκ τῶν τοῦ πατρός μου.

Q 10:23b-24
The Beatitude for the Eyes that See

Matt 13:16-17 Luke 10:23b-24

23 μακάριοι οἱ ὀφθαλμοὶ οἱ βλέποντες ἃ βλέπετε .. .
24 λέγω γὰρ ὑμῖν ὅτι πολλοὶ προφῆται καὶ βασιλεῖς …ησαν ἰδεῖν ἃ βλέπετε καὶ οὐκ εἶδαν, καὶ ἀκοῦσαι ἃ ἀκούετε καὶ οὐκ ἤκουσαν.

Q 11:2b-4
The Lord's Prayer

Matt 6:9-13a Luke 11:2b-4

2b ⟦ὅταν⟧ προσεύχ⟦η⟧σθε ⟦λέγετε⟧· πάτερ, ἁγιασθήτω τὸ ὄνομά σου· ἐλθέτω ἡ βασιλεία σου·
3 τὸν ἄρτον ἡμῶν τὸν ἐπιούσιον δὸς ἡμῖν σήμερον·
4 καὶ ἄφες ἡμῖν τὰ ὀφειλήματα ἡμῶν, ὡς καὶ ἡμεῖς ἀφήκαμεν τοῖς ὀφειλέταις ἡμῶν· καὶ μὴ εἰσενέγκῃς ἡμᾶς εἰς πειρασμόν.

Q 10:21
Thanksgiving that God Reveals Only to Children

Matt 11:25-26 Luke 10:21

At «that time» he said: I praise you, Father, Lord of heaven and earth, for you hid these things from sages and the learned, and disclosed them to children. Yes, Father, for that is what it has pleased you to do.

Q 10:22
Knowing the Father through the Son

Matt 11:27 Luke 10:22

Everything has been entrusted to me by my Father, and no one knows the Son except the Father, nor ⟦does anyone know⟧ the Father except the Son, and to whomever the Son chooses to reveal him.

Gos. Thom. 61.3b (Nag Hammadi II 2)

I was given some of that which is my Father's.

Q 10:23b-24
The Beatitude for the Eyes that See

Matt 13:16-17 Luke 10:23b-24

23 Blessed are the eyes that see what you see .. .
24 For I tell you: Many prophets and kings wanted to see what you see, but never saw it, and to hear what you hear, but never heard it.

Q 11:2b-4
The Lord's Prayer

Matt 6:9-13a Luke 11:2b-4

2b ⟦When⟧ you pray, ⟦say⟧: Father – may your name be kept holy! – let your reign come:
3 Our day's bread give us today;
4 and cancel our debts for us, as we too have cancelled for those in debt to us; and do not put us to the test!

Q 11:9-13
The Certainty of the Answer to Prayer

Matt 7:7-11 Luke 11:9-13

9 λέγω ὑμῖν, αἰτεῖτε καὶ δοθήσεται ὑμῖν, ζητεῖτε καὶ εὑρήσετε,
κρούετε καὶ ἀνοιγήσεται ὑμῖν·
10 πᾶς γὰρ ὁ αἰτῶν λαμβάνει καὶ ὁ ζητῶν εὑρίσκει καὶ τῷ
κρούοντι ἀνοιγήσεται.
11 .. τίς ἐστιν ἐξ ὑμῶν ἄνθρωπος, ὃν αἰτήσει ὁ υἱὸς αὐτοῦ ἄρτον,
μὴ λίθον ἐπιδώσει αὐτῷ;
12 ἢ καὶ ἰχθὺν αἰτήσει, μὴ ὄφιν ἐπιδώσει αὐτῷ;
13 εἰ οὖν ὑμεῖς πονηροὶ ὄντες οἴδατε δόματα ἀγαθὰ διδόναι τοῖς
τέκνοις ὑμῶν, πόσῳ μᾶλλον ὁ πατὴρ ἐξ οὐρανοῦ δώσει ἀγαθὰ τοῖς
αἰτοῦσιν αὐτόν.

Gos. Thom. 92.1 (Nag Hammadi II 2)

Λέγει Ἰησοῦς· ζητεῖτε καὶ εὑρήσετε.

Gos. Thom. 94 (Nag Hammadi II 2)

(1) [Λέγε]ι Ἰησοῦς· ὁ ζητῶν εὑρήσει,
(2) [τῷ κρούοντι] ἀνοιγήσεται.

Q 11:14-15, 17-20
Refuting the Beelzebul Accusation

Matt 9:32-34; 12:25-28 Luke 11:14-15, 17-20

14 καὶ ἐ⟦<ξέ>⟧βαλ⟦<εν>⟧ δαιμόνιον κωφόν· καὶ ἐκβληθέντος τοῦ
δαιμονίου ἐλάλησεν ὁ κωφὸς καὶ ἐθαύμασαν οἱ ὄχλοι.

15 τινὲς δὲ εἶπον· ἐν Βεελζεβοὺλ τῷ ἄρχοντι τῶν δαιμονίων
ἐκβάλλει τὰ δαιμόνια.
17 εἰδὼς δὲ τὰ διανοήματα αὐτῶν εἶπεν αὐτοῖς· πᾶσα βασιλεία
μερισθεῖσα ⟦καθ'⟧ ἑαυτῆ⟦ς⟧ ἐρημοῦται καὶ πᾶσα οἰκία μερισθεῖσα
καθ' ἑαυτῆς οὐ σταθήσεται.
18 καὶ εἰ ὁ σατανᾶς ἐφ' ἑαυτὸν ἐμερίσθη, πῶς σταθήσεται ἡ βασιλεία αὐτοῦ;
19 καὶ εἰ ἐγὼ ἐν Βεελζεβοὺλ ἐκβάλλω τὰ δαιμόνια, οἱ υἱοὶ ὑμῶν ἐν
τίνι ἐκβάλλουσιν; διὰ τοῦτο αὐτοὶ κριταὶ ἔσονται ὑμῶν.
20 εἰ δὲ ἐν δακτύλῳ θεοῦ ἐγὼ ἐκβάλλω τὰ δαιμόνια, ἄρα ἔφθασεν
ἐφ' ὑμᾶς ἡ βασιλεία τοῦ θεοῦ.

Q 11:9-13
The Certainty of the Answer to Prayer

Matt 7:7-11 Luke 11:9-13

9 I tell you: Ask and it will be given to you, search and you will find, knock and it will be opened to you.
10 For everyone who asks receives, and the one who searches finds, and to the one who knocks will it be opened.
11 .. What person of you, whose child asks for bread, will give him a stone?
12 Or again when he asks for a fish, will give him a snake?
13 So if you, though evil, know how to give good gifts to your children, by how much more will the Father from heaven give good things to those who ask him!

Gos. Thom. 92.1 (Nag Hammadi II 2)

Jesus says: Search and you will find.

Gos. Thom. 94 (Nag Hammadi II 2)

(1) Jesus [says]: The one who searches will find,
(2) [to the one who knocks] will it be opened.

Q 11:14-15, 17-20
Refuting the Beelzebul Accusation

Matt 9:32-34; 12:25-28 Luke 11:14-15, 17-20

14 And he cast out a demon «which made a person» mute. And once the demon was cast out, the mute person spoke. And the crowds were amazed.
15 But some said: By Beelzebul, the ruler of demons, he casts out demons!
17 But, knowing their thoughts, he said to them: Every kingdom divided against itself is left barren, and every household divided against itself will not stand.
18 And if Satan is divided against himself, how will his kingdom stand?

19 And if I by Beelzebul cast out demons, your sons, by whom do they cast «them» out? This is why they will be your judges.
20 But if it is by the finger of God that I cast out demons, then there has come upon you God's reign.

Mark 3:22-26

22 Καὶ οἱ γραμματεῖς οἱ ἀπὸ Ἱεροσολύμων καταβάντες ἔλεγον ὅτι Βεελζεβοὺλ ἔχει καὶ ὅτι ἐν τῷ ἄρχοντι τῶν δαιμονίων ἐκβάλλει τὰ δαιμόνια.
23 Καὶ προσκαλεσάμενος αὐτοὺς ἐν παραβολαῖς ἔλεγεν αὐτοῖς· πῶς
δύναται σατανᾶς σατανᾶν ἐκβάλλειν;
24 καὶ ἐὰν βασιλεία ἐφ' ἑαυτὴν μερισθῇ, οὐ δύναται σταθῆναι ἡ βασιλεία
ἐκείνη·
25 καὶ ἐὰν οἰκία ἐφ' ἑαυτὴν μερισθῇ, οὐ δυνήσεται ἡ οἰκία ἐκείνη
σταθῆναι.
26 καὶ εἰ ὁ σατανᾶς ἀνέστη ἐφ' ἑαυτὸν καὶ ἐμερίσθη, οὐ δύναται στῆναι
ἀλλὰ τέλος ἔχει.

Q 11:⟦21-22⟧
⟦Looting a Strong Person⟧

Matt 12:29 | Luke 11:21-22

⟦**21**⟧ ⟦< >⟧
⟦**22**⟧ ⟦< >⟧

Mark 3:27

ἀλλ' οὐ δύναται οὐδεὶς εἰς τὴν οἰκίαν τοῦ ἰσχυροῦ εἰσελθὼν τὰ σκεύη αὐτοῦ διαρπάσαι, ἐὰν μὴ πρῶτον τὸν ἰσχυρὸν δήσῃ, καὶ τότε τὴν οἰκίαν αὐτοῦ διαρπάσει.

Gos. Thom. 35 (Nag Hammadi II 2)

(1) Λέγει Ἰησοῦς· οὐ δύναταί τις εἰσελθεῖν εἰς τὴν οἰκίαν τοῦ ἰσχυροῦ βιάζεσθαι αὐτὸν εἰ μὴ δήσῃ τὰς χεῖρας αὐτοῦ.
(2) τότε τὴν οἰκίαν αὐτοῦ μεταθήσει.

Q 11:23
The One not with Me

Matt 12:30 | Luke 11:23

ὁ μὴ ὢν μετ' ἐμοῦ κατ' ἐμοῦ ἐστιν, καὶ ὁ μὴ συνάγων μετ' ἐμοῦ σκορπίζει.

Mark 9:40

ὃς γὰρ οὐκ ἔστιν καθ' ἡμῶν, ὑπὲρ ἡμῶν ἐστιν.

Mark 3:22-26

22 And the scribes who came down from Jerusalem said: He has Beelzebul, and
by the ruler of demons he casts out demons.
23 And he called them to him, and spoke to them in parables: How can Satan
cast out Satan?
24 If a kingdom is divided against itself, that kingdom cannot stand.

25 And if a household is divided against itself, that household will not be able
to stand.
26 And if Satan has risen up against himself and is divided, he cannot stand, but
his end has come.

Q 11:⟦21-22⟧
⟦Looting a Strong Person⟧

Matt 12:29 | Luke 11:21-22

⟦**21**⟧ ⟦«A strong person's house cannot be looted,»⟧
⟦**22**⟧ ⟦«but if someone still stronger overpowers him, he does get
looted.»⟧

Mark 3:27

But no one can enter a strong person's house and plunder his property without first tying up the strong person; then indeed the house can be plundered.

Gos. Thom. 35 (Nag Hammadi II 2)

(1) Jesus says: It is not possible for someone to enter the house of a strong (person) (and) take it by force unless he binds his hands.
(2) Then he will plunder his house.

Q 11:23
The One not with Me

Matt 12:30 | Luke 11:23

The one not with me is against me, and the one not gathering with me scatters.

Mark 9:40

Whoever is not against us is for us.

Q 11:24-26
The Return of the Unclean Spirit

Matt 12:43-45 Luke 11:24-26

24 ὅταν τὸ ἀκάθαρτον πνεῦμα ἐξέλθῃ ἀπὸ τοῦ ἀνθρώπου, διέρχεται δι᾽ ἀνύδρων τόπων ζητοῦν ἀνάπαυσιν καὶ οὐχ εὑρίσκει. ⟦τότε⟧ λέγει· εἰς τὸν οἶκόν μου ἐπιστρέψω ὅθεν ἐξῆλθον·
25 καὶ ἐλθὸν εὑρίσκει σεσαρωμένον καὶ κεκοσμημένον.
26 τότε πορεύεται καὶ παραλαμβάνει μεθ᾽ ἑαυτοῦ ἑπτὰ ἕτερα πνεύματα πονηρότερα ἑαυτοῦ καὶ εἰσελθόντα κατοικεῖ ἐκεῖ· καὶ γίνεται τὰ ἔσχατα τοῦ ἀνθρώπου ἐκείνου χείρονα τῶν πρώτων.

Q 11:?27-28?
?Hearing and Keeping God's Word?

Luke 11:27-28

?27-28? ..

Gos. Thom. 79.1-2 (Nag Hammadi II 2)

(1) Εἶπεν αὐτῷ γυνή τις ἐκ τοῦ ὄχλου· μακαρία ἡ κοιλία ἡ βαστάσασά σε καὶ οἱ μαστοὶ οἱ θρέψαντές σε.
(2) Εἶπεν αὐτ[ῇ]· μακάριοι οἱ ἀκούσαντες τὸν λόγον τοῦ πατρὸς (καὶ) ἀληθῶς φυλάξαντες αὐτόν.

Q 11:16, 29-30
The Sign of Jonah for This Generation

Matt 12:38-40 Luke 11:16, 29-30

16 τινὲς ⟦δὲ⟧ .. ἐζήτουν παρ᾽ αὐτοῦ σημεῖον.
29 ⟦ὁ⟧ δὲ .. ⟦εἶπεν⟧ ..· ἡ γενεὰ αὕτη γενεὰ πονηρά .. ἐστιν· σημεῖον ζητεῖ, καὶ σημεῖον οὐ δοθήσεται αὐτῇ εἰ μὴ τὸ σημεῖον Ἰωνᾶ.
30 ⟦καθ⟧ὼς γὰρ ἐγένετο Ἰωνᾶς τοῖς Νινευίταις σημεῖον, οὕτως ἔσται ⟦καὶ⟧ ὁ υἱὸς τοῦ ἀνθρώπου τῇ γενεᾷ ταύτῃ.

Mark 8:11-12

11 Καὶ ἐξῆλθον οἱ Φαρισαῖοι καὶ ἤρξαντο συζητεῖν αὐτῷ, ζητοῦντες παρ᾽ αὐτοῦ σημεῖον ἀπὸ τοῦ οὐρανοῦ, πειράζοντες αὐτόν.
12 καὶ ἀναστενάξας τῷ πνεύματι αὐτοῦ λέγει· τί ἡ γενεὰ αὕτη ζητεῖ σημεῖον; ἀμὴν λέγω ὑμῖν, εἰ δοθήσεται τῇ γενεᾷ ταύτῃ σημεῖον.

Q 11:24-26
The Return of the Unclean Spirit

Matt 12:43-45 Luke 11:24-26

24 When the defiling spirit has left the person, it wanders through waterless regions looking for a resting-place, and finds none. ⟦Then⟧ it says: I will return to my house from which I came.
25 And on arrival it finds «it» swept and tidied up.
26 Then it goes and brings with it seven other spirits more evil than itself, and, moving in, they settle there. And the last «circumstances» of that person become worse than the first.

Q 11:?27-28?
?Hearing and Keeping God's Word?

Luke 11:27-28

?27-28? ..

Gos. Thom. 79.1-2 (Nag Hammadi II 2)

(1) A woman in the crowd said to him: Hail to the womb that carried you and to the breasts that fed you.
(2) He said to [her]: Hail to those who have heard the word of the Father (and) have truly kept it.

Q 11:16, 29-30
The Sign of Jonah for This Generation

Matt 12:38-40 Luke 11:16, 29-30

16 ⟦But⟧ some .. were demanding from him a sign.
29 But .. ⟦he said⟧ ..: This generation is an evil .. generation; it demands a sign, and a sign will not be given to it – except the sign of Jonah!
30 For as Jonah became to the Ninevites a sign, so ⟦also⟧ will the son of humanity be to this generation.

Mark 8:11-12

11 The Pharisees came and began to argue with him, demanding from him a sign from heaven, to test him.
12 And he sighed deeply in his spirit and said: Why does this generation demand a sign? Truly I tell you, no sign will be given to this generation.

Q 11:31-32
Something More than Solomon and Jonah

Matt 12:41-42 Luke 11:31-32

31 βασίλισσα νότου ἐγερθήσεται ἐν τῇ κρίσει μετὰ τῆς γενεᾶς ταύτης καὶ κατακρινεῖ αὐτήν, ὅτι ἦλθεν ἐκ τῶν περάτων τῆς γῆς ἀκοῦσαι τὴν σοφίαν Σολομῶνος, καὶ ἰδοὺ πλεῖον Σολομῶνος ὧδε.

32 ἄνδρες Νινευῖται ἀναστήσονται ἐν τῇ κρίσει μετὰ τῆς γενεᾶς ταύτης καὶ κατακρινοῦσιν αὐτήν, ὅτι μετενόησαν εἰς τὸ κήρυγμα Ἰωνᾶ, καὶ ἰδοὺ πλεῖον Ἰωνᾶ ὧδε.

Q 11:33
The Light on the Lampstand

Matt 5:15 Luke 11:33

οὐδεὶς καί<ει> λύχνον καὶ τίθησιν αὐτὸν ⟦εἰς κρύπτην⟧ ἀλλ' ἐπὶ τὴν λυχνίαν, ⟦καὶ λάμπει πᾶσιν τοῖς ἐν τῇ οἰκίᾳ⟧.

Mark 4:21b-c

μήτι ἔρχεται ὁ λύχνος ἵνα ὑπὸ τὸν μόδιον τεθῇ ἢ ὑπὸ τὴν κλίνην; οὐχ ἵνα ἐπὶ τὴν λυχνίαν τεθῇ;

Gos. Thom. 33.2-3 (Nag Hammadi II 2)

(2) Οὐδεὶς γὰρ λύχνον ἅψας τίθησιν ὑπὸ τὸν μόδιον οὐδὲ εἰς κρύπτην,

(3) ἀλλ' ἐπὶ τὴν λυχνίαν τίθησιν, ἵνα πάντες οἱ εἰσπορευόμενοι καὶ οἱ ἐκπορευόμενοι βλέπωσιν τὸ φῶς αὐτοῦ.

Q 11:34-35
The Jaundiced Eye Darkens the Body's Radiance

Matt 6:22-23 Luke 11:34-35

34 ὁ λύχνος τοῦ σώματός ἐστιν ὁ ὀφθαλμός. ...αν ὁ ὀφθαλμός σου ἁπλοῦς ᾖ, ὅλον τὸ σῶμά σου φωτεινόν ἐστ⟦ιν⟧· ...αν δὲ ὁ ὀφθαλμός σου πονηρὸς ᾖ, ὅλον τὸ σῶμά σου σκοτεινόν.
35 εἰ οὖν τὸ φῶς τὸ ἐν σοὶ σκότος ἐστίν, τὸ σκότος πόσον.

Q 11:31-32
Something More than Solomon and Jonah

Matt 12:41-42 | Luke 11:31-32

31 The queen of the South will be raised at the judgment with this generation and condemn it, for she came from the ends of the earth to listen to the wisdom of Solomon, and look, something more than Solomon is here!
32 Ninevite men will arise at the judgment with this generation and condemn it. For they repented at the announcement of Jonah, and look, something more than Jonah is here!

Q 11:33
The Light on the Lampstand

Matt 5:15 | Luke 11:33

No one light<s> a lamp and puts it ⟦in a hidden place⟧, but on the lampstand, ⟦and it gives light for everyone in the house⟧.

Mark 4:21b-c

Is a lamp brought in to be put under the bushel basket, or under the bed, and not on the lampstand?

Gos. Thom. 33.2-3 (Nag Hammadi II 2)

(2) For no one, kindling a lamp, puts it under a bushel, nor does one put it in a hidden place.
(3) Rather, one puts it on the lampstand, so that everyone who comes in and goes out will see its light.

Q 11:34-35
The Jaundiced Eye Darkens the Body's Radiance

Matt 6:22-23 | Luke 11:34-35

34 The lamp of the body is the eye. If your eye is generous, your whole body ⟦is⟧ radiant; but if your eye is jaundiced, your whole body «is» dark.
35 So if the light within you is dark, how great «must» the darkness «be»!

Gos. Thom. 24.3 (P. Oxy. 655)

[φῶς ἐσ]τιν [ἐν ἀνθρώπῳ φ]ωτεινῷ, [καὶ φωτίζει τῷ κ]όσμῳ [ὅλῳ· ἐὰν μὴ φωτίζ]ῃ, [τότε σκοτεινός ἐ]στιν.

Gos. Thom. 24.3 (Nag Hammadi II 2)

φῶς ἐστιν ἐν ἀνθρώπῳ φωτεινῷ, καὶ φωτίζει τῷ κόσμῳ ὅλῳ· ἐὰν μὴ φωτίζῃ, σκοτεινός ἐστιν.

Q 11:?39a?, 42, 39b, 41, 43-44
Woes against the Pharisees

Matt 23:1-2a, 6-7, 23, 25, 26b-27 Luke 11:39, 41-44

?39a? ..
42 οὐαὶ ὑμῖν ⟦τοῖς⟧ Φαρισαίοι⟦ς⟧, ὅτι ἀποδεκατοῦτε τὸ ἡδύοσμον καὶ τὸ ἄνηθον καὶ τὸ κύμινον καὶ ⟦ἀφήκατε⟧ τὴν κρίσιν καὶ τὸ ἔλεος καὶ τὴν πίστιν· ταῦτα δὲ ἔδει ποιῆσαι κἀκεῖνα μὴ ⟦ἀφιέ⟧ναι.
39b οὐαὶ ὑμῖν, ⟦<τ>οἳ<ς>⟧ Φαρισαίοι⟦<ς>⟧, ὅτι καθαρίζετε τὸ ἔξωθεν τοῦ ποτηρίου καὶ τῆς παροψίδος, ἔσωθεν δὲ γέμ⟦ουσιν⟧ ἐξ ἁρπαγῆς καὶ ἀκρασίας.
41 ⟦καθαρίσ<ατε>⟧ .. τὸ ἐντὸς τοῦ ποτηρίου, .. καὶ .. τὸ ἐκτὸς αὐτοῦ καθαρόν .. .
43 οὐαὶ ὑμῖν τοῖς Φαρισαίοις, ὅτι φιλ<εῖτε> ⟦τὴν πρωτοκλισίαν ἐν τοῖς δείπνοις καὶ⟧ τὴν πρωτοκαθεδρίαν ἐν ταῖς συναγωγαῖς καὶ τοὺς ἀσπασμοὺς ἐν ταῖς ἀγοραῖς.
44 οὐαὶ ὑμῖν, ⟦<τοῖς> Φαρισαῖοι<ς>,⟧ ὅτι ⟦ἐσ⟧τὲ ⟦ὡς⟧ τὰ μνημεῖα τὰ ἄδηλα, καὶ οἱ ἄνθρωποι οἱ περιπατοῦντες ἐπάνω οὐκ οἴδασιν.

Mark 12:38c-39

38c βλέπετε ἀπὸ τῶν γραμματέων τῶν θελόντων ἐν στολαῖς περιπατεῖν καὶ ἀσπασμοὺς ἐν ταῖς ἀγοραῖς
39 καὶ πρωτοκαθεδρίας ἐν ταῖς συναγωγαῖς καὶ πρωτοκλισίας ἐν τοῖς δείπνοις,

Gos. Thom. 89.1 (Nag Hammadi II 2)

Λέγει Ἰησοῦς· (διὰ) τί νίπτετε τὸ ἔξωθεν τοῦ ποτηρίου;

Gos. Thom. 24.3 (P. Oxy. 655)

[Light] exists [inside a person] of light, [and he shines on the whole] world. [If he does not shine, then] there is [darkness].

Gos. Thom. 24.3 (Nag Hammadi II 2)

Light exists inside a person of light, and he shines on the whole world. If he does not shine, there is darkness.

Q 11:?39a?, 42, 39b, 41, 43-44
Woes against the Pharisees

Matt 23:1-2a, 6-7, 23, 25, 26b-27 — Luke 11:39, 41-44

?39a? ..
42 Woe for you, Pharisees, for you tithe mint and dill and cumin, and ⟦give up⟧ justice and mercy and faithfulness. But these one had to do, without giving up those.
39b Woe to you, Pharisees, for you purify the outside of the cup and dish, but inside ⟦they are⟧ full of plunder and dissipation.

41 ⟦Purify⟧ .. the inside of the cup, … its outside … pure.

43 Woe to you, Pharisees, for <you> love ⟦the place of honor at banquets and⟧ the front seat in the synagogues and accolades in the markets.

44 Woe to you, ⟦Pharisees,⟧ for you ⟦are like⟧ indistinct tombs, and people walking on top are unaware.

Mark 12:38c-39

38c Beware of the exegetes of the Law, who like to walk around in long robes, and accolades in the markets,
39 and to have front seats in the synagogues and places of honor at banquets!

Gos. Thom. 89.1 (Nag Hammadi II 2)

Jesus says: Why do you wash the outside of the cup?

Q 11:46b, 52, 47-48
Woes against the Exegetes of the Law

Matt 23:4, 13, 29-32 | Luke 11:46b-48, 52

46b ⟦καὶ⟧ οὐαὶ ὑμῖν τοῖς ⟦νομικ⟧οῖς, ὅτι ⟦δεσμεύ⟧<ετε> φορτία …
⟦καὶ ἐπιτίθ⟧<ετε> ⟦ἐπὶ τοὺς ὤμους τῶν ἀνθρώπων⟧, αὐτοὶ ⟦δὲ⟧ τῷ
δακτύλῳ ὑμῶν οὐ ⟦θέλ⟧<ετε> ⟦κινῆσαι⟧ αὐτά.
52 οὐαὶ ὑμῖν τοῖς ⟦νομικ⟧οῖς, ὅτι κλείετε ⟦τὴν βασιλείαν⟧ τ⟦<οῦ
θεοῦ> ἔμπροσθεν τῶν ἀνθρώπων⟧· ὑμεῖς οὐκ εἰσήλθατε ⟦οὐδὲ⟧
τοὺς εἰσερχομένους ἀφίετε εἰσελθεῖν.
47 οὐαὶ ὑμῖν, ὅτι οἰκοδομεῖτε τὰ μνημεῖα τῶν προφητῶν, οἱ δὲ
πατέρες ὑμῶν ἀπέκτειναν αὐτούς.
48 … μαρτυρ⟦εῖτε ἑαυτοῖς ὅτι υἱοί⟧ ἐστε τῶν πατέρων ὑμῶν. ..

Gos. Thom. 39.1-2 (P. Oxy. 655)

(1) [λέγει Ἰ(ησοῦ)ς· οἱ Φαρισαῖοι καὶ οἱ γραμματεῖς] ἔλ[αβον τὰς κλεῖδας] τῆς [γνώσεως. αὐτοὶ ἔ]κρυψ[αν αὐτάς.
(2) οὔτε] εἰσῆλ[θον, οὔτε τοὺς] εἰσερ[χομένους ἀφῆ]καν [εἰσελθεῖν].

Gos. Thom. 39.1-2 (Nag Hammadi II 2)

(1) Λέγει Ἰησοῦς· οἱ Φαρισαῖοι καὶ οἱ γραμματεῖς ἔλαβον τὰς κλεῖδας τῆς γνώσεως, ἔκρυψαν αὐτάς.
(2) οὔτε εἰσῆλθον καὶ τοὺς θέλοντας εἰσελθεῖν ἀφῆκαν.

Q 11:49-51
Wisdom's Judgment on This Generation

Matt 23:34-36 | Luke 11:49-51

49 διὰ τοῦτο καὶ ἡ σοφία .. εἶπεν· ἀποστελῶ ⟦πρὸς⟧ αὐτοὺς προφήτας καὶ σοφούς, καὶ ἐξ αὐτῶν ἀποκτενοῦσιν καὶ διώξουσιν,
50 ⟦ἵνα⟧ ἐκζητηθῇ τὸ αἷμα πάντων τῶν προφητῶν τὸ ἐκκεχυμένον
ἀπὸ καταβολῆς κόσμου ἀπὸ τῆς γενεᾶς ταύτης,

51 ἀπὸ αἵματος Ἅβελ ἕως αἵματος Ζαχαρίου τοῦ ἀπολομένου
μεταξὺ τοῦ θυσιαστηρίου καὶ τοῦ οἴκου· ναὶ λέγω ὑμῖν, ἐκζητηθή-
σεται ἀπὸ τῆς γενεᾶς ταύτης.

Q 11:46b, 52, 47-48
Woes against the Exegetes of the Law

Matt 23:4, 13, 29-32 Luke 11:46b-48, 52

46b ⟦And⟧ woe to you, ⟦exegetes of the Law,⟧ for <you> ⟦bind⟧ … burdens, ⟦and load on the backs of people, but⟧ <you your>selves do not ⟦want «to lift»⟧ your finger ⟦to move⟧ them.
52 Woe to you, ⟦exegetes of the Law,⟧ for you shut the ⟦kingdom of <God> from people⟧; you did not go in, ⟦nor⟧ let in those «trying to» get in.
47 Woe to you, for you build the tombs of the prophets, but your «fore»fathers killed them.
48 «Thus» ⟦you⟧ witness ⟦against yourselves that⟧ you are ⟦the sons⟧ of your «fore»fathers. ..

Gos. Thom. 39.1-2 (P. Oxy. 655)

(1) [Jesus says: The Pharisees and the scribes have received the keys] of [knowledge. They] have hidden [them].
(2) [Neither have they] entered, [nor] let [in those (trying to) get] in.

Gos. Thom. 39.1-2 (Nag Hammadi II 2)

(1) Jesus says: The Pharisees and the scribes have received the keys of knowledge, (but) they have hidden them.
(2) Neither have they gone in, nor have they let in those who wanted in.

Q 11:49-51
Wisdom's Judgment on This Generation

Matt 23:34-36 Luke 11:49-51

49 Therefore also .. Wisdom said: I will send them prophets and sages, and «some» of them they will kill and persecute,
50 so that «a settling of accounts for» the blood of all the prophets poured out from the founding of the world may be required of this generation,
51 from «the» blood of Abel to «the» blood of Zechariah, murdered between the sacrificial altar and the House. Yes, I tell you: «An accounting» will be required of this generation!

Q 12:2-3
Proclaiming What Was Whispered

Matt 10:26-27 Luke 12:2-3

2 οὐδὲν κεκαλυμμένον ἐστὶν ὃ οὐκ ἀποκαλυφθήσεται καὶ κρυπτὸν
ὃ οὐ γνωσθήσεται.
3 ὃ λέγω ὑμῖν ἐν τῇ σκοτίᾳ εἴπατε ἐν τῷ φωτί, καὶ ὃ εἰς τὸ οὖς
ἀκούετε κηρύξατε ἐπὶ τῶν δωμάτων.

Mark 4:22

οὐ γάρ ἐστιν κρυπτὸν ἐὰν μὴ ἵνα φανερωθῇ, οὐδὲ ἐγένετο ἀπόκρυφον ἀλλ᾽ ἵνα ἔλθῃ εἰς φανερόν.

Gos. Thom. 5.2 (P. Oxy. 654)

[οὐ γάρ ἐσ]τιν κρυπτὸν ὃ οὐ φανε[ρὸν γενήσεται], καὶ τεθαμμένον ὃ ο[ὐκ ἐγερθήσεται].

Gos. Thom. 6.5 (P. Oxy. 654)

[οὐδὲν γάρ ἐστι]ν ἀ[π]οκεκρ[υμμένον ὃ οὐ φανερὸν ἔσται].

Gos. Thom. 33.1 (P. Oxy. 1)

λέγει Ἰ(ησοῦ)ς· <ὃ> ἀκούεις [ε]ἰς τ̣ὸ ἐ̣ν̣ ᾠ̣τ̣ίον σ̣ο̣υ, τ̣ο̣[ῦτο κήρυξον ...]

Gos. Thom. 5.2=6.5 (Nag Hammadi II 2)

5.2=6.5 οὐ γάρ ἐστιν κρυπτὸν ὃ οὐ φανερὸν γενήσεται.

Gos. Thom. 33.1 (Nag Hammadi II 2)

Λέγει Ἰησοῦς· ὃ ἀκούσεις εἰς τὸ οὖς σου, εἰς τὸ ἄλλο οὖς κήρυξον ἐπὶ τῶν δωμάτων ὑμῶν.

Q 12:4-5
Not Fearing the Body's Death

Matt 10:28 Luke 12:4-5

4 καὶ μὴ φοβεῖσθε ἀπὸ τῶν ἀποκτε⟦ν⟧νόντων τὸ σῶμα, τὴν δὲ
ψυχὴν μὴ δυναμένων ἀποκτεῖναι·
5 φοβεῖσθε δὲ .. τὸν δυνάμενον καὶ ψυχὴν καὶ σῶμα ἀπολέσαι ἐν
τ<ῇ> γεέννῃ.

Q 12:2-3
Proclaiming What Was Whispered

Matt 10:26-27 Luke 12:2-3

2 Nothing is covered up that will not be exposed, and hidden that will not be known.
3 What I say to you in the dark, speak in the light; and what you hear «whispered» in the ear, proclaim on the housetops.

Mark 4:22

For there is nothing hidden, except to be disclosed; nor is anything secret, except to come to light.

Gos. Thom. 5.2 (P. Oxy. 654)

[For there is nothing] hidden that [will] not [become] manifest, [nor] buried that [will not be raised].

Gos. Thom. 6.5 (P. Oxy. 654)

[For nothing is] concealed [that will not be manifest].

Gos. Thom. 33.1 (P. Oxy. 1)

Jesus says: <What> you (sg.) hear (whispered) in one of your (sg.) ears, [proclaim …]

Gos. Thom. 5.2=6.5 (Nag Hammadi II 2)

5.2=6.5 For there is nothing hidden that will not become manifest.

Gos. Thom. 33.1 (Nag Hammadi II 2)

Jesus says: What you will hear (whispered) in your ear, proclaim on your rooftops in (someone) else's ear.

Q 12:4-5
Not Fearing the Body's Death

Matt 10:28 Luke 12:4-5

4 And do not be afraid of those who kill the body, but cannot kill the soul.
5 But fear .. the one who is able to destroy both the soul and body in Gehenna.

Q 12:6-7
More Precious than Many Sparrows

Matt 10:29-31 Luke 12:6-7

6 οὐχὶ ⟦πέντε⟧ στρουθία πωλοῦνται ἀσσαρί⟦ων δύο⟧; καὶ ἓν ἐξ αὐτῶν οὐ πεσεῖται ἐπὶ τὴν γῆν ἄνευ τοῦ ⟦πατρὸς ὑμῶν⟧.
7 ὑμῶν ⟦δὲ⟧ καὶ αἱ τρίχες τῆς κεφαλῆς πᾶσαι ἠριθμη⟦μέναι εἰσίν⟧. μὴ φοβεῖσθε· πολλῶν στρουθίων διαφέρετε ὑμεῖς.

Q 12:8-9
Confessing or Denying

Matt 10:32-33 Luke 12:8-9

8 πᾶς ὃς ⟦ἂν⟧ ὁμολογήσ⟦η⟧ ἐν ἐμοὶ ἔμπροσθεν τῶν ἀνθρώπων, κα⟦ὶ ὁ υἱὸς τοῦ ἀνθρώπου⟧ ὁμολογήσ⟦ει⟧ ἐν αὐτῷ ἔμπροσθεν τῶν ἀγγέλων ..·
9 ὃς δ᾽ ἂν ἀρνήσηταί με ἔμπροσθεν τῶν ἀνθρώπων, ἀρνη⟦θήσεται⟧ ἔμπροσθεν τῶν ἀγγέλων .. .

Mark 8:38

ὃς γὰρ ἐὰν ἐπαισχυνθῇ με καὶ τοὺς ἐμοὺς λόγους ἐν τῇ γενεᾷ ταύτῃ τῇ μοιχαλίδι καὶ ἁμαρτωλῷ, καὶ ὁ υἱὸς τοῦ ἀνθρώπου ἐπαισχυνθήσεται αὐτόν, ὅταν ἔλθῃ ἐν τῇ δόξῃ τοῦ πατρὸς αὐτοῦ μετὰ τῶν ἀγγέλων τῶν ἁγίων.

Q 12:10
Speaking against the holy Spirit

Matt 12:32a-b Luke 12:10

καὶ ὃς ἐὰν εἴπῃ λόγον εἰς τὸν υἱὸν τοῦ ἀνθρώπου ἀφεθήσεται αὐτῷ· ὃς δ᾽ ἂν ⟦εἴπ⟧ῃ εἰς τὸ ἅγιον πνεῦμα οὐκ ἀφεθήσεται αὐτῷ.

Mark 3:28-29

28 Ἀμὴν λέγω ὑμῖν ὅτι πάντα ἀφεθήσεται τοῖς υἱοῖς τῶν ἀνθρώπων τὰ ἁμαρτήματα καὶ αἱ βλασφημίαι ὅσα ἐὰν βλασφημήσωσιν·
29 ὃς δ᾽ ἂν βλασφημήσῃ εἰς τὸ πνεῦμα τὸ ἅγιον, οὐκ ἔχει ἄφεσιν εἰς τὸν αἰῶνα, ἀλλὰ ἔνοχός ἐστιν αἰωνίου ἁμαρτήματος.

Q 12:6-7
More Precious than Many Sparrows

Matt 10:29-31 Luke 12:6-7

6 Are not ⟦five⟧ sparrows sold for ⟦two⟧ cents? And yet not one of them will fall to earth without ⟦your Father's⟧ «consent».
7 But even the hairs of your head all are numbered. Do not be afraid, you are worth more than many sparrows.

Q 12:8-9
Confessing or Denying

Matt 10:32-33 Luke 12:8-9

8 Anyone who ⟦may⟧ speak out for me in public, ⟦the son of humanity⟧ will also speak out for him before the angels .. .

9 But whoever may deny me in public ⟦will be⟧ den⟦ied⟧ before the angels .. .

Mark 8:38

Those who are ashamed of me and of my words in this adulterous and sinful generation, of them the Son of Humanity will also be ashamed when he comes in the glory of his Father with the holy angels.

Q 12:10
Speaking against the holy Spirit

Matt 12:32a-b Luke 12:10

And whoever says a word against the son of humanity, it will be forgiven him; but whoever ⟦speaks⟧ against the holy Spirit, it will not be forgiven him.

Mark 3:28-29

28 Truly I tell you, everything will be forgiven to the sons of humanity for their sins and whatever blasphemies they utter;
29 but whoever blasphemes against the Holy Spirit can never have forgiveness, but is guilty of an eternal sin.

Gos. Thom. 44 (Nag Hammadi II 2)

(1) Λέγει Ἰησοῦς· ὃς ἂν βλασφημήσῃ εἰς τὸν πατέρα, ἀφεθήσεται αὐτῷ.
(2) καὶ ὃς ἂν βλασφημήσῃ εἰς τὸν υἱόν, ἀφεθήσεται αὐτῷ.
(3) ὃς δ' ἂν βλασφημήσῃ εἰς τὸ πνεῦμα τὸ ἅγιον, οὐκ ἀφεθήσεται αὐτῷ οὔτε ἐπὶ τῆς γῆς οὔτε ἐν τῷ οὐρανῷ.

Q 12:11-12
Hearings before Synagogues

Matt 10:19 | Luke 12:11-12

11 ὅταν δὲ εἰσφέρωσιν ὑμᾶς ⟦<εἰς>⟧ τὰς συναγωγάς, μὴ μεριμνήσητε πῶς ἢ τί εἴπητε·
12 ⟦τὸ⟧ γὰρ ⟦ἅγιον πνεῦμα διδάξει⟧ ὑμ⟦ᾶς⟧ ἐν ...ῃ τῇ ὥρᾳ τί εἴπ<ητε>.

Mark 13:9-11

9 Βλέπετε δὲ ὑμεῖς ἑαυτούς· παραδώσουσιν ὑμᾶς εἰς συνέδρια καὶ εἰς συναγωγὰς δαρήσεσθε καὶ ἐπὶ ἡγεμόνων καὶ βασιλέων σταθήσεσθε ἕνεκεν ἐμοῦ εἰς μαρτύριον αὐτοῖς.
10 καὶ εἰς πάντα τὰ ἔθνη πρῶτον δεῖ κηρυχθῆναι τὸ εὐαγγέλιον.
11 καὶ ὅταν ἄγωσιν ὑμᾶς παραδιδόντες, μὴ προμεριμνᾶτε τί λαλήσητε, ἀλλ' ὃ ἐὰν δοθῇ ὑμῖν ἐν ἐκείνῃ τῇ ὥρᾳ τοῦτο λαλεῖτε· οὐ γάρ ἐστε ὑμεῖς οἱ λαλοῦντες ἀλλὰ τὸ πνεῦμα τὸ ἅγιον.

Q 12:33-34
Storing up Treasures in Heaven

Matt 6:19-21 | Luke 12:33-34

33 «μὴ θησαυρίζετε ὑμῖν θησαυροὺς ἐπὶ τῆς γῆς, ὅπου σὴς καὶ βρῶσις ἀφανίζει καὶ ὅπου κλέπται διορύσσουσιν καὶ κλέπτουσιν·» θησαυρίζετε δὲ ὑμῖν θησαυρο... ἐν οὐραν⟦ῷ⟧, ὅπου οὔτε σὴς οὔτε βρῶσις ἀφανίζει καὶ ὅπου κλέπται οὐ διορύσσουσιν οὐδὲ κλέπτουσιν·
34 ὅπου γάρ ἐστιν ὁ θησαυρός σου, ἐκεῖ ἔσται καὶ ἡ καρδία σου.

Mark 10:21b

ἕν σε ὑστερεῖ· ὕπαγε, ὅσα ἔχεις πώλησον καὶ δὸς τοῖς πτωχοῖς, καὶ ἕξεις θησαυρὸν ἐν οὐρανῷ, καὶ δεῦρο ἀκολούθει μοι.

Gos. Thom. 76.3 (Nag Hammadi II 2)

ζητεῖτε καὶ ὑμεῖς τὸν θησαυρὸν αὐτοῦ τὸν ἀνέκλειπτον (καὶ) μένοντα ὅπου οὐ σὴς εἰς βρῶσιν ἐγγίζει οὐδὲ σκώληξ ἀφανίζει.

Gos. Thom. 44 (Nag Hammadi II 2)

(1) Jesus says: Whoever blasphemes against the Father, it will be forgiven him.
(2) And whoever blasphemes against the Son, it will be forgiven him.
(3) But whoever blasphemes against the Holy Spirit, it will not be forgiven him, neither on earth nor in heaven.

Q 12:11-12
Hearings before Synagogues

Matt 10:19 Luke 12:11-12

11 When they bring you before synagogues, do not be anxious about how or what you are to say;
12 for ⟦the holy Spirit will teach⟧ you in that .. hour what you are to say.

Mark 13:9-11

9 As for yourselves, beware; for they will hand you over to councils; and you will be beaten in synagogues; and you will stand before governors and kings because of me, as a testimony to them.
10 And the good news must first be proclaimed to all nations.
11 When they take you to trial and hand you over, do not be anxious beforehand about what you are to speak; but speak whatever is given you at that time, for it is not you who speak, but the Holy Spirit.

Q 12:33-34
Storing up Treasures in Heaven

Matt 6:19-21 Luke 12:33-34

33 «Do not treasure for yourselves treasures on earth, where moth and gnawing deface and where robbers dig through and rob,» but treasure for yourselves treasure«s» in heaven, where neither moth nor gnawing defaces and where robbers do not dig through nor rob.

34 For where your treasure is, there will also be your heart.

Mark 10:21b

You lack one thing; go, sell what you own, and give the money to the poor, and you will have treasure in heaven; then come, follow me.

Gos. Thom. 76.3 (Nag Hammadi II 2)

You too search for his treasure which does not perish, which stays where moth cannot reach (it) for food nor worm deface (it).

Q 12:22b-31
Free from Anxiety like Ravens and Lilies

Matt 6:25-33 Luke 12:22b-31

22b διὰ τοῦτο λέγω ὑμῖν· μὴ μεριμνᾶτε τῇ ψυχῇ ὑμῶν τί φάγητε,
μηδὲ τῷ σώματι ὑμῶν τί ἐνδύσησθε.
23 οὐχὶ ἡ ψυχὴ πλεῖόν ἐστιν τῆς τροφῆς καὶ τὸ σῶμα τοῦ ἐνδύματος;
24 κατανοήσατε τοὺς κόρακας ὅτι οὐ σπείρουσιν οὐδὲ θερίζουσιν
οὐδὲ συνάγουσιν εἰς ἀποθήκας, καὶ ὁ θεὸς τρέφει αὐτούς· οὐχ
ὑμεῖς μᾶλλον διαφέρετε τῶν πετεινῶν;
25 τίς δὲ ἐξ ὑμῶν μεριμνῶν δύναται προσθεῖναι ἐπὶ τὴν ἡλικίαν
αὐτοῦ πῆχυν ..;
26 καὶ περὶ ἐνδύματος τί μεριμνᾶτε;
27 κατα⟦μάθε⟧τε τὰ κρίνα πῶς αὐξάν⟦ει⟧· οὐ κοπι⟦ᾷ⟧ οὐδὲ νήθ⟦ει⟧·
λέγω δὲ ὑμῖν, οὐδὲ Σολομὼν ἐν πάσῃ τῇ δόξῃ αὐτοῦ περιεβάλετο
ὡς ἓν τούτων.
28 εἰ δὲ ἐν ἀγρῷ τὸν χόρτον ὄντα σήμερον καὶ αὔριον εἰς κλίβα-
νον βαλλόμενον ὁ θεὸς οὕτως ἀμφιέ⟦ννυσιν⟧, οὐ πολλῷ μᾶλλον
ὑμᾶς, ὀλιγόπιστοι;
29 μὴ ⟦οὖν⟧ μεριμνήσητε λέγοντες· τί φάγωμεν; ⟦ἤ⟧· τί πίωμεν;
⟦ἤ⟧· τί περιβαλώμεθα;
30 πάντα γὰρ ταῦτα τὰ ἔθνη ἐπιζητοῦσιν· οἶδεν ⟦γὰρ⟧ ὁ πατὴρ
ὑμῶν ὅτι χρῄζετε τούτων ⟦ἁπάντων⟧.
31 ζητεῖτε δὲ τὴν βασιλείαν αὐτοῦ, καὶ ταῦτα ⟦πάντα⟧ προστεθήσεται ὑμῖν.

Gos.Thom. 36.1 (P. Oxy. 655)

[λέγει Ἰ(ησοῦ)ς· μὴ μεριμνᾶτε ἀ]πὸ πρωῒ ἕ[ως ὀψέ, μήτ]ε ἀφ’ ἑσπ[έρας ἕως π]ρωΐ, μήτε [τῇ τροφῇ ὑ]μῶν τί φά[γητε, μήτε] τῇ στ[ολῇ ὑμῶν] τί ἐνδύ[ση]σθε.

Gos.Thom. 36.1 (Nag Hammadi II 2)

Λέγει Ἰησοῦς· μὴ μεριμνᾶτε ἀπὸ πρωῒ ἕως ὀψὲ καὶ ἀφ’ ἑσπέρας ἕως πρωῒ τί ἐνδύσεσθε.

Gos. Thom. 36.4 (P. Oxy. 655)

τίς ἂν προσθ<εί>η ἐπὶ τὴν εἱλικίαν ὑμῶν; αὐτὸ[ς δ]ώσει ὑμεῖν τὸ ἔνδυμα ὑμῶν.

Q 12:22b-31
Free from Anxiety like Ravens and Lilies

Matt 6:25-33 Luke 12:22b-31

22b Therefore I tell you: Do not be anxious about your life, what you are to eat, nor about your body, with what you are to clothe yourself.
23 Is not life more than food, and the body than clothing?

24 Consider the ravens: They neither sow nor reap nor gather into barns, and yet God feeds them. Are you not better than the birds?

25 And who of you by being anxious is able to add to one's stature a .. cubit?
26 And why are you anxious about clothing?
27 ⟦Observe⟧ the lilies, how they grow: They do not work nor do they spin. Yet I tell you: Not even Solomon in all his glory was arrayed like one of these.
28 But if in the field the grass, there today and tomorrow thrown into the oven, God clothes thus, will he not much more clothe you, persons of petty faith!
29 ⟦So⟧ do not be anxious, saying: What are we to eat? ⟦Or:⟧ What are we to drink? ⟦Or:⟧ What are we to wear?
30 For all these the Gentiles seek; ⟦for⟧ your Father knows that you need them ⟦all⟧.
31 But seek his kingdom, and ⟦all⟧ these shall be granted to you.

Gos.Thom. 36.1 (P. Oxy. 655)

[Jesus says, Do not be anxious] from morning [to late nor] from evening [to] morning, either [about] your [food], what [you are to] eat, [or] about [your robe], with what you [are to] clothe yourself.

Gos.Thom. 36.1 (Nag Hammadi II 2)

Jesus says: Do not be anxious from morning to late and from evening to morning with what you will clothe yourself.

Gos. Thom. 36.4 (P. Oxy. 655)

Who might add to your stature? That one will [give] you your clothing.

Gos. Thom. 36.2-3 (P. Oxy. 655)

(2) [πολ]λῷ κρεί[σσον]ές ẹ[στε] τῶν [κρί]νων, ἅτι[να ο]ὐ ξα[ί]νει οὐδὲ ν[ήθ]ει.
(3) κ̣[αὶ] ἓν ἔχọντ[ες ἔ]νδ[υ]μα, τί ἐν[.....].αι ὑμεῖς;

Q 12:39-40
The Son of Humanity Comes as a Robber

Matt 24:43-44 | Luke 12:39-40

39 ⟦ἐκεῖν⟧ο δὲ γινώσκετε ὅτι εἰ ᾔδει ὁ οἰκοδεσπότης ποίᾳ φυλακῇ ὁ κλέπτης ἔρχεται, οὐκ ἂν ⟦εἴασ⟧εν διορυχθῆναι τὸν οἶκον αὐτοῦ.
40 καὶ ὑμεῖς γίνεσθε ἕτοιμοι, ὅτι ᾗ οὐ δοκεῖτε ὥρᾳ ὁ υἱὸς τοῦ ἀνθρώπου ἔρχεται.

Mark 13:35a-b

γρηγορεῖτε οὖν· οὐκ οἴδατε γὰρ πότε ὁ κύριος τῆς οἰκίας ἔρχεται,

Gos. Thom. 21.5 (Nag Hammadi II 2)

διὰ τοῦτο λέγω· εἰ μανθάνει ὁ οἰκοδεσπότης ὅτι ἔρχεται ὁ κλέπτης γρηγορήσει πρὶν ἐλθεῖν αὐτὸν καὶ οὐκ ἐάσει αὐτὸν διορύξαι τὴν οἰκίαν αὐτοῦ τῆς βασιλείας αὐτοῦ τοῦ αἶρειν τὰ σκεύη αὐτοῦ.

Gos. Thom. 103 (Nag Hammadi II 2)

Λέγει Ἰησοῦς· μακάριος ὁ ἄνθρωπος, ὃς οἶδεν [ποίῳ] μέρει οἱ λῃσταὶ εἰσέρχονται, ἵνα ἀναστὰς συναγάγῃ τὴν [βασιλείαν] αὐτοῦ καὶ περιζώσῃ τὴν ὀσφὺν αὐτοῦ πρὶν εἰσπορεύεσθαι αὐτούς.

Q 12:42-46
The Faithful or Unfaithful Slave

Matt 24:45-51 | Luke 12:42-46

42 τίς ἄρα ἐστὶν ὁ πιστὸς δοῦλος ⟦καὶ⟧ φρόνιμος ὃν κατέστησεν ὁ κύριος ἐπὶ τῆς οἰκετείας αὐτοῦ τοῦ δο⟦ῦ⟧ναι ⟦αὐτοῖς⟧ ἐν καιρῷ τὴν τροφήν;
43 μακάριος ὁ δοῦλος ἐκεῖνος, ὃν ἐλθὼν ὁ κύριος αὐτοῦ εὑρήσει οὕτως ποιοῦντα·
44 ⟦ἀμὴν⟧ λέγω ὑμῖν ὅτι ἐπὶ πᾶσιν τοῖς ὑπάρχουσιν αὐτοῦ καταστήσει αὐτόν.
45 ἐὰν δὲ εἴπῃ ὁ δοῦλος ἐκεῖνος ἐν τῇ καρδίᾳ αὐτοῦ· χρονίζει ὁ κύριός μου, καὶ ἄρξηται τύπτειν τοὺς ⟦συνδούλους αὐτοῦ⟧, ἐσθί⟦ῃ⟧ δὲ καὶ πίν⟦ῃ μετὰ τῶν⟧ μεθυ⟦όντων⟧,

Gos. Thom. 36.2-3 (P. Oxy. 655)

(2) [You are] far better than the [lilies] which do not card nor spin.

(3) [And] having *one* clothing, … you …?

Q 12:39-40
The Son of Humanity Comes as a Robber

Matt 24:43-44 Luke 12:39-40

39 But know this: If the householder had known in which watch the robber was coming, he would not have let his house be dug into.
40 You also must be ready, for the Son of Humanity is coming at an hour you do not expect.

Mark 13:35a-b

Therefore, keep awake – for you do not know when the master of the house is coming,

Gos. Thom. 21.5 (Nag Hammadi II 2)

That is why I say: When the householder learns that the robber is coming, he will be on guard before he comes (and) will not let him dig into his house, his domain, to carry away his possessions.

Gos. Thom. 103 (Nag Hammadi II 2)

Jesus says: Blessed is the person who knows at [which] point (of the house) the robbers are going to enter, so that [he] may arise to gather together his [domain] and gird his loins before they enter.

Q 12:42-46
The Faithful or Unfaithful Slave

Matt 24:45-51 Luke 12:42-46

42 Who then is the faithful ⟦and⟧ wise slave whom the master put over his household to give ⟦them⟧ food on time?

43 Blessed is that slave whose master, on coming, will find so doing.

44 ⟦Amen⟧, I tell you: He will appoint him over all his possessions.

45 But if that slave says in his heart: My master is delayed, and begins to beat ⟦his fellow slaves⟧, and eats and drinks ⟦with the⟧ drunk⟦ards⟧,

46 ἥξει ὁ κύριος τοῦ δούλου ἐκείνου ἐν ἡμέρᾳ ᾗ οὐ προσδοκᾷ καὶ ἐν ὥρᾳ ᾗ οὐ γινώσκει, καὶ διχοτομήσει αὐτόν καὶ τὸ μέρος αὐτοῦ μετὰ τῶν ἀπίστων θήσει.

Mark 13:36

μὴ ἐλθὼν ἐξαίφνης εὕρῃ ὑμᾶς καθεύδοντας.

Q 12:⟦49⟧, 51, 53
Children against Parents

Matt 10:34-35 Luke 12:49, 51, 53

⟦49⟧ ⟦«πῦρ ἦλθον βαλεῖν ἐπὶ τὴν γῆν, καὶ τί θέλω εἰ ἤδη ἀνήφθη.»⟧
51 ⟦δοκεῖ⟧τε ὅτι ἦλθον βαλεῖν εἰρήνην ἐπὶ τὴν γῆν; οὐκ ἦλθον βαλεῖν εἰρήνην ἀλλὰ μάχαιραν.
53 ἦλθον γὰρ διχάσαι υἱὸν ⟦κατὰ⟧ πατρ⟦ὸς καὶ⟧ θυγατέρα ⟦κατὰ⟧ τῆ⟦ς⟧ μητρ⟦ὸς⟧ αὐτῆς, ⟦καὶ⟧ νύμφην ⟦κατὰ⟧ τῆ⟦ς⟧ πενθερᾶ⟦ς⟧ αὐτῆς.

Mark 13:12

καὶ παραδώσει ἀδελφὸς ἀδελφὸν εἰς θάνατον καὶ πατὴρ τέκνον, καὶ ἐπαναστήσονται τέκνα ἐπὶ γονεῖς καὶ θανατώσουσιν αὐτούς·

Gos. Thom. 10 (Nag Hammadi II 2)

Λέγει Ἰησοῦς· ἔβαλον πῦρ εἰς τὸν κόσμον. καὶ ἰδοὺ τηρῶ αὐτό, ἕως ἂν πυροῖ.

Gos. Thom. 16.1-2, 3b (Nag Hammadi II 2)

(1) Λέγει Ἰησοῦς· τάχα δοκοῦσιν οἱ ἄνθρωποι ὅτι ἦλθον βαλεῖν εἰρήνην ἐπὶ τὸν κόσμον,
(2) καὶ οὐκ οἴδασιν ὅτι ἦλθον βαλεῖν διαμερισμοὺς ἐπὶ τὴν γῆν, πῦρ, μάχαιραν, πόλεμον.
(3b) ὁ πατὴρ ἐπὶ τῷ υἱῷ καὶ ὁ υἱὸς ἐπὶ τῷ πατρί.

Q 12:⟦54-56⟧
⟦Judging the Time⟧

Matt 16:2-3 Luke 12:54-56

⟦54⟧ ⟦... ὀψίας γενομένης λέγετε· εὐδία, πυρράζει γὰρ ὁ οὐρανός·⟧

46 the master of that slave will come on a day he does not expect and at an hour he does not know, and will cut him to pieces and give him an inheritance with the faithless.

Mark 13:36

or else, on coming suddenly, he may find you asleep.

Q 12:⟦49⟧, 51, 53
Children against Parents

Matt 10:34-35 | Luke 12:49, 51, 53

⟦**49**⟧ ⟦«Fire have I come to hurl on the earth, and how I wish it had already blazed up!»⟧
51 ⟦Do you⟧ think that I have come to hurl peace on earth? I did not come to hurl peace, but a sword!
53 For I have come to divide son against father, ⟦and⟧ daughter against her mother, ⟦and⟧ daughter-in-law against her mother-in-law.

Mark 13:12

Brother will betray brother to death, and a father his child, and children will rise against parents and have them put to death;

Gos. Thom. 10 (Nag Hammadi II 2)

Jesus says: I have hurled fire on the world, and see, I am guarding it until it blazes up.

Gos. Thom. 16.1-2, 3b (Nag Hammadi II 2)

(1) Jesus says: Perhaps people think that I have come to hurl peace on the earth.

(2) But they do not know that I have come to hurl dissension on the earth: fire, sword, war.
(3b) father against son and son against father.

Q 12:⟦54-56⟧
⟦Judging the Time⟧

Matt 16:2-3 | Luke 12:54-56

⟦**54**⟧ ⟦«But he said to them:» When evening has come, you say: Good weather! For the sky is flame red.⟧

⟦**55**⟧ ⟦καὶ πρωΐ· σήμερον χειμών, πυρράζει γὰρ στυγνάζων ὁ οὐρανός·⟧
⟦**56**⟧ ⟦τὸ πρόσωπον τοῦ οὐρανοῦ οἴδατε διακρίνειν, τὸν καιρὸν δὲ οὐ δύνασθε;⟧

Gos. Thom. 91.2 (Nag Hammadi II 2)

λέγει αὐτοῖς· τὸ πρόσωπον τοῦ οὐρανοῦ καὶ τῆς γῆς πειράζετε, τὸν δὲ κατὰ πρόσωπον ὑμῶν οὐκ οἴδατε καὶ τὸν καιρὸν τοῦτον οὐκ οἴδατε πειράζειν.

Q 12:58-59
Settling out of Court

Matt 5:25-26 Luke 12:58-59

58 ⟦ἕως ὅτου⟧ ... μετὰ τοῦ ἀντιδίκου σου ἐν τῇ ὁδῷ, δὸς ἐργασίαν ἀπηλλάχθαι ἀπ᾽ αὐτοῦ, μήποτέ σε παραδῷ ⟦ὁ ἀντίδικος⟧ τῷ κριτῇ καὶ ὁ κριτὴς τῷ ὑπηρέτῃ καὶ ⟦ὁ <ὑπηρέτης> σε⟧ β⟦α⟧λ⟦εῖ⟧ εἰς φυλακήν.
59 λέγω σοι, οὐ μὴ ἐξέλθῃς ἐκεῖθεν, ἕως τὸ⟦ν⟧ ἔσχατον ⟦κοδράντην⟧ ἀποδῷς.

Q 13:18-19
The Mustard Seed

Matt 13:31-32 Luke 13:18-19

18 τίνι ὁμοία ἐστὶν ἡ βασιλεία τοῦ θεοῦ καὶ τίνι ὁμοιώσω αὐτήν;
19 ὁμοία ἐστὶν κόκκῳ σινάπεως, ὃν λαβὼν ἄνθρωπος ἔβαλεν εἰς ⟦κῆπ⟧ον αὐτοῦ· καὶ ηὔξησεν καὶ ἐγένετο εἰς δένδρον, καὶ τὰ πετεινὰ τοῦ οὐρανοῦ κατεσκήνωσεν ἐν τοῖς κλάδοις αὐτοῦ.

Mark 4:30-32

30 Καὶ ἔλεγεν· πῶς ὁμοιώσωμεν τὴν βασιλείαν τοῦ θεοῦ ἢ ἐν τίνι αὐτὴν παραβολῇ θῶμεν;
31 ὡς κόκκῳ σινάπεως, ὃς ὅταν σπαρῇ ἐπὶ τῆς γῆς, μικρότερον ὂν πάντων τῶν σπερμάτων τῶν ἐπὶ τῆς γῆς,
32 καὶ ὅταν σπαρῇ, ἀναβαίνει καὶ γίνεται μεῖζον πάντων τῶν λαχάνων καὶ ποιεῖ κλάδους μεγάλους, ὥστε δύνασθαι ὑπὸ τὴν σκιὰν αὐτοῦ τὰ πετεινὰ τοῦ οὐρανοῦ κατασκηνοῦν.

⟦55⟧ ⟦And at dawn: Today «it's» wintry! For the lowering sky is flame red.⟧
⟦56⟧ ⟦The face of the sky you know «how» to interpret, but the time you are not able to?⟧

Gos. Thom. 91.2 (Nag Hammadi II 2)

He said to them: You test the face of sky and earth; but the one who is before you, you have not recognized, and you do not know how to test this opportunity.

Q 12:58-59
Settling out of Court

Matt 5:25-26 Luke 12:58-59

58 ⟦While⟧ you «go along» with your opponent on the way, make an effort to get loose from him, lest ⟦the opponent⟧ hand you over to the judge, and the judge to the assistant, and ⟦the <assistant>⟧ throw ⟦you⟧ into prison.
59 I say to you: You will not get out of there until you pay the last ⟦penny⟧!

Q 13:18-19
The Mustard Seed

Matt 13:31-32 Luke 13:18-19

18 What is the kingdom of God like, and with what am I to compare it?
19 It is like a seed of mustard, which a person took and threw into his ⟦garden⟧. And it grew and developed into a tree, and the birds of the sky nested in its branches.

Mark 4:30-32

30 And he said: With what can we compare the kingdom of God, or what parable will we use for it?
31 It is like a seed of mustard, which, when sown upon the ground, is the smallest of all the seeds on earth;
32 yet when it is sown it grows up and develops into the greatest of all shrubs, and puts forth large branches, so that the birds of the sky can nest in its shade.

Gos. Thom. 20 (Nag Hammadi II 2)

(1) Εἶπον οἱ μαθηταὶ τῷ Ἰησοῦ· εἰπὲ ἡμῖν, τίνι ὁμοία ἐστὶν ἡ βασιλεία τῶν οὐρανῶν.
(2) εἶπεν αὐτοῖς· ὁμοία ἐστὶν κόκκῳ σινάπεως.
(3) μικρός ἐστιν παρὰ πάντα τὰ σπέρματα.
(4) ὅταν δὲ πέσῃ ἐπὶ τὴν γῆν τὴν ἐργαζομένην, ποιεῖ κλάδον μέγαν καὶ γίνεται σκέπη τοῖς πετεινοῖς τοῦ οὐρανοῦ.

Q 13:20-21
The Yeast

Matt 13:33 | Luke 13:20-21

20 ⟦καὶ πάλιν⟧· τίνι ὁμοιώσω τὴν βασιλείαν τοῦ θεοῦ;
21 ὁμοία ἐστὶν ζύμῃ, ἣν λαβοῦσα γυνὴ ἐνέκρυψεν εἰς ἀλεύρου
σάτα τρία ἕως οὗ ἐζυμώθη ὅλον.

Gos. Thom. 96.1-2 (Nag Hammadi II 2)

(1) Λ[έγε]ι Ἰησοῦς· ἡ βασιλεία τοῦ πατρὸς ὁμοία ἐστὶν γυναικί [τινι].
(2) ἔλαβεν μικρόν τι ζύμης (καὶ) ἔκρυ[ψεν] αὐτὴν εἰς ἄλευρον (καὶ) ἐποίησεν αὐτὸ ἄρτους μεγάλους.

Q 13:24-27
I Do Not Know You

Matt 7:13-14, 22-23; 25:10-12 | Luke 13:24-27

24 εἰσέλθατε διὰ τῆς στενῆς θύρας, ὅτι πολλοὶ ζητήσουσιν
εἰσελθεῖν καὶ ὀλίγοι ⟦εἰσὶν οἱ <εἰσερχόμενοι δι’> αὐτῆ<ς>⟧.
25 ἀφ’ οὗ ἂν ⟦ἐγερθῇ⟧ ὁ ⟦οἰκοδεσπότης⟧ καὶ κλείσ⟦ῃ τ⟧ὴ⟦ν⟧
θύρα⟦ν καὶ ἄρξησθε ἔξω ἑστάναι καὶ κρούειν τὴν θύραν⟧ λέγοντες· κύριε, ἄνοιξον ἡμῖν, καὶ ἀποκριθεὶς ἐρεῖ ὑμῖν· οὐκ οἶδα ὑμᾶς,
26 τότε ἄρξεσθε λέγειν· ἐφάγομεν ἐνώπιόν σου καὶ ἐπίομεν καὶ ἐν
ταῖς πλατείαις ἡμῶν ἐδίδαξας·
27 καὶ ἐρεῖ λέγων ὑμῖν· οὐκ οἶδα ὑμᾶς· ἀπόστητε ἀπ’ ἐμοῦ ⟦οἱ⟧
ἐργαζόμενοι τὴν ἀνομίαν.

Gos. Thom. 20 (Nag Hammadi II 2)

(1) The disciples said to Jesus: Tell us, what is the kingdom of heaven like!

(2) He said to them: It is like a seed of mustard.
(3) <It> is the smallest of all seeds.
(4) But when it falls on cultivated soil, it (the soil) produces a large branch (and) becomes shelter for the birds of the sky.

Q 13:20-21
The Yeast

Matt 13:33 Luke 13:20-21

20 ⟦And again⟧: With what am I to compare the kingdom of God?
21 It is like yeast, which a woman took and hid in three measures of flour until it was fully fermented.

Gos. Thom. 96.1-2 (Nag Hammadi II 2)

(1) Jesus [says]: The kingdom of the Father is like [a] woman.
(2) She took a little bit of yeast. [She] hid it in dough (and) made it into huge loaves of bread.

Q 13:24-27
I Do Not Know You

Matt 7:13-14, 22-23; 25:10-12 Luke 13:24-27

24 Enter through the narrow door, for many will seek to enter and few ⟦are those who <enter through> it⟧.
25 When the ⟦householder has arisen⟧ and locked the door, ⟦and you begin to stand outside and knock on the door⟧, saying: Master, open for us, and he will answer you: I do not know you,
26 then you will begin saying: We ate in your presence and drank, and «it was» in our streets you taught.
27 And he will say to you: I do not know you! Get away from me, ⟦«you» who⟧ do lawlessness!

Q 13:29, 28
Many Shall Come from Sunrise and Sunset

Matt 8:11-12 Luke 13:28-29

29 ⟦καὶ πολλοὶ⟧ ἀπὸ ἀνατολῶν καὶ δυσμῶν ἥξουσιν καὶ ἀνακλιθή-
σονται
28 μετὰ Ἀβραὰμ καὶ Ἰσαὰκ καὶ Ἰακὼβ ἐν τῇ βασιλείᾳ τοῦ θεοῦ,
⟦ὑμ<εῖ>ς⟧ δὲ ἐκβλ⟦ηθήσ<εσθε> εἰς τὸ σκότος τὸ⟧ ἐξώ⟦τερον⟧·
ἐκεῖ ἔσται ὁ κλαυθμὸς καὶ ὁ βρυγμὸς τῶν ὀδόντων.

Q 13:⟦30⟧
⟦The Reversal of the Last and the First⟧

Matt 20:16 Luke 13:30

⟦.. ἔσονται οἱ ἔσχατοι πρῶτοι καὶ οἱ πρῶτοι ἔσχατοι.⟧

Mark 10:31

πολλοὶ δὲ ἔσονται πρῶτοι ἔσχατοι καὶ οἱ ἔσχατοι πρῶτοι.

Gos. Thom. 4.2 (P. Oxy. 654)

ὅτι πολλοὶ ἔσονται π[ρῶτοι ἔσχατοι καὶ] οἱ ἔσχατοι πρῶτοι,

Gos. Thom. 4.2 (Nag Hammadi II 2)

ὅτι πολλοὶ ἔσονται πρῶτοι ἔσχατοι,

Q 13:34-35
Judgment over Jerusalem

Matt 23:37-39 Luke 13:34-35

34 Ἰερουσαλὴμ Ἰερουσαλήμ, ἡ ἀποκτείνουσα τοὺς προφήτας καὶ
λιθοβολοῦσα τοὺς ἀπεσταλμένους πρὸς αὐτήν, ποσάκις ἠθέλησα
ἐπισυναγαγεῖν τὰ τέκνα σου, ὃν τρόπον ὄρνις ἐπισυνάγει τ⟦ὰ⟧
νοσσία αὐτῆς ὑπὸ τὰς πτέρυγας, καὶ οὐκ ἠθελήσατε.
35 ἰδοὺ ἀφίεται ὑμῖν ὁ οἶκος ὑμῶν. λέγω .. ὑμῖν, οὐ μὴ ἴδητέ με ἕως
⟦ἥξει ὅτε⟧ εἴπητε· εὐλογημένος ὁ ἐρχόμενος ἐν ὀνόματι κυρίου.

Mark 11:9c

εὐλογημένος ὁ ἐρχόμενος ἐν ὀνόματι κυρίου·

Q 13:29, 28
Many Shall Come from Sunrise and Sunset

Matt 8:11-12 Luke 13:28-29

29 ⟦And many⟧ shall come from Sunrise and Sunset and recline

28 with Abraham and Isaac and Jacob in the kingdom of God, but ⟦you will be⟧ thrown out ⟦into the⟧ out⟦er darkness⟧, where there will be wailing and grinding of teeth.

Q 13:⟦30⟧
⟦The Reversal of the Last and the First⟧

Matt 20:16 Luke 13:30

⟦.. The last will be first, and the first last.⟧

Mark 10:31

But many who are first will be last, and the last will be first.

Gos. Thom. 4.2 (P. Oxy. 654)

For many who are [first] will become [last, and] the last will be first,

Gos. Thom. 4.2 (Nag Hammadi II 2)

For many who are first will become last,

Q 13:34-35
Judgment over Jerusalem

Matt 23:37-39 Luke 13:34-35

34 O Jerusalem, Jerusalem, who kills the prophets and stones those sent to her! How often I wanted to gather your children together, as a hen gathers her nestlings under «her» wings, and you were not willing!

35 Look, your House is forsaken! .. I tell you: You will not see me until ⟦«the time» comes when⟧ you say: Blessed is the one who comes in the name of the Lord!

Mark 11:9c

Blessed is the one who comes in the name of the Lord!

Q 14:⟦11⟧
⟦The Exalted Humbled and the Humble Exalted⟧

Matt 23:12 Luke 14:11

⟦πᾶς ὁ ὑψῶν ἑαυτὸν ταπεινωθήσεται, καὶ ὁ ταπεινῶν ἑαυτὸν ὑψωθήσεται.⟧

Q 14:16-18, ?19-20?, 21, 23
The Invited Dinner Guests

Matt 22:2-10 Luke 14:16-21, 23

16 ἄνθρωπός τις ἐποίει δεῖπνον ⟦μέγα, καὶ ἐκάλεσεν πολλοὺς⟧
17 καὶ ἀπέστειλεν τὸν δοῦλον αὐτοῦ ⟦τῇ ὥρᾳ τοῦ δείπνου⟧ εἰπεῖν
τοῖς κεκλημένοις· ἔρχεσθε, ὅτι ἤδη ἕτοιμά ἐστιν.
18 … ἀγρόν, ..
?19? ..
?20? ..
21 «καὶ < > ὁ δοῦλος < > τῷ κυρίῳ αὐτοῦ ταῦτα.» τότε ὀργισθεὶς ὁ
οἰκοδεσπότης εἶπεν τῷ δούλῳ αὐτοῦ·
23 ἔξελθε εἰς τὰς ὁδοὺς καὶ ὅσους ἐὰν εὕρ<ῃς> καλέσ<ον>, ἵνα
γεμισθῇ μου ὁ οἶκος.

Gos. Thom. 64 (Nag Hammadi II 2)

(1) Λέγει Ἰησοῦς· ἀνθρώπῳ τινὶ ξένοι ἦσαν· καὶ ἑτοιμάσας τὸ δεῖπνον ἀπέστειλεν τὸν δοῦλον αὐτοῦ ἵνα καλέσῃ τοὺς ξένους.
(2) ἦλθεν πρὸς τὸν πρῶτον (καὶ) εἶπεν αὐτῷ· ὁ κύριός μου καλεῖ σε.
(3) εἶπεν· ἀργύρια ἐδάνεισα ἐμπόροις, οἳ ἐλεύσονται τῆς ἑσπέρας· πορεύσομαι ἐπιτάσσειν αὐτοῖς, παραιτοῦμαι περὶ τοῦ δείπνου.
(4) ἐλθὼν πρὸς ἕτερον εἶπεν αὐτῷ· ὁ κύριός μου ἐκάλεσέν σε.
(5) εἶπεν αὐτῷ· οἰκίαν ἠγόρασα καὶ αἰτοῦσίν με ἡμέραν· οὐκ εὐκαιρῶ.

(8) ἐλθὼν πρὸς ἕτερον εἶπεν αὐτῷ· ὁ κύριός μου καλεῖ σε.
(9) εἶπεν αὐτῷ· κώμην ἠγόρασα (καὶ) πορεύομαι λαβεῖν τὸν μισθόν· οὐ δυνήσομαι ἐλθεῖν, παραιτοῦμαι.
(6) ἐρχόμενος πρὸς ἕτερον εἶπεν αὐτῷ· ὁ κύριός μου καλεῖ σε.
(7) εἶπεν αὐτῷ· ὁ φίλος μου γαμήσει καὶ ἐγὼ δεῖπνον ποιήσω· οὐ δυνήσομαι ἐλθεῖν, παραιτοῦμαι περὶ τοῦ δείπνου.
(10) ἐρχόμενος ὁ δοῦλος εἶπεν τῷ κυρίῳ αὐτοῦ· οὓς ἐκάλεσας εἰς τὸ δεῖπνον παρῃτήσαντο.
(11) εἶπεν ὁ κύριος τῷ δούλῳ αὐτοῦ· ἔξελθε ἔξω εἰς τὰς ὁδοὺς (καὶ) ὅσους ἐὰν εὕρῃς εἰσάγαγε ἵνα δειπνήσωσιν.

Q 14:⟦11⟧
⟦The Exalted Humbled and the Humble Exalted⟧

Matt 23:12 Luke 14:11

⟦Everyone exalting oneself will be humbled, and the one humbling oneself will be exalted.⟧

Q 14:16-18, ?19-20?, 21, 23
The Invited Dinner Guests

Matt 22:2-10 Luke 14:16-21, 23

16 A certain person prepared a ⟦large⟧ dinner, ⟦and invited many⟧.
17 And he sent his slave ⟦at the time of the dinner⟧ to say to the invited:
Come, for it is now ready.
18 «One declined because of his» farm.
?19? «Another declined because of his business.»
?20?..
21 «And the slave, <on coming, said> these things to his master.» Then
the householder, enraged, said to his slave:
23 Go out on the roads, and whomever you find, invite, so that my house
may be filled.

Gos. Thom. 64 (Nag Hammadi II 2)

(1) Jesus says: A person had guests. And when he had prepared the dinner, he sent his slave so that he might invite the guests.
(2) He came to the first (and) said to him: My master invites you.
(3) He said: I have bills for some merchants. They are coming to me this evening. I will go (and) give instructions to them. Excuse me from the dinner.
(4) He came to another (and) said to him: My master has invited you.
(5) He said to him: I have bought a house, and I have been called (away) for a day. I will not have time.
(8) He came to another (and) said to him: My master invites you.
(9) He said to him: I have bought a village. Since I am going to collect the rent, I will not be able to come. Excuse me.
(6) He went to another (and) said to him: My master invites you.
(7) He said to him: My friend is going to marry, and I am the one who is going to prepare the meal. I will not be able to come. Excuse me from the dinner.
(10) The slave, on coming, said to his master: Those whom you invited to dinner have asked to be excused.
(11) The master said to his slave: Go out on the roads. Bring (back) whomever you find, so that they might have dinner.

Q 14:26
Hating One's Family

Matt 10:37 Luke 14:26

⟦<ὃς>⟧ οὐ μισεῖ τὸν πατέρα καὶ τὴν μητέρα οὐ <δύναται εἶναί> μου <μαθητής>, καὶ ⟦<ὃς>⟧ <οὐ μισεῖ> τ<ὸ>ν υἱὸν καὶ τ<ὴν> θυγατέρα οὐ δύναται εἶναί μου μαθητής.

Mark 10:29b

οὐδείς ἐστιν ὃς ἀφῆκεν οἰκίαν ἢ ἀδελφοὺς ἢ ἀδελφὰς ἢ μητέρα ἢ πατέρα ἢ τέκνα ἢ ἀγροὺς ἕνεκεν ἐμοῦ καὶ ἕνεκεν τοῦ εὐαγγελίου,

Gos. Thom. 55 (Nag Hammadi II 2)

(1) Λέγει Ἰησοῦς· ὅστις οὐ μισήσει τὸν πατέρα αὐτοῦ καὶ τὴν μητέρα αὐτοῦ οὐ δυνήσεται εἶναί μου μαθητής.
(2) καὶ ὅστις οὐ μισήσει τοὺς ἀδελφοὺς αὐτοῦ καὶ τὰς ἀδελφὰς αὐτοῦ καὶ οὐ βαστάσει τὸν σταυρὸν αὐτοῦ ὡς ἐγώ, οὐ γενήσεταί μου ἄξιος.

Gos. Thom. 101.1-2 (Nag Hammadi II 2)

(1) Ὅστις οὐ μισήσει τὸν πα[τέρα] αὐτοῦ καὶ τὴν μητέρα αὐτοῦ ὡς ἐγὼ οὐ δυνήσεται εἶναί μου μ[αθητ]ής.
(2) καὶ ὅστις [οὐ] φιλήσει τὸν [πατέρα] αὐτοῦ [κα]ὶ τὴν μητέρα αὐτοῦ ὡς ἐγὼ οὐ δυνήσεται εἶναί μου μ[αθητής].

Q 14:27
Taking One's Cross

Matt 10:38 Luke 14:27

.. ὃς οὐ λαμβάνει τὸν σταυρὸν αὐτοῦ καὶ ἀκολουθεῖ ὀπίσω μου, οὐ δύναται εἶναί μου μαθητής.

Mark 8:34b

εἴ τις θέλει ὀπίσω μου ἀκολουθεῖν, ἀπαρνησάσθω ἑαυτὸν καὶ ἀράτω τὸν σταυρὸν αὐτοῦ καὶ ἀκολουθείτω μοι.

Gos. Thom. 55.2 (Nag Hammadi II 2)

καὶ ὅστις οὐ μισήσει τοὺς ἀδελφοὺς αὐτοῦ καὶ τὰς ἀδελφὰς αὐτοῦ καὶ οὐ βαστάσει τὸν σταυρὸν αὐτοῦ ὡς ἐγώ, οὐκ γενήσεταί μου ἄξιος.

Q 14:26
Hating One's Family

Matt 10:37 | Luke 14:26

26 ⟦<The one who>⟧ does not hate father and mother <can>not <be> my <disciple>; and ⟦<the one who>⟧ <does not hate> son and daughter cannot be my disciple.

Mark 10:29b

there is no one who has left house or brothers or sisters or mother or father or children or fields, for my sake and for the sake of the good news,

Gos. Thom. 55 (Nag Hammadi II 2)

(1) Jesus says: Whoever will not hate one's father and one's mother will not be able to become a disciple of mine.
(2) And whoever will not hate one's brothers and one's sisters and will not take up one's cross as I do, will not be worthy of me.

Gos. Thom. 101.1-2 (Nag Hammadi II 2)

(1) Whoever will not hate his [father] and his mother as I do, cannot be my [disciple].
(2) And whoever will [not] love his [father and] his mother as I do, cannot become a [disciple] of mine.

Q 14:27
Taking One's Cross

Matt 10:38 | Luke 14:27

.. The one who does not take one's cross and follow after me cannot be my disciple.

Mark 8:34b

If anyone wants to follow after me, let one deny oneself and take up one's cross and follow me.

Gos. Thom. 55.2 (Nag Hammadi II 2)

And whoever will not hate one's brothers and one's sisters and will not take up one's cross as I do, will not be worthy of me.

Q 17:33
Finding or Losing One's Life

Matt 10:39 Luke 17:33

⟦ὁ⟧ εὑρ⟦ὼν⟧ τὴν ψυχὴν αὐτοῦ ἀπολέσει αὐτήν, καὶ ⟦ὁ⟧ ἀπολέσ⟦ας⟧ τὴν ψυχὴν αὐτοῦ ⟦ἕνεκεν ἐμοῦ⟧ εὑρήσει αὐτήν.

Mark 8:35

ὃς γὰρ ἐὰν θέλῃ τὴν ψυχὴν αὐτοῦ σῶσαι ἀπολέσει αὐτήν· ὃς δ᾽ ἂν ἀπολέσει τὴν ψυχὴν αὐτοῦ ἕνεκεν ἐμοῦ καὶ τοῦ εὐαγγελίου σώσει αὐτήν.

Q 14:34-35
Insipid Salt

Matt 5:13 Luke 14:34-35

34 ⟦καλὸν⟧ τὸ ἅλας· ἐὰν δὲ τὸ ἅλας μωρανθῇ, ἐν τίνι ⟦ἀρτυ⟧θήσεται;
35 οὔτε εἰς γῆν οὔτε εἰς κοπρίαν ⟦εὔθετόν ἐστιν⟧, ἔξω βάλλουσιν αὐτό.

Mark 9:49-50a

49 Πᾶς γὰρ πυρὶ ἁλισθήσεται.
50a καλὸν τὸ ἅλας· ἐὰν δὲ τὸ ἅλας ἄναλον γένηται, ἐν τίνι αὐτὸ ἀρτύσετε;

Q 16:13
God or Mammon

Matt 6:24 Luke 16:13

οὐδεὶς δύναται δυσὶ κυρίοις δουλεύειν· ἢ γὰρ τὸν ἕνα μισήσει καὶ τὸν ἕτερον ἀγαπήσει, ἢ ἑνὸς ἀνθέξεται καὶ τοῦ ἑτέρου καταφρονήσει. οὐ δύνασθε θεῷ δουλεύειν καὶ μαμωνᾷ.

Gos. Thom. 47.2 (Nag Hammadi II 2)

καὶ οὐ δύναται δοῦλος δυσὶ κυρίοις λατρεύειν. ἢ τὸν ἕνα τιμήσει καὶ τὸν ἕτερον ὑβρίσει.

Q 17:33
Finding or Losing One's Life

Matt 10:39 | Luke 17:33

⟦The one who⟧ finds one's life will lose it, and ⟦the one who⟧ loses one's life ⟦for my sake⟧ will find it.

Mark 8:35

For whoever wants to save one's life will lose it, and whoever loses one's life for my sake, and for the sake of the gospel, will save it.

Q 14:34-35
Insipid Salt

Matt 5:13 | Luke 14:34-35

34 Salt ⟦is good⟧; but if salt becomes insipid, with what will it be ⟦seasoned⟧?
35 Neither for the earth nor for the dunghill ⟦is it fit⟧ – it gets thrown out.

Mark 9:49-50a

49 For everyone will be salted with fire.
50a Salt is good; but if salt has lost its saltiness, with what can you season it?

Q 16:13
God or Mammon

Matt 6:24 | Luke 16:13

Nobody can serve two masters; for a person will either hate the one and love the other, or be devoted to the one and despise the other. You cannot serve God and Mammon.

Gos. Thom. 47.2 (Nag Hammadi II 2)

And it is not possible that a slave serve two masters. Either he will honor the one and insult the other.

Q 16:16
Since John the Kingdom of God

Matt 11:12-13 Luke 16:16

ὁ .. νόμος καὶ οἱ προφῆται ⟦ἕως⟧ Ἰωάννου· ἀπὸ τότε ἡ βασιλεία τοῦ θεοῦ βιάζεται καὶ βιασταὶ ἁρπάζουσιν αὐτήν.

Q 16:17
No Serif of the Law to Fall

Matt 5:18 Luke 16:17

⟦εὐκοπώτερον δέ ἐστιν τὸν⟧ οὐρανὸ⟦ν⟧ καὶ ⟦τὴν⟧ γῆ⟦ν⟧ παρελθ⟦εῖν ἢ ἰῶτα ἓν ἢ⟧ μία⟦ν⟧ κεραία⟦ν⟧ τοῦ νόμου ⟦πεσεῖν⟧.

Mark 13:30-31

30 Ἀμὴν λέγω ὑμῖν ὅτι οὐ μὴ παρέλθῃ ἡ γενεὰ αὕτη μέχρις οὗ ταῦτα πάντα γένηται.
31 ὁ οὐρανὸς καὶ ἡ γῆ παρελεύσονται, οἱ δὲ λόγοι μου οὐ μὴ παρελεύσονται.

Q 16:18
Divorce Leading to Adultery

Matt 5:32 Luke 16:18

πᾶς ὁ ἀπολύων τὴν γυναῖκα αὐτοῦ ⟦καὶ γαμῶν <ἄλλην>⟧ μοιχεύει, καὶ ὁ ἀπολελυμένην γαμῶν μοιχ⟦εύει⟧.

Mark 10:11b-12

11b ὃς ἂν ἀπολύσῃ τὴν γυναῖκα αὐτοῦ καὶ γαμήσῃ ἄλλην μοιχᾶται ἐπ' αὐτήν·
12 καὶ ἐὰν αὐτὴ ἀπολύσασα τὸν ἄνδρα αὐτῆς γαμήσῃ ἄλλον μοιχᾶται.

Q 17:1-2
Against Enticing Little Ones

Matt 18:7, 6 Luke 17:1-2

1 ἀνάγκη ἐλθεῖν τὰ σκάνδαλα, πλὴν οὐαὶ δι' οὗ ἔρχεται.

2 λυσιτελεῖ αὐτῷ ⟦εἰ⟧ λίθος μυλικὸς περίκειται περὶ τὸν τράχηλον αὐτοῦ καὶ ἔρριπται εἰς τὴν θάλασσαν ἢ ἵνα σκανδαλίσῃ τῶν μικρῶν τούτων ἕνα.

Q 16:16
Since John the Kingdom of God

Matt 11:12-13 | Luke 16:16

.. The law and the prophets «were» until John. From then on the kingdom of God is violated and the violent plunder it.

Q 16:17
No Serif of the Law to Fall

Matt 5:18 | Luke 16:17

⟦But it is easier for⟧ heaven and earth ⟦to⟧ pass away ⟦than for one iota or⟧ one serif of the law ⟦to fall⟧.

Mark 13:30-31

30 Truly I tell you, this generation will not pass away until all these things have taken place.
31 Heaven and earth will pass away, but my words will not pass away.

Q 16:18
Divorce Leading to Adultery

Matt 5:32 | Luke 16:18

Everyone who divorces his wife ⟦and marries another⟧ commits adultery, and the one who marries a divorcée commits adultery.

Mark 10:11b-12

11b Whoever divorces his wife and marries another commits adultery against her;
12 and if she divorces her husband and marries another, she commits adultery.

Q 17:1-2
Against Enticing Little Ones

Matt 18:7, 6 | Luke 17:1-2

1 It is necessary for enticements to come, but woe «to the one» through whom they come!
2 It is better for him ⟦if⟧ a millstone is put around his neck and he is thrown into the sea, than that he should entice one of these little ones.

Mark 9:42

Καὶ ὃς ἂν σκανδαλίσῃ ἕνα τῶν μικρῶν τούτων τῶν πιστευόντων εἰς ἐμέ, καλόν ἐστιν αὐτῷ μᾶλλον εἰ περίκειται μύλος ὀνικὸς περὶ τὸν τράχηλον αὐτοῦ καὶ βέβληται εἰς τὴν θάλασσαν.

Q 15:4-5a, 7
The Lost Sheep

Matt 18:12-13 Luke 15:4-5a, 7

4 τίς < > ἄνθρωπος ἐξ ὑμῶν < > ἔχ< > ἑκατὸν πρόβατα καὶ ⟦ἀπολέσας⟧ ἓν ἐξ αὐτῶν, οὐ⟦χὶ ἀφήσ⟧ει τὰ ἐνενήκοντα ἐννέα ⟦ἐπὶ τὰ ὄρη⟧ καὶ πορευ⟦θεὶς ζητεῖ⟧ τὸ ⟦ἀπολωλός⟧;
5a καὶ ἐὰν γένηται εὑρεῖν αὐτό,
7 λέγω ὑμῖν ὅτι χαίρει ἐπ' αὐτῷ μᾶλλον ἢ ἐπὶ τοῖς ἐνενήκοντα ἐννέα τοῖς μὴ πεπλανημένοις.

Gos. Thom. 107 (Nag Hammadi II 2)

(1) Λέγει Ἰησοῦς· ἡ βασιλεία ὁμοία ἐστὶν ἀνθρώπῳ ποιμένι ἔχοντι ἑκατὸν πρόβατα.
(2) ἓν ἐν αὐτοῖς, τὸ μέγιστον, ἐπλανήθη. κατέλιπεν τὰ ἐνενήκοντα ἐννέα (καὶ) ἐζήτησεν τὸ ἕν, ἕως εὕρῃ αὐτό.
(3) κοπιάσας εἶπεν τῷ προβάτῳ· θέλω σε παρὰ τὰ ἐνενήκοντα ἐννέα.

Q 15:⟦8-10⟧
⟦The Lost Coin⟧

Luke 15:8-10

⟦**8**⟧ ⟦«ἢ τίς γυνὴ ἔχουσα δέκα δραχμὰς ἐὰν ἀπολέσῃ δραχμὴν μίαν, οὐχὶ ἅπτει λύχνον καὶ σαροῖ τὴν οἰκίαν καὶ ζητεῖ ἕως εὕρῃ;»⟧
⟦**9**⟧ ⟦«καὶ εὑροῦσα καλεῖ τὰς φίλας καὶ γείτονας λέγουσα· χάρητέ μοι, ὅτι εὗρον τὴν δραχμὴν ἣν ἀπώλεσα.»⟧
⟦**10**⟧ ⟦«οὕτως, λέγω ὑμῖν, γίνεται χαρὰ <ἔμπροσθεν> τῶν ἀγγέλων ἐπὶ ἑνὶ ἁμαρτωλῷ μετανοοῦντι.»⟧

Q 17:3-4
Forgiving a Sinning Brother Repeatedly

Matt 18:15, 21 Luke 17:3-4

3 ἐὰν ἁμαρτήσῃ ⟦εἰς σὲ⟧ ὁ ἀδελφός σου, ἐπιτίμησον αὐτῷ, καὶ ἐὰν ⟦μετανοήσῃ⟧, ἄφες αὐτῷ.
4 καὶ ἐὰν ἑπτάκις τῆς ἡμέρας ἁμαρτήσῃ εἰς σὲ καὶ ἑπτάκις ἀφήσεις αὐτῷ.

Mark 9:42

And whoever puts an enticement before one of these little ones who believe in me, it would be better for him if a donkey-stone is put around his neck and he is cast into the sea.

Q 15:4-5a, 7
The Lost Sheep

Matt 18:12-13 Luke 15:4-5a, 7

4 Which person «is there» among you «who» has a hundred sheep, ⟦on losing⟧ one of them, ⟦will⟧ not leave the ninety-nine ⟦in the mountains⟧ and go ⟦hunt for⟧ the ⟦lost one⟧?
5a And if it should happen that he finds it,
7 I say to you that he rejoices over it more than over the ninety-nine that did not go astray.

Gos. Thom. 107 (Nag Hammadi II 2)

(1) Jesus says: The kingdom is like a shepherd who has a hundred sheep.

(2) One of them went astray, the largest. He left the ninety-nine (and) sought the one until he found it.
(3) Exhausted, he said to the sheep: I love you more than the ninety-nine.

Q 15:⟦8-10⟧
⟦The Lost Coin⟧

Luke 15:8-10

⟦8⟧ ⟦«Or what woman who has ten coins, if she were to lose one coin, would not light a lamp and sweep the house and hunt until she finds?»⟧

⟦9⟧ ⟦«And on finding she calls the friends and neighbors, saying: Rejoice with me, for I found the coin which I lost.»⟧
⟦10⟧ ⟦«Just so, I tell you: There is joy before the angels over one repenting sinner.»⟧

Q 17:3-4
Forgiving a Sinning Brother Repeatedly

Matt 18:15, 21 Luke 17:3-4

3 If your brother sins ⟦against you⟧, rebuke him; and if ⟦he repents⟧, forgive him.
4 And if seven times a day he sins against you, also seven times shall you forgive him.

Q 17:6
Faith like a Mustard Seed

Matt 17:20b | Luke 17:6

εἰ ἔχετε πίστιν ὡς κόκκον σινάπεως, ἐλέγετε ἂν τῇ συκαμίνῳ ταύτῃ· ἐκριζώθητι καὶ φυτεύθητι ἐν τῇ θαλάσσῃ· καὶ ὑπήκουσεν ἂν ὑμῖν.

Mark 11:22b-23

22b ἔχετε πίστιν θεοῦ.
23 ἀμὴν λέγω ὑμῖν ὅτι ὃς ἂν εἴπῃ τῷ ὄρει τούτῳ· ἄρθητι καὶ βλήθητι εἰς τὴν θάλασσαν, καὶ μὴ διακριθῇ ἐν τῇ καρδίᾳ αὐτοῦ ἀλλὰ πιστεύῃ ὅτι ὃ λαλεῖ γίνεται, ἔσται αὐτῷ.

Gos. Thom. 48 (Nag Hammadi II 2)

Λέγει Ἰησοῦς· ἐὰν δύο εἰρηνεύσωσιν ἐν ἀλλήλοις ἐν μιᾷ καὶ τῇ αὐτῇ οἰκίᾳ, ἐροῦσιν τῷ ὄρει· μετάβα καὶ μεταβήσεται.

Q 17:⟦20-21⟧
⟦The Kingdom of God within You⟧

Matt 24:23 | Luke 17:20-21

⟦**20**⟧ ⟦«ἐπερωτηθεὶς δὲ πότε ἔρχεται ἡ βασιλεία τοῦ θεοῦ ἀπεκρίθη αὐτοῖς καὶ εἶπεν· οὐκ ἔρχεται ἡ βασιλεία τοῦ θεοῦ μετὰ παρατηρήσεως,»⟧
⟦**21**⟧ ⟦.. ἰδοὺ ὧδε ἤ· ..., «ἰδοὺ γὰρ ἡ βασιλεία τοῦ θεοῦ ἐντὸς ὑμῶν ἐστιν.»⟧

Mark 13:21

Καὶ τότε ἐάν τις ὑμῖν εἴπῃ· ἴδε ὧδε ὁ χριστός, ἴδε ἐκεῖ, μὴ πιστεύετε·

Gos. Thom. 3.1-3 (P. Oxy. 654)

(1) λέγει Ἰ[η(σοῦ)ς· ἐὰν] οἱ ἕλκοντες <ὑ>μᾶς [εἴπωσιν ὑμῖν· ἰδοὺ] ἡ βασιλεία ἐν οὐρα[νῷ, ὑμᾶς φθήσεται] τὰ πετεινὰ τοῦ οὐρ[ανοῦ·
(2) ἐὰν δ' εἴπωσιν ὅ]τι ὑπὸ τὴν γῆν ἐστ[ιν, εἰσελεύσονται] οἱ ἰχθύες τῆς θαλά[σσης προφθάσαν]τες ὑμᾶς·
(3) καὶ ἡ βασ[ιλεία τοῦ θεοῦ] ἐντὸς ὑμῶν [ἐσ]τι [κἀκτός.]

Q 17:6
Faith like a Mustard Seed

Matt 17:20b | Luke 17:6

6 If you have faith like a mustard seed, you might say to this mulberry tree: Be uprooted and planted in the sea! And it would obey you.

Mark 11:22b-23

22b Have faith in God.
23 Truly I tell you, whoever tells this mountain: Be taken up and thrown into the sea, and does not doubt in one's heart, but believes that what one says will come to pass, it will be done for that person.

Gos. Thom. 48 (Nag Hammadi II 2)

Jesus says: If two make peace with one another in one and the same house, (then) they will say to the mountain: Move away, and it will move away.

Q 17:⟦20-21⟧
⟦The Kingdom of God within You⟧

Matt 24:23 | Luke 17:20-21

⟦**20**⟧ ⟦«But on being asked when the kingdom of God is coming, he answered them and said: The kingdom of God is not coming visibly.»⟧

⟦**21**⟧ ⟦«Nor will one say:» Look, here! or: «There! For, look, the kingdom of God is within you!»⟧

Mark 13:21

And if anyone says to you at that time: Look! Here is the Christ! or There! – do not believe it.

Gos. Thom. 3.1-3 (P. Oxy. 654)

(1) Jesus says: [If] those who entice <you> [say to you: Look,] the kingdom is in the sky, [there will precede you] the birds of the sky.
(2) [But if they say]: It is under the earth, [there will enter it] the fish of the sea [ahead of] you.
(3) And the kingdom [of God] is within you, [and outside.]

Gos. Thom. 3.1-3 (Nag Hammadi II 2)

(1) Λέγει Ἰησοῦς· ἐὰν οἱ ἡγούμενοι ὑμᾶς εἴπωσιν ὑμῖν· ἰδοὺ ἡ βασιλεία ἐν τῷ οὐρανῷ ἐστιν, φθήσεται ὑμᾶς τὰ πετεινὰ τοῦ οὐρανοῦ.
(2) ἐὰν εἴπωσιν ὑμῖν· ἐν τῇ θαλάσσῃ ἐστίν, φθήσονται ὑμᾶς οἱ ἰχθύες.
(3) ἀλλὰ ἡ βασιλεία ἐντὸς ὑμῶν ἐστιν καὶ ἐκτὸς ὑμῶν.

Gos. Thom. 113 (Nag Hammadi II 2)

(1) Εἶπον αὐτῷ οἱ μαθηταὶ αὐτοῦ· ποίᾳ ἡμέρᾳ ἔρχεται ἡ βασιλεία;
(2) οὐκ ἔρχεται μετὰ ἀποκαραδοκίας.
(3) οὐκ ἐροῦσιν· ἰδοὺ ὧδε ἢ ἰδοὺ ἐκεῖ.
(4) ἀλλὰ ἡ βασιλεία τοῦ πατρὸς ἐστρωμένη ἐστὶν ἐπὶ τῆς γῆς καὶ οἱ ἄνθρωποι οὐ βλέπουσιν αὐτήν.

Q 17:23-24
The Son of Humanity like Lightning

Matt 24:26-27 Luke 17:23-24

23 ἐὰν εἴπωσιν ὑμῖν· ἰδοὺ ἐν τῇ ἐρήμῳ ἐστίν, μὴ ἐξέλθητε· ἰδοὺ ἐν
τοῖς ταμείοις, μὴ διώξητε·
24 ὥσπερ γὰρ ἡ ἀστραπὴ ἐξέρχεται ἀπὸ ἀνατολῶν καὶ φαίνεται
ἕως δυσμῶν, οὕτως ἔσται ⟦ὁ⟧ υἱὸ⟦ς⟧ τοῦ ἀνθρώπου ⟦ἐν τῇ ἡμέρᾳ
αὐτοῦ⟧.

Mark 13:21

Καὶ τότε ἐάν τις ὑμῖν εἴπῃ· ἴδε ὧδε ὁ χριστός, ἴδε ἐκεῖ, μὴ πιστεύετε·

Gos. Thom. 3.1-2 (P. Oxy. 654)

(1) λέγει Ἰ[η(σοῦ)ς· ἐὰν] οἱ ἕλκοντες <ὑ>μᾶς [εἴπωσιν ὑμῖν· ἰδοὺ] ἡ βασιλεία ἐν οὐρα[νῷ, ὑμᾶς φθήσεται] τὰ πετεινὰ τοῦ οὐρ[ανοῦ·
(2) ἐὰν δ' εἴπωσιν ὅ]τι ὑπὸ τὴν γῆν ἐστ[ιν, εἰσελεύσονται] οἱ ἰχθύες τῆς θαλά[σσης προφθάσαν]τες ὑμᾶς·

Gos. Thom. 3.1-2 (Nag Hammadi II 2)

(1) Λέγει Ἰησοῦς· ἐὰν οἱ ἡγούμενοι ὑμᾶς εἴπωσιν ὑμῖν· ἰδοὺ ἡ βασιλεία ἐν τῷ οὐρανῷ ἐστιν, φθήσεται ὑμᾶς τὰ πετεινὰ τοῦ οὐρανοῦ.
(2) ἐὰν εἴπωσιν ὑμῖν· ἐν τῇ θαλάσσῃ ἐστίν, φθήσονται ὑμᾶς οἱ ἰχθύες.

Q 17:37
Vultures around a Corpse

Matt 24:28 Luke 17:37

ὅπου τὸ πτῶμα, ἐκεῖ συναχθήσονται οἱ ἀετοί.

Gos. Thom. 3.1-3 (Nag Hammadi II 2)

(1) Jesus says: If those who lead you say to you: Look, the kingdom is in the sky, then the birds of the sky will precede you.
(2) If they say to you: It is in the sea, then the fish will precede you.
(3) Rather, the kingdom is within you, and outside of you.

Gos. Thom. 113 (Nag Hammadi II 2)

(1) His disciples said to him: The kingdom – on what day will it come?
(2) It will not come by watching (and waiting for) it.
(3) They will not say: Look, here! or: Look, there!
(4) Rather, the kingdom of the Father is spread out upon the earth, and people do not see it.

Q 17:23-24
The Son of Humanity like Lightning

Matt 24:26-27 Luke 17:23-24

23 If they say to you: Look, he is in the wilderness, do not go out; look, he is indoors, do not follow.
24 For as the lightning streaks out from Sunrise and flashes as far as Sunset, so will the Son of Humanity be ⟦on his day⟧.

Mark 13:21

And if anyone says to you at that time: Look! Here is the Christ! or There! – do not believe it.

Gos. Thom. 3.1-2 (P. Oxy. 654)

(1) Jesus says: [If] those who entice <you> [say to you: Look,] the kingdom is in the sky, [there will precede you] the birds of the sky.
(2) [But if they say]: It is under the earth, [there will enter it] the fish of the sea, [preceding] you.

Gos. Thom. 3.1-2 (Nag Hammadi II 2)

(1) Jesus says: If those who lead you say to you: Look, the kingdom is in the sky, then the birds of the sky will precede you.
(2) If they say to you: It is in the sea, then the fish will precede you.

Q 17:37
Vultures around a Corpse

Matt 24:28 Luke 17:37

Wherever the corpse, there the vultures will gather.

Q 17:26-27,?28-29?, 30
As in the Days of Noah

Matt 24:37-39 | Luke 17:26-30

26 .. ⟦καθὼς⟧ .. ⟦ἐγένετο ἐν τ⟧αῖ⟦ς⟧ ἡμέραι⟦ς⟧ Νῶε, οὕτως ἔσται
⟦ἐν τ<ῇ> ἡμέρ<ᾳ>⟧ τοῦ υἱοῦ τοῦ ἀνθρώπου.
27 ⟦ὡς γὰρ ἦσαν ἐν ταῖς ἡμέραις ἐκείναις⟧ τρώγοντες καὶ πίνοντες, γαμοῦντες καὶ γαμίζ⟦οντες⟧, ἄχρι ἧς ἡμέρας εἰσῆλθεν Νῶε
εἰς τὴν κιβωτόν, καὶ ἦλθεν ὁ κατακλυσμὸς καὶ ἦρεν ἅπαντας,
?28-29? ..
30 οὕτως ἔσται καὶ ᾗ ἡμέρᾳ ὁ υἱὸς τοῦ ἀνθρώπου ἀποκαλύπτεται.

Q 17:34-35
One Taken, One Left

Matt 24:40-41 | Luke 17:34-35

34 λέγω ὑμῖν, ἔσονται δύο ⟦ἐν τῷ ἀγρῷ⟧, εἷς παραλαμβάνεται καὶ
εἷς ἀφίεται·
35 δύο ἀλήθουσαι ἐν τῷ μύλῳ, μία παραλαμβάνεται καὶ μία ἀφίεται.

Mark 13:16

καὶ ὁ εἰς τὸν ἀγρὸν μὴ ἐπιστρεψάτω εἰς τὰ ὀπίσω ἆραι τὸ ἱμάτιον αὐτοῦ.

Gos. Thom. 61.1 (Nag Hammadi II 2)

Λέγει Ἰησοῦς· δύο ἀναπαύσονται ἐπὶ κλίνης, ὁ εἷς ἀποθανεῖται, ὁ εἷς ζήσεται.

Q 19:12-13, 15-24, 26
The Entrusted Money

Matt 25:14-15b, 19-29 | Luke 19:12-13, 15-24, 26

12 .. ἄνθρωπός τις ἀποδημῶν
13 ἐκάλεσεν δέκα δούλους ἑαυτοῦ καὶ ἔδωκεν αὐτοῖς δέκα μνᾶς
⟦καὶ εἶπεν αὐτο<ῖ>ς· πραγματεύσασθε ἐν ᾧ ἔρχομαι⟧.
15 .. ⟦μετὰ⟧ .. ⟦πολὺν χρόνον⟧ ἔρχεται ὁ κύριος τῶν δούλων
ἐκείνων καὶ συναίρει λόγον μετ᾽ αὐτῶν.
16 καὶ ⟦<ἦ>λθ<εν>⟧ ὁ πρῶτος λέγων· κύριε, ἡ μνᾶ σου δέκα προσ-
ηργάσατο μνᾶς.
17 καὶ εἶπεν αὐτῷ· εὖ, ἀγαθὲ δοῦλε, ἐπὶ ὀλίγα ἦς πιστός, ἐπὶ
πολλῶν σε καταστήσω.

Q 17:26-27,?28-29?, 30
As in the Days of Noah

Matt 24:37-39 Luke 17:26-30

26 .. As ⟦it took place in⟧ the days of Noah, so will it be ⟦in the day<>⟧ of the Son of Humanity.
27 ⟦For as in those days, they were⟧ eating and drinking, marrying and giving in marriage, until the day Noah entered the ark and the flood came and took them all,
?28-29? ..
30 so will it also be on the day the Son of Humanity is revealed.

Q 17:34-35
One Taken, One Left

Matt 24:40-41 Luke 17:34-35

34 I tell you: There will be two «men» ⟦in the field⟧; one is taken and one is left.
35 Two «women» will be grinding at the mill; one is taken and one is left.

Mark 13:16

the one in the field must not turn back to get a coat.

Gos. Thom. 61.1 (Nag Hammadi II 2)

Jesus said: Two will rest on a bed. The one will die, the other will live.

Q 19:12-13, 15-24, 26
The Entrusted Money

Matt 25:14-15b, 19-29 Luke 19:12-13, 15-24, 26

12 .. A certain person, on taking a trip,
13 called ten of his slaves and gave them ten minas ⟦and said to them: Do business until I come⟧.
15 .. ⟦After a long time⟧ the master of those slaves comes and settles accounts with them.
16 And the first ⟦came⟧ saying: Master, your mina has produced ten more minas.
17 And he said to him: Well done, good slave, you have been faithful over little, I will set you over much.

18 καὶ ἦλθεν ὁ ⟦δεύτερος⟧ λέγων· κύριε, ἡ μνᾶ σου ἐποίησεν πέντε μνᾶς.
19 εἶπεν ⟦αὐτ⟧ῷ· ⟦εὖ, ἀγαθὲ δοῦλε, ἐπὶ ὀλίγα ἦς πιστός,⟧ ἐπὶ πολλῶν σε καταστήσω.
20 καὶ ἦλθεν ὁ ἕτερος λέγων· κύριε,
21 ⟦ἔγνων⟧ σε ὅτι σκληρὸς εἶ ἄνθρωπος, θερίζων ὅπου οὐκ ἔσπειρας καὶ συνάγων ὅθεν οὐ διεσκόρπισας, καὶ φοβ⟦ηθεὶς ἀπελθὼν⟧ ἔκρυψα ⟦<τὴν μνᾶν> σου⟧ ἐν ⟦τῇ γῇ⟧· ἴδ⟦ε⟧ ἔχεις τὸ σόν.

22 λέγει αὐτῳ· πονηρὲ δοῦλε, ᾔδεις ὅτι θερίζω ὅπου οὐκ ἔσπειρα καὶ συνάγω ὅθεν οὐ διεσκόρπισα;
23 ⟦ἔδει σε οὖν βαλεῖν⟧ μου τ⟦ὰ⟧ ἀργύρι⟦α τοῖς⟧ τραπεζ⟦ίταις⟧, καὶ ἐλθὼν ἐγὼ ἐκομισάμην ἂν τὸ ἐμὸν σὺν τόκῳ.

24 ἄρατε οὖν ἀπ' αὐτοῦ τὴν μνᾶν καὶ δότε τῷ ἔχοντι τὰς δέκα μνᾶς·

26 τῷ ⟦γὰρ⟧ ἔχοντι παντὶ δοθήσεται, τοῦ δὲ μὴ ἔχοντος καὶ ὃ ἔχει ἀρθήσεται ἀπ' αὐτοῦ.

Mark 13:34

Ὡς ἄνθρωπος ἀπόδημος ἀφεὶς τὴν οἰκίαν αὐτοῦ καὶ δοὺς τοῖς δούλοις αὐτοῦ τὴν ἐξουσίαν ἑκάστῳ τὸ ἔργον αὐτοῦ καὶ τῷ θυρωρῷ ἐνετείλατο ἵνα γρηγορῇ.

Mark 4:25

ὃς γὰρ ἔχει, δοθήσεται αὐτῷ· καὶ ὃς οὐκ ἔχει, καὶ ὃ ἔχει ἀρθήσεται ἀπ' αὐτοῦ.

Gos. Thom. 41 (Nag Hammadi II 2)

(1) Λέγει Ἰησοῦς· ὅστις ἔχει ἐν τῇ χειρὶ αὐτοῦ, δοθήσεται αὐτῷ·

(2) καὶ ὅστις οὐκ ἔχει, καὶ τὸ μικρὸν ὃ ἔχει ἀρθήσεται ἀπ' αὐτοῦ.

Q 22:28, 30
You Will Judge the Twelve Tribes of Israel

Matt 19:28 Luke 22:28, 30

28 ὑμεῖς .. οἱ ἀκολουθήσαντές μοι
30 .. καθήσεσθε ἐπὶ θρόν⟦ους⟧ κρίνοντες τὰς δώδεκα φυλὰς τοῦ Ἰσραήλ.

18 And the ⟦second⟧ came saying: Master, your mina has earned five minas.
19 He said to ⟦him: Well done, good slave, you have been faithful over little,⟧ I will set you over much.
20 And the other came saying: Master,
21 ⟦I knew⟧ you, that you are a hard person, reaping where you did not sow and gathering up from where you did not winnow; and, scared, I ⟦went «and»⟧ hid ⟦your <mina>⟧ in ⟦the ground⟧. Here, you have what belongs to you.
22 He said to him: Wicked slave! You knew that I reap where I have not sown, and gather up from where I have not winnowed?
23 ⟦Then you had to invest⟧ my money ⟦with the⟧ money ⟦changers⟧! And at my coming I would have received what belongs to me plus interest.
24 So take from him the mina and give «it» to the one who has the ten minas.
26 ⟦For⟧ to everyone who has will be given; but the one who does not have, even what he has will be taken from him.

Mark 13:34

It is like a person, on taking a trip, when he leaves home and puts his slaves in charge, each with his work, and commands the doorkeeper to be on the watch.

Mark 4:25

For to the one who has, more will be given; and the one who has nothing, even what he has will be taken from him.

Gos. Thom. 41 (Nag Hammadi II 2)

(1) Jesus says: Whoever has (something) in his hand, (something more) will be given to him.
(2) And whoever has nothing, even the little he has will be taken from him.

Q 22:28, 30
You Will Judge the Twelve Tribes of Israel

Matt 19:28 | Luke 22:28, 30

28 .. You who have followed me
30 will sit .. on thrones judging the twelve tribes of Israel.

CONCORDANCE

John S. KLOPPENBORG

Introduction

The concordance indexes only the significant vocabulary found in Q in *The Sayings Gospel Q in Greek and English*, and excludes the verb «to be,» definite articles, prepositions, most particles, personal pronouns, and relative pronouns. All verbs are marked with *v*. before the English translation. No attempt has been made to provide the full range of meanings of many of the Greek vocabulary. For such a list, one should consult Frederick William Danker, *A Greek-English Lexicon of the New Testament and Other Early Christian Literature* (third edition, based on Walter Bauer's *Griechisch-deutsches Wörterbuch zu den Schriften des Neuen Testaments und der frühchristlichen Literatur*, sixth edition; ed. Kurt Aland and Barbara Aland, with Viktor Reichmann, and on previous English editions by W. F. Arndt, F.W. Gingrich, and F.W. Danker; Chicago and London: The University of Chicago Press, 2000) or Henry George Liddell, Robert Scott and Henry Stuart Jones, *A Greek-English Lexicon* (Oxford: Clarendon Press, and New York: Oxford University Press, 1996).

The presentation of data in the Concordance allows for a simple visual identification of the various types of vocabulary present in Q:

3:7 **Bold** font marks vocabulary that occurs in both Matthew and Luke, and hence constitutes "minimal Q" vocabulary. It is not necessarily the case, however, that bolded words appear in the same inflection in Matthew and Luke.

3:7 Normal font is used for vocabulary found in either Matthew or Luke and which the International Q Project has assigned to Q with a probability of either {A} or {B}.

⟦3:7⟧ Double square brackets designate {C} vocabulary in *The Sayings Gospel Q in Greek and English* and hence in the concordance. Since it is possible for an entire verse to be assigned to Q with a probability of {C} *and* that Matthew and Luke agree on the use of the same lexeme, there are some occurrences of **bolded** numerals in double square brackets, for example, λέγω ***Q*** ⟦**12:54**⟧. Here both Matthew and Luke have λέγετε, but because the entire verse is not securely in Q, it is enclosed in ⟦ ⟧.

«12:33» Guillemets mark the vocabulary belonging to phrases for which there seems to be a Q origin, but which only reflect in a general sense what Q contained. This siglum appears normally for phrases and verses that are found in only one gospel (Q ⟦«6:29↔30/Matt 5:41»⟧; ⟦«7:29»⟧; «10:7»; ⟦«10:8»⟧; «12:33»; ⟦«12:49»⟧; «14:21»; ⟦«15:8-10»⟧; ⟦«17:20»⟧, ⟦«21»⟧). Although the verse or phrase appears to come from Q, it is impossible to achieve a fully formatted text or to determine with any degree of probability the exact wording of Q lying behind the evangelist's redaction.

3:7 *Italic* font designates vocabulary that is not printed in Q because it has been assigned either a {D} or a {U} probability. In these cases, the Matthaean {D} and Lukan {D} vocabulary is included in the concordance, and both Matthew's and Luke's words in the case of {U} vocabulary where there is text in Matthew and Luke.

The decision to include {D} and {U} vocabulary, while obviously running the risk of including redactional items in the concordance, errs on the side of inclusiveness and is preferable to excluding both sets of vocabulary. There are points at which the *sense* of Q is clear enough, even though the IQP has not been able to decide between Matthew and Luke. For example, at Q 4:2, Matthew has νηστεύσας (fasting) while Luke has οὐκ ἔφαγεν οὐδέν (and he ate nothing). The IQP found no grounds to decide between the two and so registered the variant as {U} in the text of Q. Since there *is* an agreement in basic meaning between Matthew and Luke, it seems better to include both sets of vocabulary in the concordance than to exclude both and hence to exclude a basic agreement in sense.

<16:18> The editors of *The Sayings Gospel Q in Greek and English* have occasionally found it necessary to conjecture readings, which appear in the critical text of Q and the concordance marked with pointed brackets. In most cases, such conjectures have some basis in either Matthew or Luke. For exam-

ple, at Q 16:18, Matthew has no relevant text, while Luke has ἑτέραν, which is probably Lukan. In this case, <ἄλλην> has been conjectured as Q's reading, and <16:18> appears in the Concordance under ἄλλος.

Concordance

῞Αβελ (Abel)
Q **11:51**.

᾿Αβρααμ (Abraham)
Q **3:8; 3:8; 13:28**.

ἀγαθός (good)
Q ⟦6:35⟧; **6:45**; **6:45**; **6:45**; **11:13**; 11:13; **19:17**; ⟦19:19⟧.

ἀγαλλιάω (*v*. rejoice)
Q ⟦6:23⟧.

ἀγαπάω (*v*. love)
Q **6:27**; **6:32**; **6:32**; **16:13**.

ἀγγαρεύω (*v*. conscript)
Q ⟦«6:29↔30/Mt 5:41»⟧.

ἄγγελος (angel, messenger)
Q **4:10**; **7:27**; 12:8; 12:9; ⟦«15:10»⟧.

ἁγιάζω (*v*. make holy, keep holy)
Q **11:2**.

ἅγιος (holy)
Q ⟦**3:16**⟧; ⟦*3:22*⟧; **12:10**; ⟦12:12⟧.

ἀγορά (market [place])
Q **7:32**; **11:43**.

ἀγοράζω (*v*. buy, purchase)
Q *14:18*; *14:19*; *17:28*.

ἀγρός (field)
Q **12:28**; **14:18;** ⟦17:34⟧.

ἀδελφός (brother)
Q **6:41**; **6:42**; **6:42**; **17:3**.

ἄδηλος (unseen, indistinct)
Q 11:44.

ᾅδης (Hades)
Q **10:15**.

ἄδικος (unjust)
Q ⟦6:35⟧.

ἀετός (eagle, vulture)
Q **17:37**.

ἀθετέω (*v*. reject, not recognize)
Q ⟦*7:30*⟧.

αἷμα (blood)
Q **11:50**; **11:51**; **11:51**.

αἴρω (*v*. bear, take, take from)
Q **4:11**; 17:27; **19:24**; **19:26**.

αἰτέω (*v*. ask)
Q **6:30**; **11:9**; **11:10**; **11:11**; **11:12**; **11:13**.

ἀκάθαρτος (unclean)
Q **11:24**.

ἄκανθα (thorns)
Q **6:44**.

ἀκολουθέω (*v*. follow)
Q **7:9**; **9:57**; **9:60**; 14:27; 22:28.

ἀκούω (*v*. hear, listen)
Q **6:47**; **6:49**; **7:9**; ⟦7:18⟧; **7:22**; **7:22**; ⟦*7:29*⟧; *10:23*; **10:24**; **10:24**; **10:24**; *11:28*; **11:31**; **12:3**.

ἀκρασία (dissipation)
Q 11:39.

ἅλας (salt)
Q **14:34**; **14:34**.

ἄλευρον (wheat flour)
Q **13:21**.

ἀλήθω (*v*. grind)
Q **17:35**.

ἀλλά (but)
Q **7:7**; **7:25**; **7:26**; **11:33**; **12:51**.

ἄλλος (another)
Q **6:29**; **7:8;** <16:18>.

ἅλων (threshing floor, threshed grain)
Q **3:17**.

ἀλώπηξ (fox)
Q **9:58**.

ἁμαρτάνω (*v*. sin)
Q **17:3**; **17:4**.

ἁμαρτωλός (sinner)
Q **7:34**; ⟦«15:10»⟧.

ἀμελέω (*v*. neglect)
Q *14:18*.

ἀμήν (amen)
Q ⟦12:44⟧.

ἄμμος (sand)
Q 6:49.

ἀμφιέννυμι (*v*. clothe, dress)
Q **7:25;** ⟦12:28⟧.

ἀμφότεροι (both)
Q **6:39**.

ἀναβλέπω (*v*. look at, regain sight)
Q **7:22**.

ἀνάγκη (necessity; it is necessary)
Q *14:18*; 17:1.

ἀνάγω (*v*. lead, bring up)
Q ⟦4:1⟧.
ἀνακλίνω (*v*. recline)
Q **13:29**.
ἀνάπαυσις (rest, resting place)
Q **11:24**.
ἀνάπτω (*v*. kindle, light)
Q ⟦«12:49»⟧.
ἀνατέλλω (*v*. rise up, raise)
Q 6:35.
ἀνατολή (east, sunrise)
Q **13:29**; 17:24.
ἀνεκτός (bearable, endurable)
Q **10:12**; **10:14**.
ἄνεμος (wind)
Q ⟦6:48⟧; ⟦6:49⟧; **7:24**.
ἄνηθον (dill)
Q 11:42.
ἀνήρ (man)
Q **11:32.**
ἄνθρωπος (person, humanity, whoever, anyone)
Q **4:4**; 6:22; **6:31**; **6:45**; ⟦6:45⟧; 6:48; 6:49; **7:8**; **7:25**; **7:34**; **7:34**; **9:58**; 11:11; **11:24**; **11:26**; **11:30**; 11:44; ⟦**11:46**⟧; ⟦11:52⟧; **12:8**; ⟦12:8⟧; **12:9**; **12:10**; **12:40**; **13:19**; **14:16**; **15:4**; **17:24**; **17:26**; **17:30**; **19:12**; **19:21**.
ἀνίστημι (*v*. arise, rise)
Q **11:32**.
ἀνοίγω (*v*. open)
Q ⟦3:21⟧; **11:9**; **11:10**; 13:25.
ἀνομία (lawlessness)
Q 13:27.
ἀντέχω (*v*. cling, be devoted to)
Q **16:13**.
ἀντίδικος (opponent)
Q **12:58;** ⟦12:58⟧.
ἄνυδρος (waterless, dry)
Q **11:24**.
ἀξίνη (ax)
Q **3:9**.
ἄξιος (worthy)
Q **3:8; 10:7**.
ἀπαγγέλλω (*v*. announce, report)
Q **7:22**.
ἀπαιτέω (*v*. ask, demand)
Q ⟦6:30⟧.
ἀπαλλάσσω (*v*. free, release, loose)
Q 12:58.
ἅπας (all)
Q ⟦*3:21*⟧; ⟦12:30⟧; 17:27.
ἀπέρχομαι (*v*. depart, leave, go)
Q 7:24; **9:57**; **9:59**; *14:18*; ⟦19:21⟧.
ἄπιστος (faithless)
Q 12:46.
ἁπλοῦς (simple, sincere, generous)
Q **11:34**.
ἀποδεκατόω (*v*. tithe)
Q **11:42**.
ἀποδημέω (*v*. depart, be absent, take a trip)
Q 19:12.
ἀποδίδωμι (*v*. return, give back, pay)
Q **12:59**.
ἀποθήκη (barn, storehouse, granary)
Q **3:17; 12:24**.
ἀποκαλύπτω (*v*. disclose, reveal, expose)
Q **10:21**; **10:22**; **12:2**; 17:30.
ἀποκρίνομαι (*v*. answer, tell or say [in reply])
Q **4:4**; ⟦4:8⟧; ⟦4:12⟧; 7:6; **7:22**; *11:29*; 13:25; ⟦«17:20»⟧.
ἀποκτείνω (*v*. kill)
Q 11:47; *11:48*; **11:49**; **12:4**; 12:4; **13:34**.
ἀπόλλυμι (*v*. destroy, kill, lose)
Q 11:51; 12:5; ⟦15:4⟧; ⟦15:4⟧; ⟦«15:8»⟧; ⟦«15:9»⟧; *17:29;* **17:33**; **17:33**.
ἀπολύω (*v*. release, dismiss, divorce)
Q **16:18**; **16:18**.
ἀποστέλλω (*v*. send)
Q **7:27**; **10:3**; **10:16**; **11:49**; **13:34**; **14:17**.
ἅπτω (*v*. light, take hold of)
Q ⟦«15:8»⟧.
ἄρα (therefore, then, thus)
Q **11:20**; *11:48*; **12:42**.
ἀργύριον (silver, money)
Q **19:23**.

ἀριθμέω (*v.* count, number)
Q **12:7**.

ἀρκετός (enough)
Q ⟦6:40⟧.

ἀρνέομαι (*v.* deny, refuse)
Q **12:9**; 12:9.

ἁρπαγή (robbery, plunder)
Q **11:39**.

ἁρπάζω (*v.* seize, violate, steal)
Q 16:16.

ἄρτος (bread, loaf)
Q **4:3**; **4:4**; **11:3**; 11:11.

ἀρτύω (*v.* prepare, season)
Q ⟦14:34⟧.

ἄρχομαι (*v.* begin)
Q **7:24**; **12:45**; ⟦13:25⟧; 13:26; *14:18*.

ἄρχων (ruler)
Q **11:15**.

ἄσβεστος (inextinguishable)
Q **3:17**.

ἀσθενέω (*v.* be weak, powerless, sick)
Q ⟦10:9⟧.

ἀσπάζομαι (*v.* greet)
Q 10:4.

ἀσπασμός (greeting, accolade)
Q **11:43**.

ἀσσάριον (*ass* [Roman coin])
Q **12:6**.

ἀστραπή (lightning)
Q **17:24**.

αὐλέω (*v.* play [the flute])
Q **7:32.**

αὐξάνω (*v.* grow, increase)
Q **12:27**; **13:19**.

αὔριον (tomorrow)
Q **12:28**.

ἀφανίζω (*v.* render invisible, deface)
Q «12:33»; 12:33.

ἀφίημι (*v.* leave, let, cancel, give up, forsake, forgive, turn over to)
Q 4:13; ⟦6:29⟧; **6:42**; **9:60**; **11:4**; **11:4**; ⟦11:42⟧; ⟦11:42⟧; 11:52; **12:10**; **12:10**; **13:35**; 15:4; 17:3; **17:4**; **17:34**; **17:35**.

ἀφίστημι (*v.* go away, get away)
Q 13:27.

ἄχυρον (chaff)
Q **3:17**.

βαλλάντιον (money-bag, purse)
Q ⟦10:4⟧.

βάλλω (*v.* throw, hurl, invest)
Q **3:9**; **4:9**; **12:28**; ⟦«12:49»⟧; 12:51; 12:51; **12:58**; 13:19; **14:35;** ⟦19:23⟧.

βαπτίζω (*v.* baptize)
Q 3:7; **3:16**; **3:16**; ⟦*3:21*⟧; ⟦*3:21*⟧; ⟦3:21⟧; ⟦*7:29*⟧; ⟦*7:30*⟧.

βάπτισμα (baptism)
Q ⟦*7:29*⟧.

βαρύς (deep)
Q *11:46*.

βασιλεία (kingdom, dominion, reign)
Q **4:5**; **6:20**; **7:28**; **10:9**; **11:2**; **11:17**; **11:18**; **11:20**; 11:52; **12:31**; **13:18**; **13:20**; **13:28**; **16:16**; ⟦«17:20»⟧; ⟦«17:20»⟧; ⟦«17:21»⟧; *22:30*.

βασιλεύς (king)
Q 7:25; 10:24.

βασίλισσα (queen)
Q **11:31**.

βαστάζω (*v.* carry, bear, take off)
Q 3:16; 10:4; *11:27*.

Βεελζεβούλ (Beelzebul)
Q **11:15**; **11:19**.

Βηθσαϊδά(ν) (Bethsaida)
Q **10:13**.

βιάζω (*v.* inflict violence, violate)
Q **16:16**.

βιαστής (violent)
Q 16:16.

βλέπω (*v.* look at, see)
Q **6:41**; 7:22; **10:23**; 10:23; **10:24**.

βόθυνος (pit)
Q **6:39**.

βουλή ([God's] will, decision)
Q ⟦*7:30*⟧.

βούλομαι (*v.* wish, want, choose)
Q **10:22**.

βοῦς (head of cattle)
Q *14:19*.

βρέχω (*v.* wet, rain, send rain)
Q ⟦6:35⟧; *17:29*.

βροχή (rain)
Q 6:48; 6:49.
βρυγμός (gnashing, grinding)
Q **13:28**.
βρῶσις (gnawing, rust, insect)
Q «12:33»; 12:33.
Γαλιλαία (Galilee)
Q ⟦*3:21*⟧.
γαμέω (*v.* marry)
Q *14:20*; ⟦16:18⟧; **16:18**; **17:27**.
γαμίζω (*v.* give [a woman] in marriage)
Q **17:27**.
γέεννα (Gehenna, hell)
Q **12:5**.
γείτων (neighbor)
Q ⟦«15:9»⟧.
γεμίζω (*v.* fill)
Q 14:23.
γέμω (*v.* be full)
Q **11:39**.
γενεά (generation)
Q **7:31**; 11:29; **11:29**; 11:30; **11:31**; **11:32**; 11:50; **11:51**.
γέννημα (brood, litter)
Q **3:7**.
γεννητός (offspring, descendant, litter)
Q **7:28**.
γῆ (land, ground, earth)
Q **10:21**; **11:31**; 12:6; «12:33»; ⟦«12:49»⟧; **12:51**; 14:35; **16:17**; ⟦19:21⟧.
γίνομαι (*v.* be, become, happen, take place, develop, come to pass, perform, do, come)
Q ⟦*3:21*⟧; ⟦*3:22*⟧; **4:3**; 6:35; ⟦6:36⟧; ⟦6:40⟧; ⟦7:1⟧; **10:13**; **10:13**; **10:21**; **11:26**; *11:27*; 11:30; *11:41*; **12:40**; ⟦12:54⟧; **13:19**; 15:5; ⟦«15:10»⟧; ⟦17:26⟧; *17:28*.
γινώσκω (*v.* know, recognize)
Q **6:44**; 10:22; ⟦10:22⟧; **12:2**; **12:39**; **12:46**; ⟦19:21⟧.
γραμματεύς (scribe)
Q *11:16*.
γράφω (*v.* write)
Q **4:4**; **4:8**; **4:10**; 4:12; **7:27**.
γυνή (woman, wife)
Q **7:28**; *11:27*; **13:21**; *14:20*; ⟦«15:8»⟧; **16:18**.
δαιμόνιον (demon)
Q **7:33**; 11:14; **11:14**; **11:15**; **11:15**; **11:19**; **11:20**.
δάκτυλος (finger)
Q 11:20; **11:46**.
δαν(ε)ίζω (*v.* loan, *Med.*: borrow)
Q ⟦6:30⟧; ⟦6:34⟧.
δεῖ (must, it is necessary [to], have [to])
Q **11:42**; ⟦19:23⟧.
δείκνυμι (*v.* show, point out)
Q **4:5**.
δεῖπνον (dinner, banquet)
Q ⟦11:43⟧; 14:16; ⟦14:17⟧.
δέκα (ten)
Q ⟦«15:8»⟧; 19:13; 19:13; 19:16; **19:24**.
δένδρον (tree)
Q **3:9**; **3:9**; *6:43*; *6:43*; **6:43**; **6:43**; **6:44**; **13:19**.
δέομαι (*v.* ask, beg)
Q **10:2**.
δεσμεύω (*v.* bind, tie up)
Q ⟦11:46⟧.
δεσμωτήριον (prison)
Q *7:18*.
δεύτερος (second)
Q ⟦19:18⟧.
δέχομαι (*v.* receive, take in)
Q 10:8; **10:10**; 10:16; 10:16; 10:16; 10:16.
διαβλέπω (*v.* look at intently, see clearly)
Q **6:42**.
διάβολος (devil)
Q **4:2**; 4:3; 4:5; ⟦4:9⟧; **4:13**.
διακαθαρίζω (*v.* clean out, clear)
Q 3:17.
διακρίνω (*v.* make a distinction, judge)
Q ⟦12:56⟧.
διανόημα (thought)
Q 11:17.

διασκορπίζω (*v.* scatter, winnow)
Q 19:21; 19:22.
διαφέρω (*v.* carry through, differ, be worth more, be better)
Q **12:7**; **12:24**.
διδάσκαλος (teacher)
Q **6:40**; **6:40**.
διδάσκω (*v.* teach)
Q 12:12; 13:26.
δίδωμι (*v.* give, make [an effort])
Q **4:6**; **6:30**; **11:3**; **11:9**; **11:13**; **11:13**; **11:29**; **12:42**; 12:58; **19:13**; **19:24**; **19:26**.
διέρχομαι (*v.* go through, wander through)
Q **11:24**.
δίκαιος (righteous, just, good)
Q ⟦6:35⟧.
δικαιόω (*v.* justify, vindicate)
Q ⟦*7:29*⟧; **7:35**.
διορύσσω (*v.* dig through)
Q «12:33»; 12:33; **12:39**.
διχάζω (*v.* separate, divide)
Q 12:53.
διχοτομέω (*v.* cut in pieces)
Q **12:46**.
διώκω (*v.* follow, persecute, press on)
Q ⟦6:22⟧; ⟦6:23⟧; ⟦6:28⟧; **11:49**; 17:23.
δοκέω (*v.* seem, presume, believe, suppose, think, expect)
Q 3:8; **12:40**; ⟦12:51⟧.
δοκιμάζω (*v.* examine)
Q *14:19*.
δοκός (beam [of wood])
Q **6:41**; **6:42**; **6:42**.
δόμα (gift)
Q **11:13**.
δόξα (glory, splendor)
Q **4:5**; **12:27**.
δουλεύω (*v.* serve, be a slave to)
Q **16:13**; **16:13**.
δοῦλος (slave)
Q *6:40*; *6:40*; **7:8**; 12:42; **12:43**; **12:45**; **12:46**; **14:17**; «14:21»; **14:21**; **19:13**; **19:15**; **19:17**; ⟦19:19⟧; **19:22**.
δραχμή (*drachma* [Greek coin])
Q ⟦«15:8»⟧; ⟦«15:8»⟧; ⟦«15:9»⟧.
δύναμαι (*v.* be able, can)
Q **3:8**; 6:39; *6:42*; 12:4; 12:5; **12:25**; ⟦12:56⟧; *14:20*; <14:26>; 14:26; 14:27; **16:13**; **16:13**.
δύναμις (power)
Q **10:13**.
δύο (two)
Q ⟦«6:29↔30/Mt 5:41»⟧; ⟦12:6⟧; **16:13**; **17:34**; **17:35**.
δυσβάστακτος (difficult to carry)
Q *11:46*.
δυσμή (sunset, going down)
Q **13:29**; 17:24.
δώδεκα (twelve)
Q **22:30**.
δῶμα (housetop, room)
Q **12:3**.
ἐάω (*v.* permit, let)
Q ⟦12:39⟧.
ἐγγίζω (*v.* approach, reach, produce, arise, raise)
Q **10:9**.
ἐγείρω (*v.* raise, lift up)
Q **3:8**; **7:22**; 7:28; **11:31**; ⟦13:25⟧.
ἐγκρύπτω (*v.* hide, conceal)
Q **13:21**.
ἐθνικός (pagan, Gentile [adj.])
Q ⟦6:34⟧.
ἔθνος (pagan, Gentile [n.])
Q **12:30**.
εἶπον (*v.* say, tell, order, speak [aorist])
Q ⟦3:7⟧; **4:3**; **4:3**; **4:6**; 4:8; 4:9; 4:12; ⟦6:22⟧; 6:42; **7:7**; **7:9**; ⟦7:19⟧; **7:22**; **9:57**; 9:58; **9:59**; 9:60; **10:21**; **11:15**; **11:17**; *11:27*; *11:28*; ⟦11:29⟧; *11:39*; 11:49; **12:3**; **12:10**; ⟦12:10⟧; 12:11; 12:12; **12:45**; *12:54*; 13:25; 13:27; **13:35**; **14:17**; *14:18*; *14:19*; *14:20*; 14:21; ⟦«17:20»⟧; ⟦*17:21*⟧; **17:23**; 19:12; ⟦19:13⟧; 19:17; 19:19.

εἰρήνη (peace)
Q 10:5; 10:6; **10:6**; 10:6; **12:51;** 12:51.
εἷς (one [numeral])
Q ⟦«6:29↔30/Mt 5:41»⟧; **12:6**; *12:25*; **12:27**; **15:4**; ⟦«15:8»⟧; ⟦«15:10»⟧; *14:18*; **16:13**; **16:13**; **16:17**; 16:17; **17:2**; **17:34**; 17:34; **17:35**; 17:35.
εἰσέρχομαι (*v.* enter, come, move in, go in, let go)
Q **7:1**; **7:6**; **10:5**; ⟦**10:8**⟧; 10:10; **11:26**; **11:52**; **11:52**; 11:52; **13:24**; **13:24**; <13:24>; **17:27**.
εἰσφέρω (*v.* bring in, lead into, put)
Q **11:4**; 12:11.
ἑκατόν (one hundred)
Q **15:4**.
ἑκατόνταρχος (centurion)
Q **7:3**; 7:6.
ἐκβάλλω (*v.* cast out, throw up, cast up, dispatch)
Q **6:42**; **6:42**; **6:42**; 6:45; 6:45; **10:2;** 11:14; 11:14; **11:15**; **11:19**; **11:19**; **11:20**; **13:28**.
ἐκεῖ (there)
Q 10:6; **11:26**; **12:34**; **13:28**; ⟦*17:21*⟧; **17:37**.
ἐκεῖθεν (from there)
Q **12:59**.
ἐκεῖνος (that one)
Q **6:48**; **6:49**; 10:10; 10:12; **10:12**; *10:21*; **11:26**; **11:42**; *12:12*; ⟦12:39⟧; **12:43**; **12:45**; **12:46**; ⟦17:27⟧; 19:15.
ἐκζητέω (*v.* seek out, require)
Q 11:50; 11:51.
ἐκκόπτω (*v.* cut off, cut down, chop down)
Q **3:9**.
ἐκπειράζω (*v.* test, tempt)
Q **4:12**.
ἐκριζόω (*v.* uproot)
Q 17:6.
ἐκτινάσσω (*v.* shake off)
Q 10:11.
ἐκτός (outside)
Q 11:41.
ἐκχέω (*v.* pour out)
Q **11:50**.
ἔλεος (mercy)
Q 11:42.
ἐλπίζω (*v.* hope)
Q ⟦6:34⟧.
ἐμπορία (business, trade)
Q 14:19.
ἔνδυμα (clothing)
Q **12:23**; 12:26.
ἐνδύω (*v.* clothe)
Q **12:22**.
ἐνενήκοντα (ninety)
Q **15:4**; **15:7**.
ἐννέα (nine)
Q **15:4**; **15:7**.
ἐντέλλω (*v.* command)
Q **4:10**.
ἐντός (within, inside)
Q 11:41; ⟦«17:21»⟧.
ἐξέρχομαι (*v.* leave, go out, get out, streak)
Q **7:24**; **7:25**; **7:26**; **10:10**; **11:24**; **11:24**; **12:59**; *14:18*; **14:23**; 17:23; 17:24; *17:29*.
ἐξομολογέω (*v.* confess, admit)
Q **10:21**.
ἐξουσία (authority)
Q **7:8**.
ἔξω (outside)
Q ⟦10:10⟧; ⟦13:25⟧; **14:35**.
ἔξωθεν (from outside)
Q **11:39**.
ἐξώτερος (outer)
Q ⟦13:28⟧.
ἐπαθροίζω (*v.* gather, collect besides)
Q 11:29.
ἐπαίρω (*v.* lift up, hold up, raise)
Q ⟦6:20⟧; *11:27*.
ἐπερωτάω (*v.* ask)
Q ⟦«17:20»⟧.
ἐπιδίδωμι (*v.* give, hand over)
Q **11:11**; **11:12**.
ἐπιζητέω (*v.* seek, search for, want)
Q **12:30**.

ἐπιθυμέω (*v*. desire, long for)
Q *10:24*.
ἐπιούσιος (for subsistence)
Q **11:3**.
ἐπιστρέφω (*v*. turn, return)
Q ⟦10:6⟧; 11:24.
ἐπισυνάγω (*v*. gather, collect)
Q **13:34**; 13:34.
ἐπιτίθημι (*v*. lay, put on)
Q ⟦11:46⟧.
ἐπιτιμάω (*v*. rebuke)
Q 17:3.
ἐπιτρέπω (*v*. allow, permit)
Q **9:59**.
ἑπτά (seven)
Q **11:26**.
ἑπτάκις (seventy)
Q **17:4**; **17:4**.
ἐργάζομαι (*v*. work)
Q 13:27.
ἐργασία (practice, pursuit, wages, effort)
Q 12:58.
ἐργάτης (worker)
Q **10:2; 10:2; 10:7**.
ἔρημος (deserted, desert, wilderness)
Q **4:1**; **7:24**; 17:23.
ἐρημόω (*v*. lay waste, leave barren)
Q **11:17**.
ἔρχομαι (*v*. come)
Q ⟦3:7⟧; **3:16;** ⟦*3:22*⟧; *4:16*; 6:48;
6:49; <7:3>; **7:3**; **7:8**; **7:8**;
7:19; ⟦«7:29»⟧; **7:33**; **7:34**;
11:2; **11:25**; **11:31**; **12:39**;
12:40; **12:43**; ⟦«12:49»⟧;
12:51; 12:51; 12:53; **13:35**;
14:17; *14:20*; **17:1**; **17:1**;
⟦«17:20»⟧; ⟦«17:20»⟧; **17:27;**
19:13; 19:15; ⟦<19:16>⟧;
19:18; 19:20; **19:23**.
ἐρωτάω (*v*. ask)
Q *14:18*; *14:19*.
ἐσθίω (*v*. eat)
Q ⟦*4:2*⟧; **7:33**; **7:34**; «10:7»;
⟦«10:8»⟧; **12:22**; **12:29**;
12:45; 13:26; *17:28*.
ἔσχατος (last)
Q **11:26**; **12:59**; ⟦**13:30**⟧; ⟦**13:30**⟧.
ἔσωθεν (from the inside)
Q **11:39**.
ἕτερος (other)
Q ⟦7:19⟧; ⟦7:32⟧; **9:59**; **11:26**;
14:19; *14:20*; **16:13**; **16:13**;
19:20.
ἕτοιμος (prepared, ready)
Q **12:40**; **14:17**.
εὖ (well [done])
Q 19:17; ⟦19:19⟧.
εὐαγγελίζω (*v*. bring good news, evangelize)
Q **7:22**.
εὐδία (fair weather)
Q ⟦12:54⟧.
εὐδοκία (good will, favor, to please)
Q **10:21**.
εὔθετος (well-placed, suitable, fit)
Q ⟦14:35⟧.
εὐθύς (immediately)
Q 6:49.
εὔκοπος (easy)
Q ⟦16:17⟧.
εὐλογέω (*v*. bless)
Q **13:35.**
εὑρίσκω (*v*. find)
Q **7:9**; **11:9**; **11:10**; **11:24**;
11:25; **12:43**; 14:23; **15:5**;
⟦«15:8»⟧; ⟦«15:9»⟧;
⟦«15:9»⟧; 17:33; 17:33.
ἐχθρός (enemy)
Q **6:27**.
ἔχιδνα (viper)
Q **3:7**.
ἔχω (*v*. have)
Q **3:8**; 6:32; ⟦«6:34»⟧; 7:3; **7:8**;
7:33; **9:58**; **9:58**; *14:18*;
14:18; *14:19*; 15:4;
⟦«15:8»⟧; **17:6**; 19:21;
19:24; 19:26; **19:26**; **19:26**.
Ζαχαρίας (Zechariah)
Q **11:51**.
ζάω (*v*. live)
Q **4:4**.
ζεύγη (yoke)
Q *14:19*.
ζητέω (*v*. seek, look for, hunt for, search, demand)

Q **11:9**; **11:10**; 11:16; **11:24**; 11:29; **12:31**; 13:24; ⟦15:4⟧; ⟦«15:8»⟧.

ζύμη (yeast, leaven)
Q **13:21**.

ζυμόω (*v*. leaven, ferment)
Q **13:21**.

ἤδη (already, now)
Q **3:9**; ⟦«12:49»⟧; 14:17.

ἡδύοσμον (mint)
Q **11:42**.

ἥκω (*v*. come, be present)
Q **12:46**; **13:29**; ⟦13:35⟧.

ἡλικία (age, time of life, stature)
Q **12:25**.

ἥλιος (sun)
Q 6:35.

ἡμέρα (day)
Q **4:2; 10:12**; **12:46**; 17:4; ⟦17:24⟧; **17:26**; ⟦17:26⟧; ⟦17:27⟧; **17:27**; *17:28; 17:29;* 17:30.

θάλασσα (sea)
Q **17:2**; 17:6.

θάπτω (*v*. bury)
Q **9:59**; **9:60.**

θαυμάζω (*v*. marvel, wonder, be amazed)
Q **7:9**; **11:14.**

θεάομαι (*v*. see, perceive, look at)
Q **7:24.**

θεῖον (brimstone, burning sulfur)
Q *17:29*.

θέλω (*v*. wish, want, be willing)
Q ⟦6:29⟧; **6:31**; *10:24*; ⟦11:46⟧; ⟦«12:49»⟧; **13:34**; **13:34.**

θεμελιόω (*v*. lay a foundation, found)
Q 6:48.

θεός (God)
Q **3:8**; ⟦*3:22*⟧; **4:3**; **4:8**; **4:9**; **4:12**; 6:20; 7:28; ⟦*7:29*⟧; ⟦*7:30*⟧; ⟦*7:30*⟧; 10:9; **11:20**; **11:20**; *11:28*; *11:49*; <11:52>; *12:8*; *12:9*; 12:24; **12:28**; 13:18; 13:20; 13:28; **16:13**; 16:16; ⟦«17:20»⟧; ⟦«17:20»⟧; ⟦«17:21»⟧.

θεραπεύω (heal, care for, cure)
Q 7:3; **10:9.**

θερίζω (*v*. harvest, reap)
Q **12:24**; **19:21**; **19:22.**

θερισμός (harvest)
Q **10:2**; **10:2**; **10:2.**

θηλάζω (*v*. suck)
Q *11:27*.

θησαυρίζω (*v*. store up, gather, treasure up)
Q «12:33»; 12:33.

θησαυρός (treasure, storeroom)
Q **6:45**; ⟦6:45⟧; «12:33»; **12:33**; **12:34.**

θρηνέω (*v*. sing a dirge, lament, wail)
Q **7:32.**

θρίξ (hair)
Q **12:7.**

θρόνος (throne)
Q **22:30.**

θυγάτηρ (daughter)
Q **12:53**; 14:26.

θύρα (door)
Q 13:24; **13:25**; ⟦13:25⟧.

θυσιαστήριον (altar)
Q **11:51**.

Ἰακώβ (Jacob)
Q **13:28**.

ἰάομαι (*v*. heal)
Q **7:7**.

ἴδε (see, look)
Q ⟦19:21⟧.

ἴδιος (own)
Q *14:18*.

ἰδού (look, behold)
Q ⟦*3:22*⟧; 6:42; **7:25**; **7:27**; **7:34**; **10:3**; **11:31**; **11:32**; *11:41*; **13:35**; ⟦17:21⟧; ⟦«17:21»⟧; **17:23**; **17:23**.

ἱερόν (temple, sanctuary)
Q **4:9**.

Ἰερουσαλήμ (Jerusalem)
Q 4:9; **13:34**; **13:34**.

Ἰησοῦς (Jesus)
Q ⟦<3:0>⟧; ⟦*3:21*⟧; ⟦**3:21**⟧; **4:1**; 4:4; **4:8**; **4:12**; *7:1*; **7:9**; **9:58**; *11:39*.

ἱκανός (worthy, sufficient, fit)
Q **3:16**; **7:6**.
ἱμάτιον (cloak, coat)
Q **6:29**.
ἵνα (in order to, [in order, so] that)
Q **4:3**; **6:31**; *6:37*; ⟦6:40⟧; **7:6**; *11:41*; ⟦11:50⟧; 14:23; 17:2.
Ἰορδάνης (Jordan [river])
Q **3:3**; ⟦*3:21*⟧.
Ἰσαάκ (Isaac)
Q **13:28**.
Ἰσραήλ (Israel)
Q **7:9**; **22:30**.
ἵστημι (*v.* set, establish, stand)
Q **4:9**; 11:17; **11:18**; ⟦13:25⟧.
ἰσχυρός (strong, powerful)
Q **3:16**.
ἰχθύς (fish)
Q **11:12**.
Ἰωάννης (John)
Q **3:2**; ⟦*3:21*⟧; **7:18**; **7:22**; **7:24**; **7:28**; ⟦7:29⟧; ⟦*7:29*⟧; **7:33**; **16:16**.
Ἰωνᾶς (Jonah)
Q **11:29**; **11:30**; **11:32**; **11:32**.
ἰῶτα (iota)
Q 16:17.
καθαρίζω (*v.* cleanse, purify)
Q **7:22**; **11:39;** ⟦11:41⟧.
καθαρός (clean)
Q **11:41**.
κάθημαι (*v.* sit)
Q **7:32**; **22:30**.
καθίστημι (*v.* bring, appoint, set over)
Q **12:42**; **12:44**; 19:17; 19:19.
καθώς (just as, for as)
Q 6:31; ⟦11:30⟧; ⟦17:26⟧; *17:28*.
καιρός (time)
Q *10:21*; **12:42**; ⟦**12:56**⟧.
καίω (*v.* burn, to light [with fire])
Q 11:33.
κακῶς (severely, badly)
Q ⟦7:3⟧.
κάλαμος (reed)
Q **7:24**.
καλέω (*v.* call, invite)
Q 6:46; ⟦14:16⟧; **14:17**; 14:23; ⟦<«15:9»>⟧; **19:13**.
καλός (good, beautiful, healthy)
Q **3:9;** *6:43*; *6:43*; 6:43; **6:43**; ⟦14:34⟧.
καλύπτω (*v.* hide, cover up)
Q 12:2.
καρδία (heart)
Q **6:45**; **12:34**; **12:45**.
καρπός (fruit)
Q **3:8**; **3:9**; *6:43*; *6:43*; **6:43**; **6:43**; **6:44**.
κάρφος (speck, chip)
Q **6:41**; **6:42**; **6:42**.
καταβαίνω (*v.* descend, come down, pour down [of rain])
Q 6:48; 6:49; **10:15**.
καταβολή (foundation, founding, beginning)
Q 11:50.
κατακαίω (*v.* burn up, consume)
Q **3:17**.
κατακλυσμός (cataclysm, flood)
Q **17:27**.
κατακρίνω (*v.* condemn)
Q **11:31**; **11:32**.
καταλείπω (*v.* leave behind)
Q *4:16*.
καταμανθάνω (*v.* learn, observe)
Q ⟦12:27⟧.
κατανοέω (*v.* observe, notice, consider)
Q **6:41**; 12:24.
κατασκευάζω (*v.* prepare, make ready)
Q **7:27**.
κατασκηνόω (*v.* cause to dwell, to nest)
Q **13:19**.
κατασκήνωσις (dwelling place, nest)
Q **9:58**.
καταφρονέω (*v.* despise)
Q **16:13**.
κατοικέω (*v.* settle, dwell)
Q **11:26**.
κάτω (below, down, downwards)
Q **4:9**.
Καφαρναούμ (Capernaum)
Q **7:1**; **10:15**.

κεῖμαι (*v.* lie, be destined)
Q **3:9**.
κεραία (serif, crown, hook)
Q **16:17**.
κεφαλή (head)
Q **9:58**; **12:7**.
κῆπος (garden)
Q ⟦13:19⟧.
κήρυγμα (proclamation, announcement)
Q **11:32**.
κηρύσσω (*v.* proclaim, announce)
Q **12:3**.
κιβωτός (box, chest, ark)
Q **17:27**.
κινέω (*v.* move)
Q ⟦11:46⟧.
κλάδος (branch)
Q **13:19**.
κλαίω (*v.* weep, cry)
Q 7:32.
κλαυθμός (weeping, wailing)
Q **13:28**.
κλείω (*v.* lock, shut)
Q 11:52; ⟦13:25⟧.
κλέπτης (thief, robber)
Q «12:33»; **12:33**; **12:39**.
κλέπτω (*v.* rob)
Q «12:33»; 12:33.
κλίβανος (furnace, oven)
Q **12:28**.
κλίνω (*v.* lie, recline, lay)
Q **9:58**.
κοδράντης (*quadran* [Roman coin])
Q ⟦12:59⟧.
κόκκος (seed, grain)
Q **13:19**; **17:6**.
κοιλία (womb)
Q *11:27*.
κομίζω (bring, get, receive)
Q 19:23.
κονιορτός (dust)
Q **10:11**.
κοπιάω (*v.* become weary, work hard)
Q **12:27**.
κοπρία (dunghill)
Q 14:35.
κόραξ (raven, crow)
Q 12:24.
κοσμέω (*v.* put in order, decorate, tidy up)
Q **11:25**.
κόσμος (world)
Q 4:5; 11:50.
κρίμα (dispute, lawsuit, judgment)
Q ⟦6:37⟧.
κρίνον (anemone, lily)
Q **12:27**.
κρίνω (*v.* judge)
Q ⟦6:29⟧; **6:37**; **6:37**; ⟦6:37⟧; ⟦6:37⟧; **22:30**.
κρίσις (judgment, justice)
Q **10:14**; **11:31**; **11:32**; **11:42**.
κριτής (judge)
Q **11:19**; **12:58**; **12:58**.
κρούω (*v.* strike, knock)
Q **11:9**; **11:10**; ⟦13:25⟧.
κρύπτη (cellar, hidden place)
Q ⟦11:33⟧.
κρυπτός (hidden)
Q **12:2**.
κρύπτω (*v.* hide)
Q 10:21; 19:21.
κύμινον (cummin)
Q 11:42.
κύριος (Lord, sir, master)
Q **4:8**; **4:12**; *6:40*; *6:40*; **6:46**; **6:46**; **7:6**; **9:59**; **10:2**; **10:21**; *11:39*; **12:42**; **12:43**; **12:45**; **12:46**; 13:25; **13:35**; «14:21»; **16:13**; 19:15; **19:16**; **19:18**; **19:20**.
κωφός (dumb, mute, deaf)
Q **7:22**; **11:14**; **11:14**.
λαλέω (*v.* say, speak)
Q **6:45**; **11:14**; *11:39*.
λαμβάνω (*v.* receive, take)
Q ⟦6:29⟧; ⟦6:34⟧; **11:10**; **13:19**; **13:21**; 14:27.
λάμπω (*v.* shine out, give light)
Q ⟦11:33⟧.
λαός (people)
Q ⟦*3:21*⟧; ⟦*7:29*⟧.
λατρεύω (*v.* serve)
Q **4:8**.
λέγω (*v.* say, tell, talk)
Q **3:8**; **3:8**; ⟦*3:22*⟧; **6:20**; *6:42*;

6:46; ⟦7:3⟧; ⟦7:3⟧; **7:8**; **7:9**; **7:24**; **7:26**; **7:28**; **7:32**; **7:33**; **7:34**; **10:2;** 10:5; **10:9**; **10:12**; **10:24**; ⟦11:2⟧; 11:9; **11:24**; *11:27*; *11:39*; **11:51**; 12:3; **12:22**; **12:27**; 12:29; **12:44**; ⟦*12:54*⟧; ⟦**12:54**⟧; **12:59**; 13:25; 13:26; 13:27; **13:35**; **15:7**; ⟦«15:9»⟧; ⟦«15:10»⟧; 17:6; 17:34; **19:16**; 19:18; 19:20; 19:22.

λεπρός (leper, skin-diseased person)
Q **7:22**.

λίαν (very much)
Q ⟦4:5⟧.

λιθοβολέω (*v*. stone)
Q **13:34**.

λίθος (stone, rock)
Q **3:8**; **4:3**; **4:11**; 11:11; 17:2.

λόγος (word, account, saying)
Q **6:47**; ⟦6:49⟧; 7:1; **7:7**; *11:28*; **12:10;** 19:15.

λύκος (wolf)
Q **10:3**.

λυσιτελέω (*v*. be advantageous, better)
Q 17:2.

λυχνία (lampstand)
Q **11:33**.

λύχνος (light, lamp)
Q **11:33**; **11:34**; ⟦«15:8»⟧.

Λώτ (Lot)
Q *17:28; 17:29*.

μαθητής (disciple)
Q 6:20; **6:40**; ⟦6:40⟧; **7:18**; 10:2; *11:39*; <14:26>; 14:26; 14:27.

μακάριος (blessed, happy)
Q **6:20**; **6:21**; **6:21**; **6:22**; **7:23**; **10:23**; *11:27*; *11:28*; **12:43**.

μαλακός (effiminate, soft, fine)
Q **7:25**; 7:25.

μᾶλλον (rather, more)
Q **11:13**; *12:5*; **12:24**; **12:28**; 15:7.

μαμωνᾶς (Mammon)
Q **16:13**.

μαρτυρέω (*v*. bear witness, testify)
Q ⟦11:48⟧.

μαστός (breast)
Q *11:27*.

μάχαιρα (sword)
Q 12:51.

μέγας (great, large)
Q **6:49**; **7:28**; **7:28**; ⟦14:16⟧.

μεθύω (*v*. be drunk)
Q ⟦12:45⟧.

μέλλω (*v*. be about to, impend)
Q **3:7**.

μένω (*v*. remain, stay)
Q **10:7**.

μερίζω (*v*. divide)
Q 11:17; 11:17; 11:18.

μεριμνάω (*v*. worry, be anxious)
Q **12:11**; **12:22**; **12:25**; **12:26**; 12:29.

μέρος (part, portion, inheritance)
Q **12:46**.

μέσος (middle, midst)
Q **10:3**.

μεταβαίνω (*v*. change place, move around)
Q ⟦10:7⟧.

μεταμέλομαι (*v*. regret)
Q ⟦*7:30*⟧.

μετανοέω (*v*. repent)
Q **10:13**; **11:32**; ⟦«15:10»⟧; ⟦17:3⟧.

μετάνοια (repentance)
Q **3:8**.

μετρέω (*v*. measure [out])
Q **6:38**; **6:38**.

μέτρον (measure, measurement)
Q **6:38**.

μηδέ (nor)
Q 10:4; **12:22**.

μηδείς (no one, no)
Q 10:4.

μήποτε (lest, so that… not)
Q **4:11**; **12:58**.

μήτε (and not, neither)
Q *7:33*; **7:33**.

μητήρ (mother)
Q **12:53**; **14:26**.

μήτι (surely not)
Q 6:39; 6:44.

μικρός (small, little)
Q **7:28**; **17:2**.

μίλιον ([Roman] mile)
Q ⟦«6:29↔30/Mt 5:41»⟧.

μισέω (*v*. hate)
Q 14:26; <14:26>; **16:13**.

μισθός (reward, wages)
Q **6:23**; 6:32; ⟦<6:34>⟧; 10:7.

μνᾶ (*mina* [Greek coin])
Q 19:13; 19:16; 19:16; 19:18; 19:18; ⟦<19:21>⟧; 19:24; 19:24.

μνημεῖον (monument, tomb)
Q 11:44; **11:47**.

μοιχαλίς (adulterous)
Q *11:29*.

μοιχεύω (*v*. commit adultery)
Q **16:18**; ⟦16:18⟧.

μόνος (alone, only)
Q **4:4**; **4:8**.

μυλικός (millstone)
Q 17:2.

μύλος (mill, millstone)
Q 17:35.

μωραίνω (*v*. make foolish, tasteless, become insipid)
Q **14:34**.

Ναζαρά (Nazara, Nazareth)
Q 4:16.

ναί (yes)
Q **7:26**; **10:21**; 11:51.

νεκρός (dead)
Q **7:22**; **9:60**; **9:60**.

νήθω (*v*. spin)
Q **12:27**.

νήπιος (babe, child)
Q **10:21**.

νηστεύω (*v*. fast)
Q ⟦*4:2*⟧.

Νινευίτης (Ninevite)
Q 11:30; **11:32**.

νομικός (lawyer)
Q ⟦*7:30*⟧; ⟦11:46⟧; ⟦11:52⟧.

νόμος (law, custom)
Q **16:16**; **16:17**.

νοσσίον (nestling)
Q 13:34.

νότος (South)
Q **11:31**.

νύμφη (bride, daughter-in-law)
Q **12:53**.

Νῶε (Noah)
Q **17:26**; **17:27**.

ὁδηγέω (*v*. lead, guide, show the way)
Q **6:39**.

ὁδός (road, path, way)
Q **7:27**; 10:4; **12:58**; **14:23**.

ὀδούς (tooth)
Q **13:28**.

ὅθεν (from where, whence)
Q **11:24**; 19:21; 19:22.

οἶδα (*v*. know, see, be aware)
Q **11:13**; **11:17**; 11:44; **12:30**; **12:39**; ⟦12:56⟧; 13:25; 13:27; **19:22**.

οἰκετεία (household slaves)
Q 12:42.

οἰκία (house, household)
Q **6:48**; **6:48**; **6:49**; **6:49**; **10:5**; ⟦10:7⟧; ⟦10:7⟧; ⟦10:7⟧; 11:17; ⟦11:33⟧; ⟦«15:8»⟧.

οἰκοδεσπότης (householder)
Q **12:39**; ⟦13:25⟧; 14:21.

οἰκοδομέω (*v*. build)
Q **6:48**; **6:49**; **11:47**; *11:48*; *17:28*.

οἶκος (house)
Q 7:25; ⟦10:5⟧; **11:24**; 11:51; 12:39; **13:35**; 14:23.

οἰκτίρμων (compassionate, full of pity)
Q 6:36; 6:36.

οἰνοπότης (drunkard)
Q **7:34**.

ὀλιγόπιστος (of little faith, of petty faith)
Q **12:28**.

ὀλίγος (little, few)
Q **10:2**; 13:24; 19:17; ⟦19:19⟧.

ὅλος (whole, fully)
Q **11:34**; 11:34; **13:21**.

ὅμοιος (similar, like)
Q 6:48; 6:49; 7:31; **7:32**; **13:18**; 13:19; **13:21**.

ὁμοιόω (*v*. be similar to, compare to)
Q **7:31**; 13:18; 13:20.

ὁμοίως (similarly)
Q *17:28*.

ὁμολογέω (*v*. confess, admit, agree, speak out for)
Q **12:8**; **12:8**.

ὀνειδίζω (*v*. reproach)
Q **6:22**.

ὄνομα (name)
Q **11:2**; **13:35**.

ὅπου (where, wherever [with ἐάν])
Q **9:57**; «12:33»; «12:33»; **12:33**; 12:33; **12:34**; **17:37**; 19:21; 19:22.

ὅπως (so that, that, to)
Q 6:35; *7:3*; **10:2**.

ὁράω (*v*. see, look at)
Q **7:25**; **7:26**; ⟦7:30⟧; **10:24**; **10:24**; **13:35**; *14:18*.

ὀργή (anger, wrath, rage)
Q **3:7**.

ὀργίζω (*v*. get angry, *Med*.: be enraged)
Q **14:21**.

ὄρνις (bird)
Q **13:34**.

ὄρος (hill, mountain)
Q 4:5; ⟦15:4⟧.

ὀρχέομαι (*v*. dance)
Q **7:32**.

ὅταν (when)
Q **6:22**; ⟦11:2⟧; **11:24**; *11:34*; **12:11**.

ὅτε (when)
Q ⟦7:1⟧; ⟦13:35⟧.

ὅτι (that, because, for)
Q **3:8**; 4:4; **4:10**; **6:20; 6:21**; **6:21**; 6:23; **6:35**; *10:9*; ⟦10:12⟧; **10:13**; **10:21**; **10:21**; *10:23*; *10:23*; **10:24**; **11:31**; **11:32**; 11:39; **11:42**; 11:43; **11:44**; 11:46; **11:47**; ⟦11:48⟧; *11:48*; **11:52**; **12:24**; **12:30**; **12:39**; **12:40**; **12:44**; **12:51**; **13:24**; 14:17; **15:7**; ⟦«15:9»⟧; **19:21**; **19:22**.

οὐ, οὐκ, οὐχ (not, no)
Q **3:16**; ⟦*4:2*⟧; **4:4**; **4:12**; *6:37*; **6:40**; **6:41**; **6:43**; 6:46; **6:48**; **7:6**; 7:28; ⟦*7:29*⟧; **7:32**; **7:32**; **9:58**; **10:24**; **10:24**; 11:17; 11:24; **11:29**; 11:44; **11:46**; **11:52**; **12:2**; **12:2**; **12:6**; **12:10**; **12:24**; 12:24; **12:27**; 12:28; 12:33; **12:39**; **12:40**; **12:46**; **12:46**; 12:51; ⟦**12:56**⟧; **12:59**; 13:25; 13:27; **13:34**; **13:35**; *14:20*; 14:26; 14:26; <14:26>; **14:26**; **14:27**; **14:27**; **16:13**; ⟦«17:20»⟧; **19:21**; **19:21**; **19:22**; **19:22**.

οὐαί (woe)
Q **10:13**; **10:13**; 11:39; **11:42**; 11:43; **11:44**; 11:46; **11:47**; **11:52**; **17:1**.

οὐδέ (not, neither, nor)
Q *6:40*; **6:43**; 7:9; ⟦*7:30*⟧; 10:22; ⟦11:52⟧; **12:24**; **12:24**; **12:27**; **12:27**; 12:33; ⟦*17:21*⟧.

οὐδείς (no, none, no one, nothing)
Q ⟦*4:2*⟧; **10:22**; 11:33; **12:2**; **16:13**.

οὖν (therefore, so, then)
Q **3:8**; **3:9**; ⟦*7:31*⟧; **10:2**; **11:13**; **11:35**; ⟦12:29⟧; ⟦19:23⟧; 19:24.

οὐρανός (heaven, sky)
Q ⟦3:21⟧; **6:23**; **9:58**; **10:15**; **10:21**; **11:13**; **12:33**; ⟦12:54⟧; ⟦12:55⟧; ⟦**12:56**⟧; **13:19**; **16:17**; *17:29*.

οὖς (ear)
Q *10:23*; **12:3**.

οὔτε (and not, neither, nor)
Q 12:33; 12:33; 14:35; 14:35.

οὗτος (this [one], these, it)
Q **3:8**; ⟦*3:22*⟧; **4:3**; **4:6**; 7:1; **7:8**; **7:8**; ⟦7:18⟧; 7:24; **7:27**; **7:31**; ⟦10:5⟧; *10:21*; **10:21**; **11:19**; *11:27*; 11:29; 11:30; **11:31**; **11:32**; **11:42**; **11:49**; 11:50; **11:51**; *12:12*; **12:22**; **12:27**; **12:30**; **12:30**; **12:31**; *14:20*; «14:21»; **17:2**; **17:6**.

οὕτως (so, thus, this [is how], that [is what])
Q 6:23; 6:31; **10:21**; **11:30**;

12:28; **12:43**; ⟦«15:10»⟧; **17:24**; **17:26**; 17:30.
οὐχί (not, no)
Q 6:32; 6:34; 6:39; **12:6**; 12:23; ⟦15:4⟧; ⟦«15:8»⟧.
ὀφειλέτης (debtor)
Q 11:4.
ὀφείλημα (debt)
Q 11:4.
ὀφθαλμός (eye)
Q ⟦6:20⟧; **6:41**; **6:41**; **6:42**; **6:42**; **6:42**; **6:42**; **10:23**; **11:34**; **11:34**; 11:34.
ὄφις (snake, serpent)
Q **11:12**.
ὄχλος (crowd)
Q ⟦3:7⟧; **7:24**; **11:14**; *11:27*; *11:29*; *11:39*; ⟦*12:54*⟧.
ὄψιος (late, evening)
Q ⟦12:54⟧.
παιδίον (child)
Q **7:32**.
παῖς ([serving] boy)
Q 7:3; **7:7**.
πάλαι (long ago)
Q **10:13**.
πάλιν (again, on the other hand)
Q ⟦6:43⟧; ⟦13:20⟧.
παραγίνομαι (*v*. come, arrive, be present)
Q ⟦*3:21*⟧.
παραδίδωμι (*v*. hand over, deliver, entrust)
Q **10:22**; **12:58**.
παραιτέομαι (*v*. ask for, request)
Q *14:18*; *14:18*; *14:19*.
παρακαλέω (*v*. invite, summon, comfort, console)
Q ⟦6:21⟧; 7:3.
παραλαμβάνω (*v*. receive, take along, take away, bring)
Q 4:5; **11:26**; **17:34**; **17:35**.
παρατήρησις (observation)
Q ⟦«17:20»⟧.
παρατίθημι (*v*. set before)
Q ⟦«10:8»⟧.
παρέρχομαι (*v*. go by, pass away)
Q **16:17**.
παροψίς (dish)
Q 11:39.
πᾶς (all, every, everything, anyone)
Q **3:3**; **3:9**; **4:5**; **4:6**; ⟦6:22⟧; **6:47**; ⟦6:49⟧; ⟦7:18⟧; ⟦*7:29*⟧; **10:22**; **11:10**; **11:17**; 11:17; ⟦11:33⟧; **11:50**; **12:7**; **12:8**; **12:27**; **12:30**; ⟦12:31⟧; **12:44**; ⟦14:11⟧; *14:18*; **16:18**; *17:29;* **19:26**.
πατήρ (father)
Q **3:8**; 6:35; **6:36**; **9:59**; **10:21**; **10:21**; **10:22**; **10:22**; **10:22**; **11:2**; **11:13**; **11:47**; **11:48**; ⟦12:6⟧; **12:30**; **12:53**; **14:26**.
πεινάω (*v*. be hungry, hunger)
Q **4:2**; **6:21**.
πειράζω (*v*. tempt, test)
Q **4:2**.
πειρασμός (temptation, testing)
Q **11:4**.
πέμπω (*v*. send)
Q **7:18**.
πενθερά (mother-in-law)
Q **12:53**.
πενθέω (*v*. be sad, grieve, mourn)
Q ⟦6:21⟧.
πέντε (five)
Q ⟦12:6⟧; *14:19*; 19:18.
πέρας (end, limit, boundary)
Q **11:31**.
περιβάλλω (*v*. throw, lay around, put on, array, wear [clothing])
Q **12:27**; 12:29.
περίκειμαι (*v*. lie, be put around)
Q ⟦17:2⟧.
περιπατέω (*v*. walk about, walk around)
Q **7:22**; 11:44.
περίσσευμα (abundance, fulness, exuberance)
Q **6:45**.
περισσότερος (greater, more)
Q **7:26**.
περίχωρος (area, region)
Q **3:3**.
πετεινόν (bird)
Q **9:58**; 12:24; **13:19**.

πέτρα (bedrock, stone)
Q **6:48**; 6:48.

πήρα (bag, wallet)
Q **10:4**.

πῆχυς (cubit)
Q **12:25**.

πίνω (*v*. drink)
Q **7:33**; **7:34**; «10:7»; **12:29**; **12:45**; 13:26; **17:27**; *17:28*.

πίπτω (*v*. fall, collapse)
Q **6:39**; 6:48; 6:49; 12:6; ⟦16:17⟧.

πιστεύω (*v*. believe)
Q ⟦*7:29*⟧; ⟦*7:30*⟧.

πίστις (faith, belief, faithfulness)
Q **7:9**; 11:42; **17:6**.

πιστός (faithful, trustworthy)
Q **12:42**; **19:17**; ⟦19:19⟧.

πλανάω (*v*. mislead, lead astray)
Q 15:7.

πλατεῖα (plaza, [broad] street)
Q 13:26.

πλήν (rather, yet, but)
Q **10:14**; **17:**1.

πληρόω (*v*. fill, fulfil)
Q ⟦7:1⟧.

πνεῦμα (spirit, wind)
Q **3:16**; ⟦3:22⟧; **4:1**; **11:24**; **11:26**; **12:10**; ⟦12:12⟧.

πνέω (*v*. blow)
Q ⟦6:48⟧; ⟦6:49⟧.

ποιέω (*v*. do, make, bear [fruit], prepare, earn)
Q **3:8**; **3:9**; **6:31**; **6:31**; 6:32; 6:34; *6:43*; *6:43*; **6:43**; **6:43**; **6:46**; **6:47**; **6:49**; **7:8**; **7:8**; **11:42**; **12:43**; **14:16**; 19:18.

πόλις (city, town)
Q **10:8**; 10:10; ⟦10:10⟧; **10:12**.

πολύς (many, much, more, vast)
Q **6:23**; **10:2; 10:24**; **11:31**; **11:32**; **12:7**; **12:23**; 12:28; **13:24**; ⟦13:29⟧; ⟦14:16⟧; ⟦19:15⟧; 19:17; 19:19.

πονηρός (evil, bad, wicked)
Q **6:22**; **6:35**; **6:45**; **6:45**; **6:45**; **11:13**; **11:26**; **11:29**; **11:34**; **19:22**.

πορεύομαι (*v*. go, depart)
Q **7:8**; **7:8**; **7:22**; **11:26**; *14:19*; **15:4**.

πόρνη (prostitute)
Q ⟦*7:29*⟧.

ποσάκις (how often, how many times?)
Q **13:34**.

πόσος (how great, how much?)
Q **11:13**; 11:35.

ποταμός (river, stream, flash-flood)
Q **6:48**; **6:49**.

πότε (when?)
Q ⟦«17:20»⟧.

ποτήριον (cup, drinking vessel)
Q **11:39**; 11:41.

ποῦ ([any]where)
Q **9:58**.

πούς (foot)
Q **4:11**; **10:11**.

πραγματεύομαι (*v*. conduct, do business)
Q 19:13.

πρόβατον (sheep)
Q 10:3; **15:4**.

προσδοκάω (*v*. expect, await)
Q **7:19**; **12:46**.

προσεργάζομαι (*v*. approach, come, do business)
Q 19:16.

προσεύχομαι (*v*. pray)
Q **6:28**; **11:2**.

προσκόπτω (*v*. strike against, batter)
Q **4:11;** 6:49.

προσκυνέω (*v*. worship, reverence, bow down)
Q **4:7**; **4:8**.

προσπίπτω (*v*. fall down, pound [against])
Q ⟦6:48⟧.

προστίθημι (*v*. add to, grant)
Q **12:25**; **12:31**.

προσφωνέω (*v*. address)
Q **7:32**.

πρόσωπον (face)
Q **7:27**; ⟦**12:56**⟧.

προφήτης (prophet)
Q **6:23**; **7:26**; **7:26**; **10:24**; **11:47**; **11:49**; 11:50; **13:34**; **16:16**.

πρωΐ (early in the morning, at dawn)
Q ⟦12:55⟧.
πρωτοκαθεδρία (front seat, place of honor)
Q **11:43**.
πρωτοκλισία (front couch, place of honor)
Q ⟦11:43⟧.
πρῶτος (first)
Q **6:42**; **9:59**; ⟦10:5⟧; **11:26**; *11:41*; ⟦**13:30**⟧; ⟦**13:30**⟧; *14:18*; 19:16.
πτερύγιον (pinnacle, tip)
Q **4:9**.
πτέρυξ (wing)
Q **13:34**.
πτύον (winnowing shovel, pitchfork)
Q **3:17**.
πτῶμα (corpse)
Q 17:37.
πτῶσις (collapse, fall)
Q ⟦6:49⟧.
πτωχός (poor, beggar)
Q **6:20**; **7:22**.
πῦρ (fire)
Q **3:9; 3:16; 3:17;** ⟦«12:49»⟧; *17:29*.
πυρράζω (*v.* be fiery red, be flame red)
Q ⟦12:54⟧; ⟦12:55⟧.
πωλέω (*v.* sell)
Q **12:6**; *17:28*.
πῶς (how?)
Q **6:42**; **11:18**; **12:11**; **12:27**.
ῥάβδος (staff, stick)
Q 10:4.
ῥαπίζω (*v.* strike, slap)
Q ⟦6:29⟧.
ῥίζα (root)
Q **3:9**.
ῥίπτω (*v.* throw)
Q 17:2.
σάκκος (sackcloth)
Q **10:13**.
σαλεύω (*v.* shake, move)
Q **7:24**.
σαπρός (rotten, decayed)
Q *6:43*; *6:43*; 6:43; **6:43**.
σαρόω (*v.* sweep)
Q **11:25**; ⟦«15:8»⟧.
σατανᾶς (Satan)
Q **11:18**.
σάτον (measure)
Q **13:21**.
σημεῖον (sign)
Q **11:16**; **11:29**; **11:29**; **11:29**; 11:30.
σήμερον (today)
Q 11:3; **12:28**; ⟦12:55⟧.
σής (moth, worm)
Q «12:33»; **12:33**.
σιαγών (cheek)
Q **6:29**.
Σιδών (Sidon)
Q **10:13**; **10:14**.
σίναπι (mustard)
Q **13:19**; **17:6**.
σῖτος (grain, wheat)
Q **3:17**.
σκανδαλίζω (*v.* scandalize, make stumble, offend)
Q **7:23**; **17:2**.
σκάνδαλον (offence)
Q **17:1**.
σκληρός (hard, difficult)
Q 19:21.
σκορπίζω (*v.* scatter)
Q **11:23**.
σκοτεινός (dark, darkened)
Q **11:34**.
σκοτία (darkness, dark)
Q **12:3**.
σκότος (dark, darkness)
Q **11:35**; 11:35; 13:28.
Σόδομα (Sodom)
Q **10:12**; *17:29*.
Σολομών (Solomon)
Q **11:31**; **11:31**; **12:27**.
σοφία (wisdom)
Q **7:35**; **11:31**; 11:49.
σοφός (sage)
Q **10:21**; 11:49.
σπείρω (*v.* sow [seed])
Q **12:24**; **19:21**; **19:22**.
σποδός (ashes)
Q **10:13**.

σταυρός (cross)
Q **14:27**.
σταφυλή (bunch of grapes)
Q **6:44**.
στέγη (roof)
Q **7:6**.
στενός (narrow)
Q **13:24**.
στόμα (mouth)
Q **6:45**.
στρατιώτης (soldier)
Q **7:8**.
στρέφω (*v*. turn, change, offer)
Q 6:29.
στρουθίον (sparrow)
Q **12:6**; **12:7**.
στυγνάζω (*v*. become gloomy, lower)
Q ⟦12:55⟧.
συκάμινος (mulberry tree)
Q 17:6.
σῦκον (fig)
Q **6:44**.
συλλέγω (*v*. collect, gather, pick)
Q **6:44**.
συνάγω (*v*. assemble)
Q **3:17**; **11:23**; 12:24; 17:37; 19:21; 19:22.
συναγωγή (synagogue, assembly)
Q **11:43**; 12:11.
συναίρω (*v*. settle accounts)
Q 19:15.
σύνδουλος (fellow slave)
Q ⟦12:45⟧.
συνετός (wise, intelligent, learned)
Q **10:21**.
σῶμα (body)
Q **11:34**; **11:34**; **11:34**; **12:4**; 12:5; **12:22**; **12:23**.
ταμεῖον (storeroom)
Q *12:3*; 17:23.
ταπεινόω (*v*. humble)
Q ⟦**14:11**⟧; ⟦**14:11**⟧.
τέκνον (child)
Q **3:8**; 7:35; **11:13**; **13:34**.
τελωνής (tax collector, toll collector)
Q 6:32; ⟦**7:29**⟧; **7:34**.
τεσσεράκοντα (forty)
Q **4:2**.
τίθημι (*v*. put, place, give)
Q **11:33**; **12:46**.
τις, τι (someone, something)
Q 9:57; ⟦10:22⟧; 11:15; 11:16; *11:27*; 19:12.
τίς, τί (who? what?)
Q **3:7**; 6:32; ⟦6:34⟧; **6:41**; 6:46; **7:24**; **7:25**; **7:26**; **7:31**; 7:31; **11:11**; **11:19**; **12:11**; 12:12; **12:22**; **12:22**; **12:25**; **12:26**; **12:29**; **12:29**; 12:29; **12:42**; ⟦«12:49»⟧; 13:18; 13:18; 13:20; **14:34**; **15:4**; ⟦«15:8»⟧.
τόκος (interest)
Q **19:23**.
τόπος (place, region)
Q **11:24**.
τότε (then)
Q ⟦*3:21*⟧; **6:42**; ⟦**11:24**⟧; **11:26**; *11:39*; 13:26; **14:21**; 16:16.
τραπεζίτης (banker, money-changer)
Q ⟦19:23⟧.
τράχηλος (throat, neck)
Q **17:2**.
τρεῖς (three)
Q **13:21**.
τρέφω (*v*. feed, nourish)
Q **12:24**.
τρίβολος (thistle, thorn)
Q 6:44.
τρόπος (manner, way)
Q **13:34**.
τροφή (nourishment, food)
Q **12:23**; 12:42.
τρώγω (*v*. eat, munch)
Q 17:27.
τύπτω (*v*. strike, beat)
Q **12:45**.
Τύρος (Tyre)
Q **10:13**; **10:14**.
τυφλός (blind)
Q **6:39**; **6:39**; **7:22**.
ὕδωρ (water)
Q **3:16**.

υἱός (son)
Q ⟦**3:22**⟧; **4:3**; **4:9**; 6:22; **6:35**; **7:34**; **9:58**; 10:6; **10:22**; **10:22**; **10:22**; **10:22**; **11:11**; **11:19**; **11:30**; ⟦11:48⟧; ⟦12:8⟧; **12:10**; **12:40**; **12:53;** 14:26; **17:24**; **17:26**; **17:30**.

ὑπάγω (*v*. depart, go, be on one's way)
Q ⟦«6:29↔30/Mt 5:41»⟧; 10:3; *12:58*.

ὑπακούω (*v*. obey, listen, follow)
Q 17:6.

ὑπάρχω (*v*. possess, have, exist)
Q **12:44**.

ὑπηρέτης (servant, assistant)
Q 12:58; ⟦<12:58>⟧.

ὑποδείκνυμι (*v*. show, indicate)
Q **3:7.**

ὑποδήμα (sandal)
Q **3:16**; **10:4**.

ὑποκριτής (hypocrite, actor)
Q **6:42**.

ὕστερος (last)
Q *4:2*; ⟦*7:30*⟧.

ὑψηλός (very high, tall)
Q ⟦4:5⟧.

ὑψόω (*v*. exalt, raise up)
Q **10:15**; ⟦**14:11**⟧; ⟦**14:11**⟧.

φάγος (glutton)
Q **7:34**.

φαίνω (*v*. shine, give light, flash)
Q 17:24.

Φαρισαῖος (Pharisee)
Q ⟦*7:30*⟧; *11:16*; **11:39**; **11:42**; 11:43; ⟦11:44⟧.

φεύγω (*v*. flee, run from)
Q **3:7**.

φήμι (*v*. say)
Q 7:6.

φθάνω (*v*. come before, precede, arrive, come)
Q **11:20**.

φιλέω (*v*. love, like)
Q 11:43.

φίλος (friend, chum)
Q **7:34**; ⟦«15:9»⟧.

φοβέω (*v*. fear)
Q **12:4**; **12:5**; **12:7**; **19:21**.

φορέω (*v*. bear, wear)
Q 7:25.

φορτίον (burden, cargo, load)
Q **11:46**.

φρόνιμος (prudent, wise)
Q **12:42**.

φυλακή (guard, prison)
Q 12:39; **12:58**.

φυλάσσω (*v*. guard, watch, defend)
Q *11:28*.

φυλή (tribe)
Q **22:30**.

φυτεύω (*v*. plant)
Q 17:6; *17:28*.

φωλεός (fox hole)
Q **9:58**.

φωνή (voice, sound)
Q *11:27*.

φῶς (light)
Q **11:35**; **12:3**.

φωτεινός (shining, radiant)
Q **11:34**.

χαίρω (*v*. be glad, rejoice)
Q **6:23**; **15:7;** ⟦«15:9»⟧.

χαρά (joy)
Q ⟦«15:10»⟧.

χειμών (stormy weather, winter)
Q ⟦12:55⟧.

χείρ (hand)
Q **3:17; 4:11**.

χείρων (worse, more severe)
Q **11:26**.

χιτών (tunic, shirt)
Q **6:29**.

Χοραζίν (Chorazin)
Q **10:13**.

χορτάζω (*v*. feed, satisfy)
Q **6:21**.

χόρτος (grass)
Q **12:28**.

χρῄζω (*v*. have need of)
Q **12:30**.

χρονίζω (*v*. be delayed, take time)
Q **12:45**.

χρόνος (time)
Q ⟦19:15⟧.

χωλός (lame)
Q **7:22**.

ψυχή (soul, life)
Q 12:4; 12:5; **12:22**; **12:23**; **17:33**; 17:33.

ὧδε (here)
Q **11:31**; **11:32**; ⟦17:21⟧.

ὦμος (shoulder)
Q ⟦11:46⟧.

ὥρα (hour, time)
Q *10:21*; **12:12**; **12:40**; **12:46**; ⟦14:17⟧.

RECOMMENDED READING

There is an extensive bibliography in other languages, especially German, which is omitted here, and only a selection of English literature is included. For a complete bibliography one may consult F. Neirynck, J. Verheyden, and R. Corstjens, *The Gospel of Matthew and the Gospel Source Q: A Cumulative Bibliography 1950-1995* (2 vols., BETL 140; Leuven: Leuven University Press and Uitgeverij Peeters, 1998); or D. M. Scholer, *Q Bibliography, Twentieth Century*. Documenta Q: Supplementum (Leuven: Peeters, 2001).

For the text of Q in Greek and English in the context of a synopsis of the Gospels, see James M. Robinson, Paul Hoffmann, and John S. Kloppenborg, gen. eds., Milton C. Moreland, man. ed., *The Critical Edition of Q: Synopsis, including the Gospels of Matthew and Luke, Mark and Thomas, with English, German, and French Translations of Q and Thomas* (Leuven: Peeters; Minneapolis: Fortress Press, 2000).

For the databases used in the reconstruction of the critical edition of Q, see the series Documenta Q, James M. Robinson, Paul Hoffmann, and John S. Kloppenborg, gen. eds., Stanley D. Anderson, Sterling G. Borndahl, Shawn Carruth, Robert A. Derrenbacker, Jr., Christoph Heil, Thomas Hieke, Steven R. Johnson, and Milton C. Moreland, vol. eds. (Leuven: Peeters, 1996 ff.).

Aland, K., ed. 1984. *Synopsis of the Four Gospels. Greek-English Edition of the Synopsis Quattuor Evangeliorum*. Seventh Edition. Stuttgart: German Bible Society.

Allison, Dale C. 1997. *The Jesus Tradition in Q*. Valley Forge, Penn.: Trinity Press International.

Asgeirsson, Jon, Kristin de Troyer, and Marvin W. Meyer, eds. 1999. *From Quest to Quelle: Festschrift James M. Robinson*. BETL 146. Leuven: University Press and Peeters.

Catchpole, David R. 1993. *The Quest for Q*. Edinburgh: T. & T. Clark.

Fleddermann, Harry T. 1995. *Mark and Q: A Study of the Overlap Texts*. BETL 122. Leuven: University Press and Peeters.

Harnack, Adolf. 1908. *The Sayings of Jesus: The Second Source of St. Matthew and St. Luke*. Trans. John Richard Wilkinson. New Testament Studies 2. London: Williams & Norgate; New York: G. P. Putnam's Sons.

Havener, Ivan. 1987. *Q: The Sayings of Jesus*. Good News Studies 19. Wilmington, Del.: Michael Glazier.

Jacobson, Arland D. 1992. *The First Gospel: An Introduction to Q*. Sonoma, Calif.: Polebridge.

Kirk, Alan. 1998. *The Composition of the Sayings Source: Genre, Synchrony, and Wisdom Redaction in Q*. Supplements to Novum Testamentum 91. Leiden: E. J. Brill.

Kloppenborg, John S. 1987. *The Formation of Q: Trajectories in Ancient Wisdom Collections*. Studies in Antiquity and Christianity. Philadelphia: Fortress. Reprint Harrisburg, Penn.: Trinity Press International, 2000.

—. 1988. *Q Parallels: Synopsis, Critical Notes, and Concordance*. Foundations and Facets: New Testament. Sonoma, Calif.: Polebridge.

—, ed. 1994. *The Shape of Q: Signal Essays on the Sayings Gospel*. Minneapolis, Minn.: Fortress.

—, ed. 1995. *Conflict and Invention: Literary, Rhetorical, and Social Studies on the Sayings Gospel Q*. Valley Forge, Penn.: Trinity Press International.

—, Marvin W. Meyer, Stephen J. Patterson, Michael G. Steinhauser, eds. 1990. *Q Thomas Reader*. Sonoma, Calif.: Polebridge Press.

— and Leif E. Vaage, eds. 1991. *Early Christianity, Q and Jesus*. Semeia 55. Atlanta, Ga.: Scholars Press.

Kloppenborg Verbin, John S. 2000. *Excavating Q: The History and Setting of the Sayings Gospel*. Edinburgh: T. & T. Clark; Minneapolis, Minn.: Fortress.

Lindemann, Andreas, ed. 2001. *The Sayings Source Q and the Historical Jesus*. BETL 158. Leuven: University Press and Peeters.

Mack, Burton L. 1993. *The Lost Gospel: The Book of Q and Christian Origins*. San Francisco: HarperSanFrancisco.

Neirynck, Frans. [2]1995. *Q-Synopsis. The Double Tradition Passages in Greek*. Studiorum Novi Testamenti Auxilia 13. Leuven: University Press and Peeters.

Piper, Ronald A. 1989. *Wisdom in the Q-tradition: The Aphoristic Teaching of Jesus*. SNTSMS 61. Cambridge and New York: Cambridge University Press.

—, ed. 1995. *The Gospel behind the Gospels: Current Studies on Q*. Supplements to Novum Testamentum 75. Leiden: E. J. Brill.

Robinson, James M. and Helmut Koester. 1971, paperback 1979. *Trajectories through Early Christianity*. Philadelphia, Penn.: Fortress Press.

Theissen, Gerd. 1992, 1993. *Social Reality and the Early Christians: Theology, Ethics, and the World of the New Testament*. Trans. Margaret Kohl. Minneapolis, Minn.: Fortress Press, and Edinburgh: T & T Clark.

Tuckett, Christopher M. 1983. *The Revival of the Griesbach Hypothesis: An Analysis and Appraisal*. SNTSMS 44. Cambridge and New York: Cambridge University Press.

—. 1996. *Q and the History of Early Christianity: Studies on Q*. Edinburgh: T. & T. Clark; Peabody, Mass.: Hendrickson.

Uro, Risto. 1987. *Sheep among the Wolves: A Study on the Mission Instructions of Q*. Annales Academiae Scientiarum Fennicae. Dissertationes humanarum litterarum 47. Helsinki: Suomalainen Tiedeakatemia.

—, ed. 1996. *Symbols and Strata: Essays on the Sayings Gospel Q*. Suomen Eksegeettisen Seuran Julkaisuja. Publications of the Finnish Exegetical Society of Helsinki: Finnish Exegetical Society; Göttingen: Vandenhoeck & Ruprecht.

PRINTED ON PERMANENT PAPER • IMPRIME SUR PAPIER PERMANENT • GEDRUKT OP DUURZAAM PAPIER - ISO 9706

N.V. PEETERS S.A., KLEIN DALENSTRAAT 42, B-3020 HERENT